Understanding

FRED &
ROSE
WEST

Understanding
FRED &
ROSE
WEST

Noose, Lamella and the Gilded Cage

LEO SAMUEL GOATLEY

The Book Guild Ltd

First published in Great Britain in 2019 by
The Book Guild Ltd
9 Priory Business Park
Wistow Road, Kibworth
Leicestershire, LE8 0RX
Freephone: 0800 999 2982
www.bookguild.co.uk
Email: info@bookguild.co.uk
Twitter: @bookguild

Typeset in 11pt Minion Pro

Printed and bound in the UK by TJ International, Padstow, Cornwall

ISBN 978 1912881 895

British Library Cataloguing in Publication Data.
A catalogue record for this book is available from the British Library.

To my wife Katherine who, although she did not want me to write this book, assisted me at various stages of the case and has always been a source of love and support.

CONTENTS

1.

CONTEXT

The West case was one of the most disturbing serial murder cases in British criminal history. Murder most foul, but it seems even foulness is relative. The case was appalling on a number of levels: the horrific details of the offences; the juxtaposition of ordinary day-to-day routine family life with depraved, sadistic sex, along with the torture and murder of innocent young women who were just starting out in their lives; the sheer persistence of the offending that remained undetected for so many years; and the cruel unknowing that had to be painfully borne by the victims' loved ones. The nation was scarred as the details emerged. There was a sense of an unwelcome mirror held up to society, if it ever needed to be, reminding us of just what depths humankind can sink to.

For twelve years I acted for Rose West as her solicitor and for a time represented both Rose and Fred West in relation to childcare proceedings. I acted for Rose in all stages of the numerous criminal allegations brought against her from July 1992 through to the serial murder trial at Winchester Crown

Court in October and November of 1995, then the appeal in the Lord Chief Justice's court in 1996 and a subsequent application to the Criminal Cases Review Commission in 2001. It was only Rose who stood trial and then was convicted of the murder of ten young women. Fred West committed suicide on January 1st 1995 while remanded in custody awaiting trial.

Strange as it may seem, I had always viewed Rose West as a reasonable person to deal with. If my view of her had really been so demeaning as the press has portrayed, if in my mind I had characterised her as a monster, it would have been impossible to continue to act. But that was not the view I had formed of her. She presented as sociable, usually calm and, most important of all, she vehemently denied the nightmarish catalogue of allegations set out on the indictment. She was not a difficult client. When initially remanded in custody at Pucklechurch, near Bristol, she had come under the wing of a kindly old nun, Sister Paul, whose ministry was simply to be a friend and pray with prisoners. Sister Paul was non-judgmental and I have no doubt Rose had a genuine affection for her, holding her in high esteem. It was the little nun who gave Rose the plastic rosary beads that she kept throughout her trial. Her parting from the nun was one of the reasons why she became so distressed when she was moved north to HMP Durham following the committal proceedings at Dursley magistrates' court in February 1994.

I spent hundreds of hours in interview and attendance with Rose West before, during and after her trial and appeal, travelling to Durham to visit her in prison on many occasions. Provided I did not venture to take her out of her comfort zone, she was straightforward to deal with, better than many I have represented. Therein lies one of the fault lines, both in Rose as a person, and the difficulty it presented in the preparation of her case. While over time she developed a platonic affection for me – which she sometimes expressed in her letters – she was also a woman who intuitively chose not to volunteer information about a darker side to her personality, even where I explained that it would help her case. She was content enough to engage on the level of easy conversation, but the secrets that she undoubtedly guarded remained largely locked away in some part of her mind and were only revisited by her after her trial.

While the police investigation into the West murders was thorough and deservedly earned commendation for the way it was conducted, it is fair to say that even the officers were not satisfied that the full extent of the case had been fully excavated and resolved. There is much that remains a mystery. There are many questions that will not go away. In giving my account as her defence solicitor, I revisit and review the many conversations that we had. I have also reviewed available evidence relating to the victims and have given close scrutiny to the early years and the disappearance in 1968 of Mary Bastholm, a young woman who did not appear on the indictments of either Fred or Rose West. Her file remains open as that of an unsolved missing person.

Due process in criminal law is designed to effectively and fairly bring perpetrators of offences to account for their crimes while acquitting those who are not guilty. This requires a presumption of innocence until otherwise proven guilty. The precise elements that need to be established for a jury to properly deliberate necessitate application of substantive law and the rules of evidence and procedure and an adherence to those facts that address those questions that are relevant. This means there are many questions, which though very interesting, a court of law will nevertheless not enquire into.

At the end of criminal proceedings, you often hear police officers and lawyers talking of justice being served, of drawing a line in the sand, of giving closure to the family, of being able to move on. The reality is often very different. Serious crimes change people's lives forever, sometimes victims survive, sometimes they do not, and their loved ones must carry the terrible psychological luggage for the rest of their lives. There are no winners. The families of the perpetrators are just as damaged, and the ensuing generations burdened with the chilling resonating knowledge of some terrible episode for which their relative was responsible.

It is not just DNA that parents pass onto their children; the psychological imprint of their nurturing will mediate in their lives and, in a moderated form, resonate through the generations. This of course does not mean at all that the child of a serial killer will follow suit. On the contrary, it is likely to precipitate a dialectical process where the mind-numbing knowledge of the sins of parents is the antithesis of the social norms schoolchildren may aspire to, thereby triggering an instinctive repulsion.

And there remain all the interminable, seemingly unfathomable questions that conspire to deny the closure people so long for. It is a complex process. Initially, revenge and punishment of the offender offers a sense of justice; it gives a temporary sense of relief. But this is often short-lived and the inner destruction ploughs through the living's broken lives. The possibility of healing is something that has been explored with courage and great sensitivity by Marian Partington, whose sister, Lucy, was one of the Wests' victims.

In this book I have considered the questions of how and why Fred and Rose West developed into the monsters that together committed such dreadful acts. Those are questions that a court of law does not enquire into. It is perhaps a paradox that the sharp logic and economy of the law also must serve to curtail a wider discourse.

To try and unravel these issues, principally in the section entitled 'Lamella', I adopt a discourse endeavouring to provide a glimpse into the dark recesses of Fred and Rose West's minds. This is structured approach of signification applied to psychoanalysis by Jacques Lacan in his revisiting of Freudian ideas. In so doing he adopted the structured linguistics of Saussure. There is an inherent subjectivity in such an approach, but the ideas have been devised, utilised and elaborated in so influencing Lacan by many innovative modern thinkers from Saussure to Claude Lévi-Straus and André Breton. Lacan incorporated these ideas into the rigorous method derived from his scientific background as a psychiatrist. The approach enables the conveying of meaning through such linguistic structures and in so doing it affords the opportunity to understand human action in a variety of contexts across a broad range of disciplines whether in culture, art, political history, sociology or, in this case, psychology.

Despite its subjectivity it offers a cohesive and imaginative means to peel back layers, to enquire behind the all-encompassing 'roadblock' of seemingly self-explanatory words like 'love', 'hate', 'morality' and 'evil', which are otherwise a *fait accompli* as they purport demarcation of the limits of contextual analysis. Once that happens, the discourse dries up and there remains an unsatisfied feeling that more is needed to be said.

Lacan was influenced by the surrealist capacity for ornate self-presentation and he adopted ideas from their manifesto into his method. The surrealists would use free thinking and loose imaginative ideas to mimic madness and to present visions of the unconscious mind. These highly visual representations opened up further discourse, enabling meaning to emerge by applying signification. In *How to Read Lacan*, the contemporary philosopher Slavoj Žižek demonstrates how cultural cross-referencing enables insights into Lacan's work.

Psychoanalysis explores the interconnection between the conscious and the unconscious mind: "The psychoanalytic view holds that there are inner forces outside of your awareness that are directing your behaviour." (Cherry) Breton defined surrealism as, "Pure psychic automatism, by which it is intended to express, verbally, in writing, or by other means, the real process of thought."

In using this approach I have retained a conversational style designed to signify the darker places Lacanian analysis may take us. Where intimate issues are expanded occasional mimicry and coarse vernacular is used for emphasis.

The alternative would be to reject the discourse and subscribe purely to a strict empiricism based on scientific observation and experimentation, demonstrating repeatable results as the premise to found a credible theory. But Freud and Lacan would argue that their methods were scientific, and the trace evidence gleaned by observation of the behaviours and responses of their patients was sound in revealing the workings of their unconscious mind, the dark and unknowable instinctual motive force of the unconscious.

In the Freudian unconscious there is no time; the unconscious is time independent. The unconscious is where it is, always, there is no difference between the past, present and the future. And it is to the unmediated bleeding of repressed and thereby perverted primordial drives that we must look to understand what imbued Fred and Rose West to carry out their horrific crimes.

2.

THE 1992 CHILD ABUSE ENQUIRIES

On August 3rd 1992 PC Stephen Burnside, a burly Scotsman who later became an inspector, was on the beat in Cromwell Street when some children who had been playing nearby came up to him and told the officer that one of their friends, a thirteen-year-old girl, was being interfered with by her dad. He might have easily ignored the juvenile banter and walked on, looking out for known criminals or evidence of street crime. Instead, he listened, and he took note of the plaintiff admonition that was repeated to him. He asked questions, took names, noted an address and reported the matter back to his duty sergeant. A report was filed, an inquiry was underway. As the case was referred to the child abuse investigation team the county social services department was also notified. On August 4th, the police and social services held a joint case conference and the following day, the police applied to the Gloucester magistrates and obtained a warrant to search the girl's family home.

The case involved the Gloucester builder Fred West and his wife Rosemary. They resided in the centre of the small city, near the park at 25 Cromwell Street. It was and is a neighbourhood with a transient population of bedsits and renters, as well as more established working class families, like the Wests. Their family home was a square three-storey building with a converted basement. It was made of rendered stone painted a creamy buff colour. The property had been extended with a flat roof kitchen and bathroom appended to the rear. On the right side as you faced the property from the street, this unregulated construction was cobbled onto the more recent church building next door. Apart from this extension, each floor of the property consisted of a landing and two small rooms either side, each with a window, one facing out into the street. and the other to the rear garden.

On August 6th 1992 at about 9am, the police executed the warrant. Two detectives and four uniformed officers arrived at the address to take the five younger children – Tara, Barry, Louise, Rosemary and Lucyanna – to a place of safety. Fred was at work. Rose was arrested. She objected to the police presence and wrestled with them initially. A search of the property commenced. Later in the day at about 2:30pm, Fred was located in Stroud at the property of Derek Thomson, the boss of the building company he worked for. He was arrested and brought to Gloucester police station to be interviewed. Howard Ogden, 'Ogie', was the duty solicitor acting for Fred West, a sole practitioner like myself, appointed to carry out publicly funded work.

I received a duty solicitor call in relation to Rose. She was being held on suspicion of aiding and abetting her husband in the sexual abuse of their thirteen-year-old daughter. Rose was waiting in a consultation room: a woman in her late thirties, with short dark hair and heavy black-rimmed glasses. She was a frumpy, indignant mother, plucked from mundane domesticity, dowdily attired in slacks, slippers and a loose-fitting top. She spoke in a slightly breathless, shrill way, but she was not loud. She was not a difficult client to speak to and that always remained the case. She was clearly annoyed at being detained and looked to me to explain to her what it was all about. After clarifying the allegation to her, she expressly stated that she at no time had ever sexually abused her thirteen-year-old daughter, or any of her children for that matter. Her demeanour, which translated into her instructions, was that she felt deeply wronged by the apparently speculative and misplaced intervention of the police who had so aggressively invaded her house and her space earlier in the day. Her indignation and unquestionable denial was compelling.

Rose West could be reserved and sometimes chose not to give a clear answer, preferring to tell me that I would need to ask Fred West about that one, or sometimes she would say she needed to think about a question. It never occurred to me, even for a moment, that she could be a murderer, let alone a serial killer.

The specific allegation put was that certain incidents had occurred repeatedly in the family's downstairs bathroom, which adjoined the kitchen area and part of the unregulated build that cobbled onto the back of the house. These incidents involved both Fred and Rose restraining their young daughter against her will, forcefully removing her clothing and then intimately inspecting, touching and – using some form of sharp object – penetrating her vagina. When the girl cried and objected, she was smacked, beaten and told to be quiet, that it was to help her so that she would have a better marriage. She recalled Fred undressing and forcing himself upon her, first from the front and then her parents forced her to bend over the toilet, after which she felt an excruciating pain in her anus. She recalled that this caused her to bleed.

As a result of the interviews, during which Fred stated that Louise was making it all up out of spite and jealousy because the girl thought he had more affection for her younger sister, Fred West was charged on August 7th with three counts and rape and one of buggery. Following a magistrates' court remand hearing and bail application, he was remanded in custody on August 8th. In the meantime, Rose West was bailed to return to the police station. The investigation team had a number of people to speak to. A lengthy statement running to twenty-one pages recounting the family history was provided by Fred's eldest child, Anne Marie, who by now was married and had two children of her own. They also spoke to Anne Marie's husband, Chris Davis, as well as the younger West siblings.

On August 11th 1992, I recall it was a warm summer's day in the late morning that I returned to the police cells as Rose West answered her bail. She was particularly annoyed about the mess and damage the police had caused to her home during the search. Over time this curiously remained the preoccupation of both Fred and Rose West despite the enormity of the incrementally emerging allegations.

DC Hazel Savage was involved in the police interviews. She was an experienced, intuitive cop whose deep seated misgivings about the Wests were soon to be entirely vindicated. She expressly told both Fred and Rose that the case was not just going to go away. In fact, this seemingly anonymous, hard-working, domesticated working class couple, plucked from the humdrum of their daily lives, had history that Hazel Savage was all too aware of. As part of the routine order of business, background questions were asked to establish how many children of the family there were, their ages and where they were. Inevitably questions were asked about Heather. Rose's replies would later come back to haunt her.

Rose West was joined on the indictment as aiding and abetting the rape and buggery of her daughter. In the meantime, emergency protection orders had been obtained and care proceedings commenced. The children were immediately moved into foster care. An interim care order was then made following representations from all parties. When Rose was bailed to later attend a preliminary hearing, she returned to an empty house. She felt her world falling apart. She sensed the impending momentum that was to come. She despaired at the emptiness of the house without the children around her. That night when Mae and Stephen found her, she had taken forty-eight sleeping pills. She was rushed to hospital and had her stomach pumped. This had been a serious attempt at suicide. In my view, it was totally out of character. I suspect that if Rose really had a predisposition to suicidal thoughts, then there would have been many opportunities since as time has rolled on over the past twenty-five years.

In May 1993, I attended at Gloucester Crown Court at 9:30am for the first day of the trial. After waiting for about five minutes in the unusual quiet of the carpeted corridor that provided a continuous perimeter to the circular Victorian court room, defence leading counsel, the avuncular Christopher Wilson-Smith QC, emerged from the robing room to stoically advise that the matter was being discontinued. The scheduled criminal trial collapsed when the children refused to give evidence. It transpired that they had during the intervening months regularly walked back to 25 Cromwell Street, a distance of about two miles from the foster home where they had been placed.

This left the question of care proceedings to be resolved. At this stage, I was acting for both Fred and Rose West, although at least on the surface, it was only Rose who was proactive in visiting my office and urging whatever steps were necessary to get the children back. In any event, for much of this time Fred was either remanded in custody or residing on strict conditions at a bail hostel in Birmingham. Social services viewed the case with such seriousness that the matter was transferred to the jurisdiction of the High Court in October 1992. After a number of interim hearings in Bristol, a further hearing was held on December 15th 1993. Both Fred and Rose attended on this occasion.

With hindsight, it alarms me to be reminded of the fact that my wife, Katherine, attended in a clerking capacity for me at a hearing at Bristol Family Court on a cold wet February in 1993. Counsel was also in attendance. The hearing – when it eventually occurred – was brief, but in the meantime Katherine had been sitting in the waiting room for most of the day next to Fred and Rose.

Katherine recalls that Rose remained silent for the most part while Fred was chatty for much of the time. It was not an easy time for us, as my wife was in the early months of pregnancy with our eighth child and suffering with queasiness.

Even now she remembers finding Fred creepy. Prior to the attendance, I had shown Katherine the file and she had viewed with me pornographic homemade videos, as well as photographs seized from 25 Cromwell Street. She had also read witness statements and so she was under no illusions of what territory the case encompassed. However, when Fred kept trying to spark up a conversation, she intuitively felt she had no wish to respond to or tell him anything. This related, in particular, to Fred asking questions about our family and whether we had children. He would then go into a monologue about how difficult and ungrateful children are after all that parents do for them. Katherine recalls that although he was not using swear words, what was particularly unpleasant about him was the way he would not be respectful of someone's space. He would sidle up, get too close, put his hand on her arm, be too pally, nudge her as though he was sharing a secret with her. She thought it so odd that instead of being terribly worried about the enormity of the abuse allegations and upset about losing his children, he proudly produced a bundle of photographs from his pocket showing the various DIY projects he had carried out on 25 Cromwell Street. He then went into a rant about how annoyed both he and Rose were at the way they had been treated by the police and the disrespect they had shown in getting a search warrant and pulling the panels off the walls of the downstairs bathroom.

Given the horrific revelations that subsequently unfolded, it is quite extraordinary to now read the cost draughtsman's narrative to the legal aid bill that was submitted at the conclusion of the care proceedings on February 22nd 1994:

"...This matter was fraught with extreme difficulty and sensitivity throughout; Care Orders were obtained by the Gloucestershire County Council in relation to the five children of the family in view of the allegations of abuse; those allegations were always repudiated by the Respondents and Applications were made on behalf of the Second Respondent for discharge of those Orders and for interim contact; various direction Orders were made including preparation of reports by Dr Gay and filing of guardian ad litem reports; numerous statements were filed by and behalf of all the Parties herein including the children who were separately represented in addition to the guardian ad litem.

"Attempts were made to settle the matter by way of negotiation where the Applicants offered supervised contact in view of the fact that the children were making unapproved visits and/or an Order was made for contact with the Respondents; the Respondents were so incensed by the allegations made that they felt that if they accepted supervised contact it would, in effect, be regarded as an admission of the allegations of abuse; in view thereof both Respondents rejected the question of supervised contact, instructions were received to withdraw the Applications for discharge of the Care Orders on behalf of the Second Respondent and the children were similarly granted leave to withdraw their Applications for Care Order; at the hearing on December 15th 1993 an order was made for supervised contact to be arranged by the Applicant in consultation with the guardian ad litem and Dr Gay; as previously mentioned that offer was not taken up by the Respondents and the matter came for hearing on February 22nd 1994 when the offer of supervised contact was continued and all other Applications were adjourned..."

While the criminal abuse trial did not proceed, the investigation had nevertheless thrown up a can of worms that was never just going to be filed and forgotten, not least were the jovial representations made to the foster carers by the children that their mum and dad always joked about Heather being buried at the bottom of the garden. As DC Hazel Savage's national insurance and medical enquiries about Heather had drawn a blank, the police did not find the joke at all funny.

3.

PROCEEDINGS (1994-1995)

My office was based in a small, Cotswold stone, Victorian gothic building at 4 Pitt Street in Gloucester. It had originally been built as the Diocesan Registry, but in recent years the main part housed the Gloucester Probate sub-registry. I had an upstairs office with a large crumbling stone mullioned window. On the other side was King's School and on the opposite side of the street was the Bishop's Palace, a large red brick mansion, probably built in the 1930s. Pitt Street was a narrow road in the shadow of the walls and grounds of the cathedral in the centre of the city. It was sleepy and inconspicuous. I shared the building with an elderly gentleman, Vernon Daykin, who ran a printing and billing service for quantity surveyors, who needed their huge costings sheets transcribed typed up and printed.

Vernon was a wise old man. I think he grafted hard for the sake of it. He was always at the office by seven in the morning and he drove in from Coleford in the Forest of Dean. He had initially worked in a bank but served as an intelligence officer during the second world war. When the war ended he went back to banking, but soon became bored and re-joined the RAF who, on discovering his talent for languages, sent him to the Foreign Office School of Languages in Beirut in the 1950s to learn Arabic, which he obviously mastered because he had written a book on technical Arabic. He ended up at GCHQ reading Arabic newspapers, a week's worth of which were delivered to his desk at 9am on each Monday. He recalled reading these, then doing the crossword and binning the lot by lunchtime. He decided to join his wife's printing business at Pitt Street.

Vernon had learnt a cautionary lesson while in Beirut as one of the other language students on his course was George Blake, a modest, scrupulously polite, almost obsequious individual who invariably at the end of an evening at the Foreign Office Club would wait in the foyer to offer whoever might be a little the worse for wear a lift home. Vernon was never tempted by George Blake's late-night ad lib taxi service.

As a young solicitor setting up business, I adopted the view of trusting people until they demonstrated that they were not to be trusted. Vernon assured me that he took the entirely opposite view and would did not trust anybody until they earned his approval. He was also a firm believer in neither confirming nor denying anything, which is a more formal way of saying 'no comment'. As a criminal lawyer, if someone tells you they are innocent and asks you to defend them, if I then waited for them to earn my trust by some elevated demonstration of integrity, I would have had very few clients.

I ran a small general practice which included some residential and commercial conveyancing, wills and probate, a bit of civil litigation, and some publicly funded childcare, family and criminal litigation. I had opened the office about seven years earlier and within the crime remit had dealt with a previous murder case as well as an attempted murder. Both cases produced reasonable results, with the murder charge resulting in the Crown accepting a plea to voluntary manslaughter by reason of diminished responsibility and the attempt being reduced to an assault occasioning actual bodily harm.

It was a tight ship, with my wife doing my accounts on a part-time basis and a secretary, Penny, who in March 1994, shortly after the commencement of the West case, decided to return to her home in Shropshire. She later told me that the case was giving her nightmares. She had studied Law at Liverpool University and was getting experience working in a solicitor's office. In her place, by a strange turn of events, I recruited an elderly man, by the name of David O'Connor, whom I knew from St Peter's RC Church Social Club. David had recently been dismissed from a part-time retirement job as the car park attendant at Shire Hall. Apparently, one of the local worthies on the county council had found him the worse for wear on account of imbibing a wee dram of whiskey while on duty in his hut at the entrance barrier to the rear of the County Council building and adjacent to Gloucester Crown Court. He protested his innocence, but to no avail.

David had had a varied career. Although of Irish parentage, he had been born in Cardiff in 1926. In 1944, he joined the Irish Guards and spent the rest of the war guarding Buckingham Palace. In 1947, his battalion was sent to Palestine. In the early 1950s, he joined Gloucester Constabulary, where he was a keen member and secretary of the gun club. He also recalled his undercover duties policing the raincoat brigade at the local public toilets. He was part of an elite detachment of officers so deployed. Actually, David also wore a raincoat as he would lay in wait in covert surveillance for hours at time and then, when some lonely man would find a kindred spirit, David would pounce, pulling out his police badge in skilled evidential synchronisation at the moment of buggery, then licking his pencil to meticulously record in his notebook another victory in the battle against gross indecency in a public place. This was part of the strategic push to curtail the perceived post-war depravity within the country and ensure that the nuclear family could sleep soundly in their beds.

The stress of all those cold, rainy midweek nights sitting in a toilet cubicle at Gloucester Bus Station may have eventually got to him and in 1958 he was recruited to work as secretary to Colonel Harry Llewellyn of equestrian Olympic fame in Abergavenny, Monmouthshire, where he married and remained employed until the early 1970s, when he became a pub landlord at Rodborough, near Stroud, Gloucestershire. While David always remained dapper and punctilious, it was evident that he was drinking the profits, and this resulted in his wife leaving him and taking their daughter with her to Australia. He never got over this. He left the pub business and retired to Gloucester, where he had a neat housing association apartment in Westgate Street.

David had a strong work ethic, but his leisure time would be in the social club or a town pub, smoking a cigar and drinking a pint, followed by a couple of shorts. There had been an occasion when an old Jamaican couple, who were clients of mine, decided to sell a house they owned and retire in Montego Bay. At the conclusion of the matter, they presented me with a bottle of clear, un-proofed Jamaican Rum. I tried a sip on the end of my tongue and decided to put the bottle away in an office cupboard. David obviously soon discovered this and knew I was not going to drink it and so summarily polished the bottle off. When I arrived for work the following day, he was at his desk dapper, prim and proper and apologetic, functioning. I said no more about it.

With his earnings from working for me, he decided to fly out to Australia to see if there was any way he could repair and rekindle his relationship with his ex-wife. I drove him to Heathrow in 1996 and with great excitement and some trepidation, he few off Down Under. When I collected him a couple of weeks later, he was a dejected man. Apparently, he had put on his best suit and guard's tie, ironed his shirt and bought a bunch of flowers. He walked up to the door of his ex's home and rang the doorbell and waited. And waited. Eventually, his wife opened the door. After so many years he of course instantly recognised her. He smiled and doffed his hat. But she stared blankly back at him and at first pretended not to know who he was. After a moment, a man arrived behind her and following an embarrassing interval, David turned and walked away about fifty metres, before deciding that as he had travelled so far, he could not leave the situation as it was. He walked back and rang the doorbell again. This time he did have a response and she politely explained to him that her life had moved on and it would not be possible to invite him in.

At the end of the West case, I needed to reorganise my business and there was no longer scope for David. He was disappointed when the job ended. He died in 2003. He had been in hospital. No one had visited him. I was contacted as his 'next of kin'. I contacted the Royal British Legion, who arranged someone to attend the council funeral at the crematorium, Coney Hill in Gloucester. Only my wife, myself, a member of Stroud District Council and a dour member of the RBL were present. At least someone knew who he was. At least someone knew he had died. At least he had lived a long life. At least his passing was marked with the dignity of a Christian ceremony, however brief and basic.

At lunchtime on 26th February 1994, I returned to my office after attending court. My secretary had apparently been trying to contact me. A call had come in from Cheltenham police station custody suite. My client Rose West was being detained there on suspicion of the murder of her eldest daughter Heather.

This was a bombshell. At the time it was completely unexpected. Such a prospect had never been on my radar. After all, Rose had given an account of how Heather had left home all those years earlier. I anticipated a plausible explanation whereby the whole matter would be cleared up.

Unknown to me, there was already in hand a large-scale police operation. A search warrant had been sought from and granted by Gloucester Magistrates' the day before, enabling police scenes of crime officers (SOCO) to search 25 Cromwell Street and begin to excavate the back garden. Interviewing officers had already attended upon Fred and Rose at their home to conduct informal interviews without placing them under arrest. This initial gentle nudge was the first twist of a screw that would resolutely and irreversibly keep turning for the next two years.

When I arrived at Cheltenham Police Station and was shown into the cell where Rose was being held, it was immediately evident that she was extremely distraught. If I was to select two occasions in the twelve years that I acted for her when I considered her to be inconsolable, at her most distressed and tearful, without any kind of pretence, then this was one of them; the other was twenty-two months later, in the cells at Winchester Crown Court after she had just been found guilty of murdering ten young women. Notably, informing her that Fred West had committed suicide on January 1st 1995 was not.

I recall trying to comfort her by saying that her arrest must be a terrible mistake, but that I would need to obtain her instructions and remind her of her strict legal rights, in particular her right not to answer questions Rose remained withdrawn, with her head buried in her folded arms. She was whimpering and generally incoherent. There were moments when she lifted her red, flushed and tearful face to utter a recurring sobbing theme of: "That fuckin' Fred West, if he had done anything, what had he done, what he had done, what he had put them all through?"

20

This hardly amounted to constructive instructions. Eventually, her composure improved and after about an hour and half, she had her first interview. As far as Rose was concerned, it was like she had told the police before: Heather was a difficult child; she was a lesbian in a time that didn't accept that, she was a risk to the other children, she had tried to trap their fingers in the door and had threatened to give Barry drugs. When Heather said she was leaving to work at a holiday camp, Rose thought it was a good thing too, but like a good mother made sure she had some money to take with her.

The weekend interviews, court and custody suite attendances of the weekend of the 25th, 26th and 27th were gruelling. Psychologically and intellectually I was confronted with a brief of dramatically escalating terms of reference, where one day the advice relates to proximity to murder of the client's daughter and the next day a picture emerges of something unimaginably worse.

On Saturday evening on February 26th it was evident that the normal twenty-four-hour custody period permissible for detaining suspects would run out before interviewing was concluded. The police therefore made an application to Gloucester magistrates' court for an extension in accordance with the procedure provided by the Police and Criminal Evidence Act (1984). Given that Fred West had already admitted to three murders, his solicitor did not oppose the application. However, on behalf of Rose I did oppose the application, but the magistrates determined that the case for a further thirty-six hours detention was justified, if required. It would be necessary for the police to reach some decision within that period, because without further application Rose would have to be either charged or released, with or without bail, depending on how much of the custody clock remained available.

Night time courts are strange places, reconvened after the day's list, their ambience of silent waiting rooms and empty hallways, yet faintly echoing the frantic business of the day. At night time adversaries are curiously well-disposed to each other and the justices appear more patient and courteous. There was, however, only ever going to be one outcome; even so, the law is clear that beyond these time limits the detainee must be released. Detention of any kind is oppressive and where someone has not yet been charged with any offence it would be contrary to all basic notions of justice and could amount to false imprisonment.

By the Sunday afternoon, Rose had made no admissions, whereas Fred admitted to the killing and implicated himself in others, expressly exonerating Rose from being complicit. While there was no reason for the police to delay charging Fred, they were obliged to bail Rose.

Initially she was bailed back to 25 Cromwell Street, provided her older children Mae and Stephen resided with her as a safeguarding issue. Shortly after this, the police realised the significance of the address as the crime scene of a major inquiry and Rose was required to vacate the property; she was placed in a safe house.

I recall at the time Rose was bailed, Superintendent John Bennett collared me for one of his lengthy, cosy chats. We were standing in the subdued evening light of the main foyer at Gloucester Central Police Station. I remember him holding his arm out to the wall and emphasising to me that he had absolutely no doubt that Fred and Rose West were as close as the paintwork was to the plaster. He also intimated that the bail date of April 21st was a long stop date and that, if required, she would be rearrested well before then.

With hindsight, as he was about to seek the Chief Constable's approval to instigate a covert surveillance operation at a safe house involving bugging, I do wonder whether the police could have tried harder to detain Rose for a longer period of time. The installation of bugging devices, had they reaped any meaningful evidence, would have been controversial even with the approval of the Home Secretary.

In law, the trial process commences with arrest. The proceedings are said to be 'active'. From that time, any information generated by the investigation is strictly sub judice, whereby it is protected from disclosure and gratuitous public discussion. This is essential if a defendant is to get a fair trial. In a high-profile case, the sub judice rule is constantly challenged by the need in an open democracy to respect public interest and the powerful 'fourth estate', as the media has been called, in pursuing its perceived role to get the story out there. The tabloids were full of salacious headlines with colour pictures of witnesses. This clearly risked jeopardising the integrity of the proceedings and compromising the accused's right to a fair trial.

It is the job of the Attorney General, as the government's chief law officer, to intervene when necessary to protect proceedings by seeking injunctions through the High Court. The Attorney General's office can act on its own volition, but often it will respond to matters reported to it, which are then reviewed before injunction proceedings are commenced. I found myself frequently having to contact the Attorney General's Office with complaints of published material that the defence team clearly believed undermined Rose's right to a fair trial.

This right is an obvious self-explanatory common law right. It is also guaranteed by the European Convention on Human Rights which includes:

- Article 6(1) In the determination of… civil rights and obligations or of any criminal charge… everyone is entitled to a fair and public hearing within a reasonable time by an independent and impartial tribunal established by law. Judgment shall be pronounced publicly but the press and public may be excluded from all or part of the trial in the interest of morals, public order... or the extent strictly necessary in the opinion of the court in special circumstances where publicity would prejudice the interests of justice.

- 6(2) 'Everyone charged with a criminal offence shall be presumed innocent until proven guilty according to law.'

The Attorney General's interventions are invariably made pursuant to the Contempt of Court Act 1981 which I found was the most effective means of safeguard, surprisingly more so than the case law and jurisprudence that had evolved in the European Court of Human Rights. It states, among other things, as follows:

- In this Act '...the strict liability rule' means the rule of law whereby conduct may be treated as a contempt of court as tending to interfere with the course of justice in particular legal proceedings regardless of intent to do so.
- The strict liability rule applies only to publications, and for this purpose the publication includes any speech, writing (programme included in a cable programme service) or other communication in whatever form, which is addressed to the public at large or any section of the public. Strict liability applies only to a publication which creates a substantial risk that the course of justice in the proceedings in question will be seriously impeded or prejudiced. The strict liability applies to a publication only if the proceedings

in question are active within the meaning of this section at the time of publication. Schedule 1(4) specifies proceedings to be active from the date of arrest without warrant.

If matters were already in the public domain, the injunction would be futile. Protecting the proceedings felt like walking on quicksand. I responded by proactively stating Rose West's innocence. It would mean that the sub judice rule designed to protect the defendant seemed unable to quell the open season on Rose in the press scrum and so long as she remained silent, it could have the effect of working against her.

There was a toxic, insatiable mix of deviant sadomasochistic sex, child abuse, threesomes, prostitution, abduction, torture and murder all inextricably mixed and emanating from the parents of an ostensibly ordinary, functioning nuclear family. The deceptive illusion Fred and Rose West had created as the smokescreen for their deeply warped and dysfunctional life was irresistible for the tabloids. The unremitting onslaught of prurient and salacious reporting feeding the public appetite for gruesome details not only, in my view, undermined the trial process, it also reflected something in society, in the collective psyche, that I remember at the time felt was disturbing. I would look out from my office window or walk through town and see the crowds and the television crews setting up their antenna systems in the Cromwell Street area. At times, helicopters hovered overhead. When the emerging investigation took some new twist, I would awake in the morning to find reporters camped outside my front door. It was a sense of 'this is where it is at'. This is what everybody could not get enough of. And I would think, why? It is all so bloody awful; why is this not happening as some subdued dignified thorough process of determination, bringing to account, but most of all having sympathy and remembrance of the victims? And yet my overriding professional duty was fairly and squarely to defend Rose West. And if I was to remain her solicitor, I reminded myself that that was what I should keep firmly in my mind.

There was always the prospect of abuse of process applications that can be made at any stage of the proceedings.

Various counsel came and went both from the prosecution and the defence. The shifting briefs occurred with the prosecution as Neil Butterfield QC withdrew following his appointment to the High Court. His junior Andrew Chubb was then led by Brian Leveson QC, who had recently had an unsuccessful outcome before the jury in Liverpool when Ken Dodd was acquitted on charges of tax evasion.

On the respective defence teams, Howard Ogden originally instructed Charles Barton QC as leading counsel and Martin Steen as junior from Albion Chambers in Bristol. For Rose, I initially instructed Christopher Wilson-Smith QC as leading counsel and Neil Ford as junior, also of Albion Chambers. For a time, I also retained Brendan Shiner, an old barrister practising from Queens Square Chambers in Bristol, specifically to assist with attendance at police interviews with Rose West.

Howard Ogden found himself in a compromised position, following his former client and then clerk Scott Canavan offering the Fred West interviews for sale to the press for £100,000. Ogden himself had been coaxed into a book deal following Fred's grisly admissions and his client had signed an authority for Ogden to do a deal. The hapless sole practitioner then had the Law Society come down on him like a ton of bricks. In the unreality of the media hype Howard Ogden was for a moment drawn in and lost the professional compass to carry on with the case preparation. He did not go looking for a book deal but had journalists telephoning and knocking on his door every hour of the day helping him to deconstruct and reinterpret how he might progress the situation. I think he allowed himself to be exploited. He did tell me that he became convinced by the assurances given to him by a crime writer.

In any event the debacle necessitated Ogden's departure and Fred West changed his solicitor. Tony Miles of Bobbetts McCann took over and appointed Michael Ogden QC as leading counsel with Martin Picton as his junior.

With the inescapable glare of national and international publicity, I felt the pressure to ensure that Rose had and was seen to have the best representation available. With hindsight, after over thirty-five years as a practising solicitor, I have no doubt of the comparable quality and competence of barristers practising from provincial chambers. As a local sole practitioner, I was probably drawn to the value of having on board players with kudos and a track record in handling major cases in the London criminal courts. I was so steered after consultation with a number of professionals. For this reason, my initial enquiry in April 1994 was to the chambers of George Carmen QC. I was advised that he would very much like to take the case, but because of other cases he was involved in, he would be unable to travel to HMP Pucklechurch to meet and speak to Rose until August. The pressure for hard work and active defence meant hitting the ground running and such a wait would be unacceptable, not least for Rose. She needed to know who her leading counsel was going to be; who it was who would be presenting her defence in court.

And so after a number of enquiries, I was put in touch with Patrick Duane, who was the chambers clerk to Richard Ferguson QC at 1 Crown Office Row, Temple Bar. At this time, Patrick also recommended an up-and-coming junior in the same set called Sasha Wass, whom he confirmed Ferguson would have every confidence in having on board. I accepted his advice and agreed that this would facilitate communication and co-operation.

Richard Ferguson had a track record at least as illustrious as George Carmen. He was a charismatic Ulsterman with a smooth

Irish lilt. His practice was forged in the uncompromising arena of Belfast during the troubles. His father had been a police sergeant in the Ulster constabulary. He was brought up a Methodist and studied at Trinity College Dublin. He had a great love of Irish literature. His strong principles as a lawyer placed his duty to his client above any question of religion or political views. While he was Protestant, who had been brought up a Methodist and had been a member of an Orange Lodge as well – for a while, an MP in the DUP – he also unusually had the trust of Republicans as well as Unionists. Over time this would prove to be a volatile and unsustainable position.

He left the Orange Lodge and removed himself from the frontline of politics. But the invidious cloud of rumour made life precarious and placed an enormous strain on his marriage, which eventually collapsed after his house was firebombed in an act of sectarian hatred. By this time, Dick had taken silk in Northern Ireland, but by 1972 life was too dangerous for him to continue to practise in the Province and he relocated to London with his new wife. He had to start again as a junior counsel in criminal courts of England. In 1984 the IRA planted a bomb at the hotel where the Conservative Party Conference was taking place in Brighton. While Margaret Thatcher survived unscathed, the bomb did terrible damage and caused a number of fatalities and serious injury to a number of senior Tories. Dick received the brief to act on behalf of two suspectd terrortsts.

By 1986, Richard Ferguson had taken silk in London and was building a considerable reputation.

Like all top silks, he had a sense of the theatrical and knew where his audience was with the jury and how to perform for the greatest impact. It was instructive how in a matter of such dreadful enormity, he was able to accurately assess and respond to the general scheme of public interest.

Prior to committal, while he was content to agree to judicial review of the prosecution's attempt to accelerate the matter by preferring a voluntary bill of indictment, at the same time he assured me that the old-style committal would make no difference and the case was irresistibly heading for trial in the Crown Court. At old-style committals, which are now a thing of the past in the British justice system, it was required for the Crown to show that they had a prima facie case, that is, it had to satisfy examining magistrates that there was sufficient evidence to provide a reasonable prospect of conviction. Often counsel would advise against an old-style committal because it provided an opportunity to test witnesses.

In any event the Chief Metropolitan Stipendiary Magistrate, Peter Badge, was appointed to hear the committal. He was a dour, slim, unemotional man, grey with a calm authority. Sasha Wass told me that his favourite pastime outside of the law was making and sailing coracles, which for the uninitiated, are circular boats made of split and interwoven willow rods used through the ages on rivers in the Celtic fringes of the British Isles. There are similar flimsy vessels in Asia. The argument goes that by binding sufficient willow together, the boat becomes watertight. This of course echoes the prosecution case for similar fact evidence.

Mr Badge sat at Dursley courthouse, Gloucestershire to hear the committal between February 6th and 14th 1995.

Dursley is a scenic little town located south of Gloucester and about fifteen miles from Bristol. The court is attached to the police station next to Rednock School. While there is only one courtroom, it is surprisingly spacious and well-designed. On account of it being less of problem to reschedule routine business at Dursley than at Gloucester or Cheltenham and the facilities and parking area being regarded as adequate, it was determined as a suitable venue for the committal hearing.

The hearing opened with an application by Sasha Wass, counsel for the defence, to stay the proceedings on the basis of abuse of process. The arguments she put forward in support were several and dealt with the lapse of time in bringing proceedings, loss of written evidence and prejudicial publicity.

Neil Butterfield QC and Andrew Chubb presented the prosecution evidence. There was no desire to rehearse witnesses and cross-examining them would only serve to steal the thunder and impact of the counsel's presentation at trial. The mass of media interest continued when the world's press descended on the little Gloucestershire market town with outside broadcast vehicles, satellite dishes and radar scanners parked in the adjoining farmer's field. As the prison wagon carrying Rose West arrived from Pucklechurch, sixth formers from the adjoining school, as well as many locals from the town lined the court entrance road. At one point, the prison vehicle was splattered with eggs. I later heard that a journalist from a tabloid had provided the school students with the eggs and arranged the staging of the demonstration as a way of ensuring some value was added to his story.

At the end of the hearing, the stipendiary magistrate decided that he had heard sufficient evidence from the prosecution to commit the case to Winchester Crown Court for trial. Rose West was remanded into custody for arraignment and eventual trial.

The high-profile spectacle that descended on Dursley marked a closing chapter for Dursley Magistrates' Court. Shortly thereafter, with review and rationalisation by both the Ministry of Justice and Gloucestershire Constabulary, firstly, Dursley police station ceased to be a twenty-four-hour station, which meant that suspects would no longer be detained there, even though it had a more than adequate custody suite and then secondly, the courthouse itself was moth-balled with the result that in the last couple of decades no case has been heard there. The situation in 2019 is that the only magistrates' court venue in Gloucestershire is at Cheltenham.

On May 12th 1995, the plea and directions hearing for Rose West took place at Winchester before the appointed trial judge, Mr Justice Mantell. The judge was a large man with slightly wavy white hair and glasses. His complexion had a ruddy hue. He had, as might be expected from a senior member of judiciary, a studied posture of impartiality, and was astute and cautious in his choice of words. When he spoke, his vowels rolled and echoed richly in the chamber of his vocal chords. I heard that he had been appointed senior presiding judge on the Western circuit after a distinguished career on the northern circuit. Apparently, he had gone to the Bar after University in Manchester, followed by national service where he was commissioned as an officer in the educational branch of the RAF.

At the arraignment, fourteen counts on the indictment were put to Rose West and she duly pleaded not guilty to all matters. In addition to the ten counts of murder, there were four counts of rape.

The counts were that Rose West did commit murder between dates ranging from 1971 to 1994.

Murder is a common law offence stated to be constituted where a person of sound mind and discretion unlawfully kills a reasonable creature in being and under the Queen's peace with intent to kill or commit grievous bodily harm with death resulting within a year and a day (prior to 1996).

A further hearing was held at Winchester Crown Court on July 7th before the trial judge to consider the defence application; firstly for severance of the four counts of rape on the indictment on the basis that these would unnecessarily confuse and add to the risk of prejudice as the jury had to consider the evidence relating to the murder charges. The judge agreed that there should be severance.

At this time, consideration of an abuse of process argument founded on delay, press intrusion of prejudicial tabloid headlines, witnesses selling stories and the quality of witness statements on matters from so many years ago, tainted by cross contamination and suggestion. While the judge acknowledged that the situation was far from ideal, he concluded that he would nevertheless be possible to conduct a fair trial and that he would ensure the clearest possible direction be given to the jury. In any event, it would always be possible to refresh such an application at any stage of the proceedings as further unfair interference occurred. He also made it clear that ten girls had been murdered and that it would be unthinkable to stop the trial.

I recall Dick Ferguson assuring me on more than one occasion that this case was not going to go away, that the trial and any subsequent appeal would not be the end. Other lawyers would take up the cudgels, fresh evidence would come to light, points of law and fact would need to be revisited, new witnesses would be found. No doubt his experience as counsel for the Birmingham Six had tempered his intuition. Twenty-five years later, it is apparent that his instinct was wrong. But then times have changed and legal aid become increasingly curtailed. It is no longer possible for solicitors to routinely apply, even in serious cases, to get two legal aid certificates, one for leading counsel and one for a junior, let alone apply for a certificate for replacement counsel, where for whatever reason counsel handed the initial brief then hands over to someone else.

Notwithstanding his confidence and easy manner before any court in the land, there was, thankfully, a human fallibility about Dick Ferguson. He reminded me that it was about giving the case your best shot, and not taking things for granted. Overconfidence at the Bar, I suspect, can very rapidly turn victory into defeat. At the trial, it was impressive to observe first-hand the quality of his cross-examination.

He would remind us of the time he needed to read the brief and would waive the two essential evidence files and say this was what he needed to know. The other 146 files of taped interviews and further file of unused statements were for myself and Sasha to peruse and flag up anything useful. When Dick and Sasha travelled up to HMP Durham in the months of pre-trial preparation to meet and discuss the case with the client, we would lunch in a local pub before wandering up to the prison. He would have with him a slim volume of literary work as a pleasant distraction from business. At the time, he was in the process of being nominated to membership of the Garrick Club.

When it was decided, after some debate, to play the tapes of Fred West admitting his guilt and exonerating Rose, I think Dick was acutely aware of the impact and courtroom drama that would result, as indeed it did. Extracts of these tapes were played on a Friday afternoon and probably represented the high point of the defence case. We all, however, knew there was nothing to get cheerful about, because by playing the tapes we were inviting the prosecution to respond with extracts of other later taped interviews where, after he had changed his solicitor, Fred fairly and squarely placed the blame for most of the killings on Rose. All he did was cut the dead bodies up and bury them. While reminding Rose that she did not have to give evidence if she did not want to, in deciding tactics, Dick was quick to point out that without Rose West getting in the witness box and without the defence playing the Fred West tapes, there was precious little for the defence to actively rely on. The rest of the case was about undermining the prosecution's similar fact evidence and demonstrating to the jury that most of the key witnesses had sold stories to the press and were inherently unreliable.

4.

SIMILAR FACT EVIDENCE

The West trial turned on the admissibility of similar fact evidence.

Criminal law is administered on the basis of a presumption of innocence. The rules of evidence evolved to be sensitive to this sacrosanct principle and in so doing would not permit the admissibility of facts that were highly prejudicial to the defendant yet did not specifically prove commission of the offence in question; for example where the prejudicial facts related to an entirely separate incident, time, place or victim (Lord Herschell in Makin v Attorney General for New South Wales, 1894 (AC 57, 65)).

The probative power of similar fact evidence is illustrated in two old cases.

In Makin, a husband and wife were accused of murdering a baby they had fostered. The prosecution offered evidence of a number of other murders that they had committed on account of the bodies of twelve other fostered babies buried in the gardens of houses previously owned by the defendants.

This similar fact evidence was allowed because of the improbability of any other explanation for the presence of the multiple bodies.

In the 'brides in the bath' case, R v Smith, 1915 (11 Cr App R, 229), the accused was indicted of one count of murder. The prosecution sought the admission of evidence that two previous women had similarly gone through a marriage ceremony with him and had then made financial arrangements with the defendant as beneficiary and then drowned in the bath. The improbability that these three separate incidents could all be accidents meant that the evidence was admissible. The strikingly similar facts could have no other rational explanation and it was therefore just that it should be admitted.

Judgments of the House of Lords (now known as the Supreme Court) and Appeal Court have refined and verified the requirements as to when this similar fact evidence can be admitted in a criminal trial.

In the leading case of DPP v Boardman, 1975 (AC 457) the general principle was cautious, requiring the weighing of the probative value of the similar fact evidence against its prejudicial effect. This test in the opinion of their lordships needed to be buttressed by stressing the requirement for 'striking similarity' between the case before the court and the facts being sought to be admitted.

Even then the law lords emphasised the need for safeguards where the evidence was weak, unreliable or maybe contaminated and in such cases should be excluded. This took account of the of the risk inherent in extending the principle, as had happened in DPP v Sims (1946) where Lord Denning had ruled that previous mere allegations by a number of witnesses in addition to previous proven cases could nevertheless be admissible.

So by this judicial calculus how did the similar fact evidence in the West case shape up?

At this stage it is instructive to consider only the details of the witness statements as made to police. The surrounding circumstances that spearheaded much of the defence challenge to this testimony will be considered in the chapter dealing with the trial.

Caroline Owens

At the time of moving to 25 Cromwell Street in 1972, Fred owned a dinky beige, two-door four-seater Ford Popular motor vehicle, hardly the most prepossessing set of wheels on the road, but it was a car; it meant the freedom of the highways. Fred's ownership of a car had always been one of the boxes Fred ticked on young Rose's list of must-haves for a boyfriend. He was older, he worked, had some money, had a car, desired her sexually and offered her unbounded liberty. What more could a girl ask for?

Driving the country roads in a car was a better way of exploring places and seeing what opportunities there were to pick up young women. Fred had been at it for years, on his own, trying whatever means he could to tempt attractive-looking girls to go for a ride with him. In Fred's mind, they were all desperate for 'it' and could not wait to get their knickers off. The truth was that his deluded assessment was often appallingly wrong and resulted in numerous young women making complaints to the police. It appears that none of these were ever followed up.

And it has to be said that Fred West was far from being the only young man behind the wheel of a car or on a motorbike in the early 1970s, hoping to get lucky with some young woman he might come across. The power play between having a car and not having a car was significant. Hitchhikers were in abundance, as were people waiting for a bus. The vulnerability of young women was never considered. In the male-dominated promiscuous society of the time, such a modus operandi was commonplace and almost ritualised as part of the popular means of meeting and courtship; maybe not so different from Tinder on mobile phones today.

On an October evening in 1972, Fred and Rose had gone for a drive which had taken them to Tewkesbury. There outside a pub, Gupshill Manor, on the outskirts of the town, they saw a pretty young woman hitchhiking. The young woman was sixteen-year-old Caroline Owens, who was hitching back to her home in Cinderford after visiting her boyfriend. They offered her a lift. As it was ten-thirty at night, she was glad to get in and felt safe because there was both a man and women in the vehicle.

Fred and Rose asked what she was doing, and Caroline said she was unemployed. They offered her a job as their nanny and, observing all the formalities and pleasantries, arranged to meet her parents a few days later. They brought Anne Marie, Heather and Mae with them. Caroline thought they were cute, and all was agreed. She would share a bedroom with Anne Marie and be paid three pounds a week.

At first Caroline thrived in the free and easy atmosphere at 25 Cromwell Street. She was a young woman away from home for the first time who was sexually active; life was great. She was able to have her boyfriend come and stay once a week and when a former boyfriend turned up, Fred and Rose gave them their double bed for the night. She later recalled it being the hippie era, when people were more friendly and did as they liked. She also had sex with a couple of the other lodgers, Ben Stanniland and Dapper Davies. On the negative side she felt uneasy that there were no locks on the bathroom door and Rose had a habit of walking in whenever she was in the bath. On these occasions Rose would take the liberty of stroking Caroline's hair and making suggestive compliments. Caroline also found the perpetual arguing that seemed to go on between Fred and Rose difficult to cope with. The reason for the acrimony she could not be sure of, other than she felt that Fred was a persistent bully. So after six weeks, Caroline decided to move back in with her parents in Cinderford. Rose was not happy about this, but Fred, at least, pretended not to be concerned.

Caroline reverted to the routine of visiting her boyfriend in Tewkesbury and then hitchhiking back to Cinderford in the evening. It was on December 6th, as she was trying to flag a lift from the same spot outside Gupshill Manor, that lo and behold, a beige Ford Popular pulled up with Rose winding the window down to ask if she wanted a lift. With reluctance, Caroline agreed. She was bundled into the backseat and Rose followed and sat next to her. From the outset, Fred and Rose started talking in a smutty way and asked her if she had had sex with her boyfriend that evening. When she said no, Fred asked Rose to check and Rose immediately grabbed at Caroline's crotch over her trousers. Rose had her arm around Caroline and was trying to fondle her breasts. Fred asked, "What's her tits like?" They drove towards Gloucester and then headed out towards the Forest of Dean. Fred stopped the car and turned round and repeatedly punched Caroline in the face until she passed out. When she woke up petrified, her hands were bound behind her back and Fred was winding brown tape around her head so that she could not see and could just breathe through her nose.

On arriving at Cromwell Street, she was bundled out of the car and up to the first floor front bedroom that had a sofa and a mattress on the floor. Fred agreed to remove the tape from her mouth but cut her cheek with a knife in so doing. Fred then sat Caroline down on the sofa. Rose sat next to her and started touching her and trying to kiss her. Caroline resisted, asking her to get off and leave her alone. At this point, Fred untied her hands and went and made her a cup of tea.

When she finished her tea, the nightmare only got worse as she was stripped completely naked and again bound, blindfolded and gagged and made to lie on her back on the mattress on the floor. They then proceeded to closely examine her vagina, prodding and poking her and inserting fingers inside. Fred commented on her chubby 'lips' and advised treatment to make her clitoris more prominent. This was to be achieved by belting her between the legs with a two-inch wide leather belt with a metal buckle. Caroline recalls that Fred then hit her between the legs about ten times. When he had finished, Rose knelt down and performed oral sex on her. As she did this, Fred knelt down behind his wife and started having sexual intercourse with her.

Sex is the only pastime in which people consensually engage where the great enjoyment and fun of the moment does not give rise to laughter. Here, Rose, while Fred was penetrating her from behind, was grinning and laughing in Caroline's face as she licked her vagina. It does provide evidence of Rose's 'fun' being in the abusive performance rather than in the ecstasy of the sex, certainly with Fred.

As for Fred, the self-confessed semi-impotent, premature ejaculator, if what Caroline Owens recalled was correct, then he was humping his missus from behind for ten to fifteen minutes and then straightaway, when Rose briefly left the room, was again erect and sexually charged enough to rape the hapless young woman on the mattress, who recalled him ejaculating after about a minute of intercourse. She later described the event as 'a dabble'. This may suggest that he had not ejaculated at all while coupled to his wife from the rear. If he had, from a physiological perspective he would have lasted a lot longer before ejaculating again as described by Caroline.

What does this tell us, bearing in mind that in 1972 Fred and Rose were at the height of their depraved potency? She was nineteen and he was twenty-nine years old. Well, it tends to support the fact that whatever Fred and Rose had in common, it was not great sex. It also demonstrates that Fred liked his women bound and trussed, if he was to have an orgasm.

Caroline then recalled Fred getting tearful and apologising. Rose then returned to the room and Fred nodded off to sleep next to the still-bound hostage on the sofa. Caroline could not sleep and made a tentative move to escape but was unable to open the window and so spent the rest of the night awake next to her attacker. At seven the next morning, someone came to the door and Fred got up and went downstairs at which point Caroline started making a noise to draw attention to her plight, but Rose stifled this by sitting on her head on a cushion. When Fred came back, they were both angry. Fred said he would keep her in the cellar and let his 'black friends' use her, and when they were finished, he would bury her under the streets of Gloucester. He told her hundreds of girls were buried there.

However, ludicrously, Fred West then offered Caroline her old job back as though nothing untoward had happened. She managed to control her utter disgust and in survival mode agreed to the proposal, as she realised it would give her time to form a plan of escape.

When Rose left the room to see the children, Fred again raped Caroline before again crying and apologising and asking her not to tell Rose, as the whole point of her being there was for Rose's enjoyment.

This pathetically contrived little scenario, with crocodile tears and all, was a curious attempt by Fred to justify the serious offence he had just committed. It was the most bizarre self-serving mitigation or, in his mind, even a defence exonerating himself. It was of the same category of playacting that he employed years earlier as a teenager in Much Marcle, when he would force himself on a girl, have his way and then apologise, telling the young woman that he had had a blackout and did not know what he had done; asserting some involuntary act in absolution. It also indicates that he knew he had done something very wrong, that he fully understood right from wrong and was aware of the boundaries of reasonable conduct, even if he merely played lip service to them and was free to break the rules at will.

Caroline told Fred that she would need to collect some things from Cinderford. Fred then told her to have a bath. Rose then brought the children upstairs and Caroline helped tidy the house before Rose said she was going to the laundrette and needed some help. Caroline went with her, when by chance, Ben Stanniland walked into the laundrette and Rose started chatting to him, Caroline made her escape, eventually making her way back to Cinderford. The following day after composing herself, though still battered and bruised, she told her mother and stepfather what had happened and the police were called.

Fred and Rose were arrested on December 9th 1972 on suspicion of the rape and abduction of Caroline Owens. The Wests tried to fob the matter off as kinky consensual sex. This was, after all, the 1970s and anything went. The police viewed Caroline as in some way complicit because she had slept with a couple of the other lodgers. She dreaded being cross-examined in court and accused of being a slut. It would have been too embarrassing for both her and her family. Eventually, Fred and Rose were charged with summary offences of indecent assault and assault, occasioning actual bodily harm and a rape charge was not preferred. They appeared at Gloucester Magistrates' in January 1973 and after mitigation, where the bench was told that Fred and Rose were a happily married couple with three children and that Rose was pregnant. With Fred smiling obsequiously with cap in hand, they were each fined twenty-five pounds.

MISS A

Miss A was from a broken home. Her mother resided in Tewkesbury. She had been abused by her father and her brother; at the age of thirteen, she had been placed in care at Russet House in Gloucester. When she reached the age of fifteen years, she was placed at Jordan's Brook House. This establishment was for wayward teenage girls who had been expelled or absconded from other homes. The regime there, while constructive and working in the best interests of the children, inevitably placed restrictions on liberty. Privileges had to be earned and the girls were not routinely free to come and go as they wished. Many would abscond to chance their luck, maybe meet a boy in a car cruising the surrounding lanes. Miss A had initially become acquainted with Cromwell Street while at Russet House, and for a short time in 1975 after absconding, she lived in a flat in Cheltenham with Rose West's younger brother Graham. She later denied making the connection between Graham and Rose, but this seems fanciful.

Rose and Fred gained a reputation for offering a safe haven with tea and sympathy – more usually described as orange juice, biscuits and a place to stay – among the wayward girls from Jordan's Brook. Miss A regularly visited during 1976. Rose was usually on hand to offer an understanding shoulder to lean on, as she would always explain that she too had spent time in care as a teenager. And then on one visit, Rose put her arm around Miss A and began trying to fondle her breasts and kiss her. Miss A was confused and embarrassed and wriggled away. She slept at Cromwell Street that night, then returned to Jordan's Brook the following day and decided for the next month or so to avoid visiting the Wests.

However, rather foolishly, when Miss A next earned the privilege of a home visit away from Jordan's Brook, it was to

Cromwell Street she ventured again. When she arrived in the evening, Rose answered the door in a see-through blouse. She was shown into the lounge where she would sleep. Rose came in and also slept in the lounge. At some point, Miss A got up to use the toilet; Rose followed her and she could hear Rose calling out to Fred. When she left the bathroom, Rose jostled her forcefully into another room, she was cajoling Miss A and urging her that it was all right to touch each other and display affection. Rose had progressed rapidly from friendly girlie mate to close physical contact, hugging, caressing, kissing and then scratching at Miss A's breasts in an aggressive and uncomfortable manner, and all the while imploring Miss A to enjoy it; that it was all right to do whatever you like.

In the room, Miss A saw two other girls naked: one on the floor and the other on a bed.

One was fair and looked about fourteen years old. The other girl had a darker complexion and looked slightly older. Fred was also in the room, still dressed at this time. Rose then started stripping Miss A's clothes off her until she was completely naked. Rose then did a striptease for Fred's titillation. Rose then got on the bed where one of the girl's was sitting. Fred then bound the girl's wrists and Rose turned her onto her stomach; with her legs splayed open, each ankle was tightly bound with the adhesive tape. Miss A then observed Fred and Rose kissing. Rose picked up a vibrator and a candle, together with a tube of lubricant. She then inserted the vibrator into the girl's anus, at which the helpless victim screeched. Rose then took Fred's clothes off him; he bent down and kissed the girl's anus before then pulling her bottom up and entering her from behind. Rose knelt behind Fred, stroking his backside. When Fred ejaculated, Rose asked him if he enjoyed it. She then ripped the tape off the girl, who sat in total despair, sucking her hair.

It was now Miss A's turn. She sat on the bed, self-conscious and humiliated; Rose had continued with the threatening entreaties to touch, feel and enjoy as she stroked and caressed Miss A's body. Rose then bound Miss A's wrists together with masking tape and then bound her ankles with tape, as had occurred to the preceding victim.

Miss A heard a buzzing sound as a vibrator entered her vagina. She could then feel smooth female hands and then scratchy nails inside her vagina. She then felt the pain of a candle being inserted into her back passage. This was followed by Fred West raping her. All the while Rose and Fred kept up a dialogue with Rose asking Fred if he was enjoying himself and she smiled in a maniacal way saying what fun it all was. Fred was giving a commentary on his progress with up to date reports on whether he was about to ejaculate. Rose reminded him to withdraw when he came, which after a short while he did over Miss A's back. Rose then brusquely cut the tape from Miss A's hands and ankles.

It is this evidence that provides signification of the respective mindsets of Fred and Rose, with the roleplaying more by Rose than by Fred. Fred was the architect of the situation, like the moronic contrived plot of a cheap pornographic movie to satisfy his distorted lust. Rose was his sergeant at arms, *aide-de-camp*, the able assistant, facilitator. She was the custodian of the vibrators, dildos and tubes of lubricant. She was parading around, cruelly grabbing and molesting young women, scratching their breasts, fingering their vaginas with sharp fingernails and all the while she laughed and played with a gormless grin stretched across her face. And her actions were punctuated by frequent deferrals to Fred to ask if he was enjoying himself and asking him when he was going to ejaculate. Whatever else may be gleaned, he sure was not turning Rose on. She was speaking from a script, she was doing Fred's bidding, yet it was evident that in this role she was crueller than she needed to be. In perusing this evidence, it is difficult to perceive her as sexually stimulated by what she was doing. Rose's reality was that from a very young age she obtained approval from her father by doing his bidding and performing by laughing and playing as she masturbated him and then had full sex with him, something she continued to do with Fred's approval even after she was married. The cruelty and the unbridled sadism emanated from an open valve of seething anger; the symptom of the repressed pain consequent upon the destruction of innocence in the disguise of parental love and affection. The role of the mean, vile beast was not difficult for her. She had watched her father at close quarters all her life.

ANNE MARIE DAVIS

Anne Marie made her first statement in August 1992 in relation to allegations against Fred and Rose of the rape and buggery of their thirteen-year-old daughter, Louise. By the time of Rose's trial for murder in October 1995, she had made twenty more statements, many of them more than a dozen pages in length. Her testimony spanned the full experience of her life growing up in the West household with intricate details of the manner of her abuse at the hands of her father and stepmother.

Rose consistently denied each and every allegation made by Anne Marie. It was essential ground I had to cover with my client and often Rose would become agitated and emotional in expressing her disgust at the way Anne Marie had behaved and the way, after all they had done for her, that she had treated them. More so than any of her half-siblings, the lines were drawn for a battle. None of the other children wished to give evidence against their mother. They had all walked away from the 1993 abuse trial, causing it to collapse and apparently had no wish to testify at the 1995 trial. There was much that Mae and Stephen, and the younger ones for that matter, could have said, but in cold legal logic it would only have added texture by illustrating incidents of violence and sexual abuse. It did not go to the central plank of system, of similar fact, of a tell-tale recurring modus operandi that was sufficiently resonant in its character to validate in the minds of the jury the prosecution's theory of how the victims met their deaths.

After Fred West hanged himself on New Year's Day 1995 the DPP, Barbara Mills, reviewed the evidence before deciding to charge Rose West with an additional murder count relating to Charmaine. It was at this time that the DPP also decided that three counts relating to rape of the other West children, which Rose had been jointly charged along with a number of older West Indian men from the neighbourhood would be dropped. Anne Marie was the principal victim of these rapes.

Those proceedings were formally discontinued at the committal proceedings at Dursley Magistrates' Court during the second week of February 1995. In acceding to the application by leading counsel for the Crown, Neil Butterfield QC, that the counts remain on the file, the presiding stipendiary magistrate, Mr Peter Badge, then upon hearing from Conrad Sheward, solicitor for one of the Jamaican defendants, known by the *nom de plume*, 'Suncu', a defence costs order was made. There is perhaps some irony that Sheward was the solicitor who had acted for Fred and Rose West way back in the summer of 1972 when they pleaded guilty summarily at Gloucester Magistrates' to sexual assault and actual bodily harm on Caroline Owens.

A charge of rape of the West children, some as young as eight years old, would nevertheless be preferred against Fred's brother John West. As it turned out, he also chose to hang himself rather than face justice.

As Rose had so vehemently denied everything that Anne Marie was alleging, I obtained legal aid for an expert to assess whether there was any element of false memory. I travelled up to the Institute of Psychiatry on Denmark Hill, opposite to King's College Hospital in South West London. Dr Gísli Gudjónsson had already had an opportunity to peruse the statements and assured me with a certainty beyond doubt that there was no false memory, that what was contained in the statements was clear with precise dates and places and was consistent over time in describing the method of abuse. Also, as I already realised, the tone had been set in Anne Marie's first statement, long before the hue and cry of the media scrum had started. They lent credibility to all the broadly consistent succeeding statements. There could be no realistic accusation of contamination by other stories or financial incentive to embellish.

After the trial, there was a complete volte-face by Rose in relation to Anne Marie. Somehow, and I do not know how, they were for a time reconciled. Rose calmly said to me on a visit to HMP Durham, "Yeah, well, all that stuff about Anne Marie, what she was saying was true, all that did happen."

At this point in time, no one in the world would have doubted what Anne Marie had said. What was significant was Rose admitting to the truth of Anne Marie's evidence, evidence that she had received as written depositions, evidence I had spent hours reading through to her, evidence of facts, incidents and allegations that collectively made a hugely damning indictment.

By that simple admission, Rose was admitting to being a cruel, sadistic paedophile. She was admitting to forcing a twelve-year-old girl to prostitute herself in threesomes with much older men; she was admitting to driving out with Fred in his van to abduct, beat, gag, bind and sexually abuse. She was admitting to a ferocious temper; she was admitting to not thinking anything about picking up a knife to uncontrollably stab anyone (including Fred) who might get her riled.

While Anne Marie had not falsely remembered things that did not happen, I am quite certain that there are many things that did happen and that she did witness but does not remember, particularly when she was very young. This is a well-known coping mechanism. It is not deliberate. It is not her fault.

At the age of eight, she recalls arriving home from school to discover that Charmaine had gone. There must have been some antecedent narrative for Rose to decide to keep the little girl off from school, if that is what happened. In March 1971, Rose had taken Charmaine to the hospital with a puncture wound to her foot, probably caused by a knife. In the following months, what greater harm may have befallen her that kept her off school, and yet was not a cause for a further visit to the hospital? Whatever, sadly it would have been the last time little Charmaine was ever seen alive? What is it that Anne Marie may have blocked out?

Fred treated Anne Marie as his little wife and shared her out with his father-in-law, Bill Letts, as well his brother, John West. She was also made available to a number of West Indian men who regularly visited the house for sex, principally with Rose. They were not the only visitors to abuse Anne Marie and her sisters. In the early morning breakfast time, Fred's mates from Wingate's would turn up for a spot of breakfast before giving Fred a lift to work. While they were waiting, Fred would invite them into the children's bedroom next to the kitchen extension, where they would routinely touch the little girls intimately.

Anne Marie recalled how when she was eight years old, she was taken down into the dingy cellar of 25 Cromwell Street and raped by her parents. Fred had constructed a metal contraption on his workbench at Wingate's. It was an arch of metal about four feet long with little metal arms protruding at one end. Anne Marie was told to undress, but before she could, Rose had grabbed and ripped her garments off. She was then made to lie naked on an old mattress and her arms and legs spread and tied to the metal frame with duct-tape and pieces of cut cloth. She was gagged with tape across her mouth. Nearby was a glass bowl of water and a plastic object, which unbeknown to the innocent little girl was a dildo. As Anne Marie helplessly wriggled and wrestled in panic, Rose sat on her head so that she could hardly breathe. Rose was at the same time scratching at Anne Marie's chest. She then felt an excruciating pain as the plastic object was inserted into her vagina. She lost all sense of time but remembered seeing the water discoloured and red.

They then removed the tape and without saying a word, both left the cellar leaving her tied up. She was both petrified and relieved that the torture had ceased, but after a few minutes she heard them both returning, whereupon they repeated the dreadful abuse a second time. They then ripped the gag from her mouth and undid her bindings.

When she plaintively had protested as to why they were doing what they were, Fred said, "Shut up. It is going to help you in later life. I'm just doing what all fathers have to do. It's a normal thing, so stop carrying on. This will make sure that you get a husband when you are older. You'll be ready for him and you'll be able to have children."

This statement, although self-evidently contrived by Fred as an excuse for grotesque abuse, also has a frightening scintilla of truth in it. A researcher in psychology once suggested to me that the next time I was in a second-hand book shop to try and find an old family health manual from Edwardian times, in any event prior to the second world war. I followed this up and was amazed to find a passage about young pubescent girls. There, in clear print, was the suggestion that the father could, and often does, take a leading role, rather than the child's mother in helping explain and physically intervene with the practicalities when she starts menstruating. There followed a discussion of sanitary towels and intimate issues about the hymen and virginity. By all reasonable standards, this is outrageous, yet there was the conventional wisdom of yesteryear lending succour to the depraved obsessions of Fred and Rose West. It was one of Fred's mantras, which he asserted was handed down from his own father, that it was a father's right to take the virginity of his teenage daughters, as though it was part of the established order of things; a rite of passage.

But then I am reminded, on a tangential tack, even as recently as the early 1990s, during a debate in the House of Commons when a Tory MP got to his feet to state that in his view it was no one else's business if a man beat his wife. The entrenched powerplay of male dominance in a patriarchal society will perhaps inevitably invite abuse.

Anne Marie then described how after this she became her father's little workmate, going out in his green A47 van on his calls as a jobbing builder. He had a mattress in the back of the van and from this time he was regularly having full sexual intercourse with her. He would passionately kiss her on the lips, which she hated. She felt an impossible confusion of paternal affection, of being his daughter and also being his girlfriend, and she admitted that part of her felt that she was getting one over on her wicked stepmother.

From about the age of twelve years, she found herself groomed and cajoled to enter Rose's special room while Rose was entertaining men. These were usually Jamaican men who Fred was friendly with. Anne Marie's entrée started with Fred making her look through a peephole in the bedroom door so that she could see Rose having sex. She was then dressed up to look older and made to join in the bedroom romp, regularly having sexual intercourse with big Jamaican men, who assumed she was older.

At the age of thirteen, Anne Marie was curiously invited for a night out with her stepmother. Fred had said he did not want to go out and suggested that Anne Marie went with Rose. They got dressed up and put make-up on. Fred drove them to a pub on the outskirts of Gloucester where Rose bought Anne Marie a cherry brandy, which she did not like but was forced to drink and then another and another. Men in the bar were buying them drinks. Anne Marie soon began to feel wobbly and inebriated. At the end of the evening, she was unsteady on her feet when Rose said it was time to go. They started walking along the road when Fred arrived in his van to pick them up. Rose suddenly turned on Anne Marie and laid into her, bundled her into the back of the van, jumped in after her and continued to beat her as Fred drove off. Eventually, Fred pulled in and Anne Marie thought he would stop the assault. Instead he joined in to give his hapless a daughter a good hiding.

KATHRYN HALLIDAY

Kathryn Halliday moved to Cromwell Street in 1988. She was thirty-one years old and had weathered with the vicissitudes of life. She was divorced and had later settled into a lesbian relationship. She was now co-habiting with her partner.

She met Fred West when he was recommended as a local builder and he called round to repair a leaking ceiling. She found him helpful, friendly and engaging, someone she felt she could trust. He chatted away and while some of his banter was quite smutty, it was nothing Halliday could not handle or indeed, had not heard before. Somehow, Fred established that Halliday was a lesbian and was quick to point out that Rose was bisexual, as he said, "She likes a bit of the other." In the 1980s, gay love was still largely in the closet and it would have made Kathryn Halliday feel at ease to know that there were kindred spirits living just yards away. Fred invited her to call by to meet Rose, an offer that within a few days Halliday had taken up.

When she arrived, she was invited up to a first floor living room where Fred poured her a drink and asked her if she'd like to view a pornographic movie. He described the extensive depraved variations on offer. Halliday requested just a straight blue movie, nothing too extreme. She was not into animals, bondage or paedophilia. About ten minutes later Rose walked in wearing her signature heavy-rimmed glasses, a see-through blouse and a short miniskirt without knickers. She sat down next to Halliday, immediately cosying up as she introduced herself. Within minutes, she was kissing and fondling the visitor. Barely were the pleasantries of verbal introductions complete before Rose had taken her clothes off and was earnestly stripping her new friend naked. Fred and Rose then jostled and ushered the mesmerised Halliday to a room on the top floor and lay her down on a double bed.

Rose commenced a very physical sexual encounter, actually violent, where Halliday felt Rose was more interested in inflicting pain than sensuous pleasure. Fred, who had been filming the action, then stripped off and joined in. He turned Halliday onto her stomach and, lifting her up at the hips, had intercourse with her from behind while Rose romped next to her, continuing to fondle her intimately.

It seems there must have been some connection, because while Halliday felt that the encounter was not what she would describe as making love, she nevertheless returned again and again. Each time Rose would incrementally test Halliday's limits by going just a little further with the pain threshold, the size of the dildos being used, the sheer aggression in the act of sexual romping. Halliday realised that Rose was actually physically very strong and would often keep up a verbal tirade during what could only euphemistically be called lovemaking. Rose would screech, "What's the matter, ain't you woman enough to take it?"

Kathryn Halliday was smacked and beaten and bound tightly with nylon cord. On one occasion Fred used a belt with a buckle on her. Fred was usually present as a voyeur but rarely joined in. On the few occasions that he did, he ejaculated prematurely into Halliday, although apparently rarely penetrated Rose. Halliday recalls one occasion where he did have intercourse with Rose and finished within a minute, whereupon Rose told him he might as well not have bothered.

The escalating torment and physical intensity of this *ménage à trois* reached a new level when one evening, as the three of them lay naked on the bed, Fred got up and ushered them into another room, wherein he opened a cupboard and unpacked a case full of black rubber masks and full body suits, some of which had slits to enable breathing through the nose, others had no means of breathing at all. There was a small layer of sweat on them, indicating that they had been used.

Kathryn Halliday provided a narrative of an experienced woman who apparently was clearly tolerating, if not expressly consenting to her subjection to sexual abuse. Her account was with eyes wide open and up close and personal, unlike the accounts given by young, naïve girls who were bewildered and traumatised by the horror of the episodes they were subjected to. Their accounts echoed overwhelming anxiety and panic that they naturally felt.

For that reason, Halliday gives a valuable insight into the extent of their depraved restless sex drive.

What we do not have is Fred and Rose resting on their bed, sharing a fag with each other, asking the other how it was for them, like the essential pillow talk with a Gauloises cigarette in hand in a bad French movie.

It does seem that for Fred and Rose, any sexual pleasure in these manically severe restless romps was short-lived, rather like a crack addict who always needs another and more extreme hit to get the optimal feeling he may have experienced in the past.

The instability necessitating some constant new permutation demonstrates that both were dangerously addicted to a highly toxic repertoire.

SHARON COMPTON
THE SIMILAR FACT EVIDENCE THAT WAS NEVER HEARD

Superintendent Bennett has stated that Sharon Compton was unknown at 25 Cromwell Street and therefore her nebulous association further undermined the validity of her extensive testimony; nevertheless there is no doubt he believed in what she was saying for many months based on her initial statements. Sharon Compton was Alison Chambers' roommate at Jordan's Brook House. This is a fact verifiable by social services records. Alison Chambers certainly visited Cromwell Street, because her remains were dug up in the garden in March 1994. Objectively and with hindsight and relief at the securing of Rose West's conviction, I suspect DS Bennett would concede that whatever else he might believe about her, Sharon Compton was very much a visitor at 25 Cromwell Street.

Compton's evidence was withdrawn by the prosecution at a very late stage because of the incremental, apparently wild and florid extensions to the narrative that occurred with each statement that she made. She descended from star witness to non-person following a legal assessment of her lengthy evidence. Upon notification of the removal of her statements from the evidence pack, I recall observing Brian Leveson's demeanour at court. The assiduous and cautious silk clearly had a heavy brow and must have viewed the loss of one of the key strands binding the circumstantial rope of similar fact evidence as a serious blow to the Crown's case.

As vivid and as explicit as any of the other 'surviving' witnesses, Sharon Compton's evidence confirmed the sadistic non-consensual repertoire that the Wests subjected their victims to. However, it was when she then went on to mention other people being involved and attending violent sex parties in the basement that the Crown felt that her testimony was becoming ludicrous, dreamlike and flaky. She described some of the people present at these parties, including a man whom she described as looking like the television actor Brian Blessed, who actually had a close resemblance to John West. John West was someone who routinely visited 25 Cromwell Street, often stopping off with his crew when he was with his council dustbin lorry. John West was later charged with the rape of two of the Wests' daughters.

Of more concern, she stated that she saw a uniformed police officer at one of these sadistic sex parties. She mentioned a police inspector who was actively involved in abusing girls in the cellar. This was one bizarre revelation too many and Compton's evidence was withdrawn from the Crown's bundle.

On one level, the involvement of other people detracted from the essential prosecution case against Fred and Rose acting together as a pair; it muddied the water, and to a point supported a defence contention that other people may have been responsible. In terms of the truth, what Sharon Compton disclosed was alarmingly close to the kind of sex parties that Fred had described attending many years earlier when he was with Rena, when young women were taken to squalid sex clubs in Bristol where they were abused and exploited in basement shebeens.

I have also spoken to Derek Myatt, whose brother Rob Myatt had been a member of the Scorpion Motorcycle gang and used to hang out at the Pop In Cafe on Southgate Street, Gloucester. At one point, a number of Scorpions dossed down at 25 Cromwell Street and had a gang bang with Rose West. Rob Myatt was also a bin man on the same crew as John West and frequently visited Cromwell Street. One of their mates was a lad called Noddy Dix, who was also in the Scorpions. He was called Noddy because he had a slight twitch. His mother, Margaretta, gave evidence at Rose West's trial. The Dix family were close neighbours of the Wests. They recalled an occasion when Noddy was up on the roof of his family house with an air rifle shooting at pigeons, which was one of his favourite pastimes. He recalled seeing Fred West digging up his back garden and burying a number of bags. Noddy mentioned this to his mates and it was discussed locally.

I am reminded of a statement in the unused material where Fred had got up onto an adjoining roof in Cromwell Street to help with the repair of a chimney. He suddenly stopped and looked around and said, "What a good place to bury a body." The two neighbours looked at each other in puzzlement and then carried on working. Could Fred have volunteered to assist in the task because he needed to check what the view was from that vantage point to the graveyard that was his own back garden?

At this time, a Police Inspector by the name of Don Howe was apparently minding Fred West who, even though known to be a petty criminal, was also identified as a useful nark (police informant), as he regularly informed on drug dealers and drug users in the neighbourhood. It was known that Don Howe was often seen at 25 Cromwell Street. It was presumed this was in the line of duty. However, around this time, Don Howe left the Gloucestershire Constabulary and became a store detective at Bon Marche in Gloucester. Nevertheless, it was Don Howe who attended at Noddy Dix's house and warned him against spreading malicious gossip about Fred West and 25 Cromwell Street. As Noddy was not always on the right side of the law, he left Gloucester soon after. It is understood that he moved to Plymouth, where he met a girl and settled down.

Painful as it may be, the prospect of aberrant individual police collusion in the comings and goings from the West household cannot be entirely ruled out. Too many people knew about it and were sufficiently concerned over the years to comment about Fred and Rose West – who were clearly, for various reasons, on the police radar – and yet the abominable offending continued. This is not to suggest that police officers were gratuitously in concert with the Wests in their bloodlust, but consider an officer visiting the libertine household awash with fecund young women who were often tempted there themselves by the lax sexual environment. Some of the young lodgers were, in any event, engaged in prostitution. The police officer perhaps starts asking questions about drugs or stolen goods; comments that he has heard about noises in the night or girls who have gone missing. Fred first soft soaps the officer with a cup of tea and some useful information about a lodger dealing in cannabis. Rose then walks past with a see-through blouse and no bra. The officer is then left alone in a room and a couple of young women come in, close the door and, without saying a word, undress and have sex with the officer. Is he going to file a report back with his Duty Sergeant? No chance. Life happens. Police officers are not immune from the frailties of human nature.

Even during the 1994/95 West inquiry, a West family member told me that the police liaison officer assigned to her cultivated his relationship with her and when the opportunity arose, had sex with her. It is difficult to see how this could have been in the line of duty.

5.

VICTIMS: FACTS AND HISTORICAL OPINION

ANNE MCFALL

For a brief period Anne McFall secured her place as Fred's woman, his lover and the carer for Charmaine and Anne Marie. She had been keen to please him and assume a privileged place in the chaotic state of flux that was West's underwhelming life. Whether the young woman was infatuated or if the grim prospect of a return to an alcoholic mother in a dilapidated tenement in Glasgow made the life with Fred at a Gloucester caravan site seem idyllic cannot be known. Perhaps there was an element of both.

The truth was, it was not long before Fred West grew tired of her; her dependence on him and her romantic ideas of settling down with him agitated him. The last thing he wanted was another child. His life was becoming unbearably complicated. The hollow words of false affection uttered to facilitate seduction evaporated as frustration turned to violence. He was having to pay to keep Rena, who had turned up from Scotland at the Watermead caravan park at Brockworth near Gloucester and Anne at the caravan at Sandhurst. She was young, she was needy, she now knew the beast in Fred, but he was all she had. Fred's mind was, in a way, inexplicable even to himself; he was conflicted and confused. These women were taking him out of his comfort zone, interfering with his space and distorted peace of mind. He needed the freedom to roam in the quest for the materialisation of his perverted fantasies. The emerging narrative of his life was to spin a web from a false romantic yarn which he soon became bored with. It made him deeply at odds with himself. He needed to find perfunctory solutions to absolve himself of the emotional demands young women placed on him as a result of his encouraging them in the first place. He would progressively have to lie to relate to his family, and Charmaine and Anne Marie were still on the radar of social services, who Fred had only recently been able to placate by telling them that Rena had returned, and they could once again be one big happy family.

Fred believed he was able to carry out abortions. In some misguided, convoluted way, the recent press about the legalisation of abortion in 1967 would have given Fred fresh impetus to attempt a procedure on the unwitting Anne, who would never have volunteered to abort her child, whether legally through the NHS or otherwise. If Anne's baby was to be aborted as Fred wished, he would have to use force. He may have tried putting something in her tea, he may have shouted at her and punched her hard in the stomach, just as Rena had recalled him doing when she miscarried before conceiving Anne Marie.

Ultimately at some stage, probably late at night, he bound her hands to restrain her from fighting back while he attempted to abort the baby. Bindings on an eight-month pregnant woman would not have facilitated sexual intercourse, even if Anne initially consented to be tied up; but even then, each limb would need to be secured, not to each other but at points to make her outstretched. I believe Fred wanted to abort the baby, not kill Anne. Tragically and horrifically, he succeeded in doing both. Intent to kill Anne was absent from this offence, however what he did would amount to intent to commit grievous bodily harm and the ensuing death would have justified an indictment for murder.

While it is not impossible that he then dismembered Anne McFall's heavily pregnant body in the caravan, Fred West said during police interviews that he cut her body after he had driven to Letterbox Field, Much Marcle in Herefordshire. If the dismemberment had taken place in the caravan there would have been huge amount of blood and gore, but then if she had died as a result of being butchered in a botched abortion, West would already have had a lot of mess to clear up and as he had tools in hand he may just have carried on situ. My view, however, is that the tangible evidence supports dismemberment in the field at Much Marcle.

In 1994, with great persistence and accomplishment, Gloucestershire police found the young Scottish woman's remains in the field, together with the slight skeletal print of her infant next to her. There were bindings on the bones of the feet and a large rope binding. There was also a little blue cardigan that the tragic young woman had been wearing and also a quilt, presumably from the caravan.

The larger piece of rope supports the account of dismemberment taking place in the remote field. While the petite Anne McFall, even with a nearly full-term baby, would not have weighed much more than a hundred pounds, it would have been difficult for Fred West to walk across the rough, hard surface of the field carrying the body in his arms. Fred was used, in his job as a lorry driver for an agricultural company, to carrying bags of grain slung over his shoulder. The longer piece of cord would, following death, have tied both hands and feet together and then with her body wrapped in the quilt, he would have then wrapped the cord also around the quilt and slung the bundle over his shoulder.

Even though it was summer and the ground was hard, Fred would have known the field and where there would have been a moist depression sufficient to enable a hole to be dug. The dismemberment on one level was a practical solution to ensure the bodies could be buried in the most compact and economic space, with depth rather than shallow scattering foremost in his mind. Beavering away as a solitary figure in the middle of the night, attending the practical necessities for murderous despatch would become a recurrent toil for Fred, even to the moment of his own self-administered demise.

It might be wished that the narrative was so completed, but regrettably, the depraved repertoire and modus operandi of Fred West requires plunging into much greater depths.

When the eminent Home Office Pathologist Professor Bernard Knight examined the remains of Anne McFall, as indeed he was called on to do with eleven other victims, he found that there were thirty-two bones missing. Most of these were small bones from the hands and feet, but also missing was a long thin bone from the shin, as well as a rib. Given the boundless depravity of Fred West's conduct, the prospect of one of the victim's calf muscles being sliced off in a cannibalistic act has to be a possibility. His total intrusion into and assumption of the physical being that had been Anne McFall, along with his persisting power by planting her remains in his well-trodden territory at Much Marcle are consistent with his eating part of her. In discussions I had with Mae and Stephen before the case came to trial, they both confirmed their memories of weird, foul-smelling pieces of meat occasionally being in the kitchen fridge.

The defence position that I put forward on this aspect of the case, as it applied equally to Rose West, was that the passage of time, the movement of soil, the activity of burrowing rodents, the effects of atmospheric damp and erosion, as well as inadvertent dispersal during the recovery process accounted for the disparity.

As defence solicitor, obtaining necessary expert reports on many areas of the investigation was always at the forefront of my thinking. On the question of the excavation of remains, in the weeks prior to the police excavation in the fields at Much Marcle, I was, as indeed was the world, only too aware of the frenetic activity as the police dug in the garden at 25 Cromwell Street, with hard grafting big burly officers in size twelve wellington boots digging and sifting and sorting through tons of waste. My enquiries to several universities had brought an overwhelming view that to properly excavate the sites, forensic archaeologists should have been employed. The express advice I received was that the fact that smaller bones constituted the predominant number of missing skeletal remains was itself an indicator that despite the genuine best efforts of conscientious and hardworking teams of police officers, these delicate remnants could easily have been obliterated under the tread and smudge of heavy boots.

Professor Knight, who personally oversaw the digging, did not accept this view. He was present to advise and observe and expressed himself fully satisfied at all times with the integrity of the recovery process. In support of the Professor's view was the overriding pattern of recurrence in all the victims, a system that did not allow for random dispersal. In addition, it has to be accepted that if the delicate little bones of the unborn child survived, then so should the smaller bones of the hands and feet of the mother, let alone larger bones. And in some cases, fingernails were recovered but not the bones of the hands they were attached to.

So, all these years on, I must accept that these bones were missing because Fred West, in the process of cutting up the bodies, had taken parts as mementos. It is a chilling prospect to realise that beyond death there was a ritual that he desired, that he imagined, that he longed for, that held an integral fascination in his overall repertoire. The process of tidying up the incriminating consequences, getting rid of the bodies, 'sorting it out', was no unwanted loose end; on the contrary, it gave this psychopath some kind of primal satisfaction.

MARY BASTHOLM

Mary Bastholm was an innocent young teenager who was fifteen years old at the time she disappeared from a bus stop on Bristol Road in Janaury 1968. She was on the way to visit her boyfriend in the village of Hardwicke, about five miles away. They were going to play Monopoly. The Monopoly set she was carrying was found scattered near the bus stop. Mary was never seen again.

In October 1967, Anne McFall had disappeared. At the caravan park at Sandhurst, Gloucester, Fred explained to the site manager that she had gone back to Scotland and handed the keys back. He then moved Rena and the two babies, Charmaine and Anne Marie, from the Watermead caravan park to a caravan park at Stoke Orchard near Bishop's Cleeve, Cheltenham. He obtained work locally at Oldacres Mill.

The reconstituted nuclear family did not last long. Fred was violent when he was at home but worked long hours. Rena was not the stay-at-home, childminder type. She decided to move back to Scotland.

Fred and Rose later claimed that they first met at the Royal Well Bus Station in Cheltenham town centre. It would be natural for a couple who had been together for a long time to be asked by their children and others they may come into contact with how they met. The account of the Royal Well Bus Station meeting was therefore well rehearsed and had been repeated and probably embellished many times over the years. It patently was not the truth. There was a reason for the lie.

Fred always denied having anything to do with Mary's disappearance. And the account of when and where he met Rose would always put her beyond suspicion. This silence is a signification of another narrative strand within the grim West saga.

Why did Fred need to continue to lie? Firstly, he would have needed to invent a new version of events so as to exclude Rose and there was nothing to connect him to the disappearance, as Mary was as much a stranger to him as other victims who had been abducted in a similar way. He also knew, of course, that there was no way her remains would be found at Cromwell Street, or Midland Road for that matter. And there was always the risk, as they discovered with Heather, that invention would catch them out. So why stick your neck out? That is the simple calculus for denial.

The location of Mary's remains is not known. Fred took that secret to the grave with him, but I believe Rose West does know and could shed light on the mystery of this unsolved murder.

It may be justified to in some way incentify her, possibly give her the prospect of earning privileges within the prison regime in order to obtain her co-operation. The reality is that this would be immensely difficult because it is a phase of Rose's life that she has closed a very solid door on. She does not want to go there. It should be kept in mind that Rose's brain works in a very different way to Fred's. She is not driven and preoccupied with perverted sexual fantasies. She was an ever-ready nymphomaniac who, from an early age, was programmed to respond to other people's sexual desires. On this level, she would submit herself willingly to whatever anybody wanted to do, no holds barred. Paradoxically, this sexual submissiveness meant that with a partner like Fred, she was also an agent for the infliction of sadistic sex with other young women.

A hypothesis I proffer is that if the killing of Mary Bastholm was the first joint enterprise, the initiating *folie à deux*, where Fred introduced his new compliant and willing partner, the juvenile Rose West, to the horrors of sadistic murder, then it must also remain questionable whether Rose was truly equally guilty of the murders of many of the other victims. I do not doubt that she was a killer, but the modus operandi, the system, the pattern may have been more nuanced than the neatly packaged similar fact evidence that the prosecution presented.

The following facts indicate that Fred and Rose were together and jointly murdered Mary Bastholm.

Let us first look more closely at the contention that the story Fred and Rose told about how they met was contrived and fictitious. How and why could Rose assert she was so prim and proper in her posturing in the opening gambit of courting when she had already built up a reputation for dropping her knickers for every Tom, Dick and Harry who wanted it? And got it. And one after the other, as her brother-in-law, Jim Tyler recalls of Rose's dalliances with pipe layers up on the Cirencester Road at Seven Springs where Rose was supposed to be selling hot dogs in her sister, Gleny's maternity absence. The gratuitous bonking was probably at the insistence of Fred, who told his young apprentice how much it would please him for her to get as much experience as possible.

The bus stop banter and beckoning where Fred, so totally out of character, follows the courtly gestures of a trying to win the young maiden's heart, rather than relying on route one and just

UNDERSTANDING FRED & ROSE WEST

grabbing her and doing as he pleased. The scenario simply does not ring true and it conceals how they actually got to know each other at least a year earlier, when Rose was just fourteen years old.

The recollections that Rose has of being raped by at least two men, who were strangers, one of whom she thought might kill her, were fictitious. She is actually probably recalling early occasions of rape by her father, Bill Letts and then sessions of rough predatory sex by and with Fred. In these sessions, Fred realised Rose could accommodate and identify with his desires. He needed to find out more about her sexual limits; his daily, hourly, continual fantasies drove in him a need to test her in a wider repertoire of threesomes, bondage, lesbianism, sadism. What was this young woman really capable of? Could he use her sexually extravagant pliability and her plasticity of character to make her an active instrument of his sordid dreams? This was the forming of their bond. Her will was subsumed in his narcissistic will. His mind was her mind. With her he was complete. The ideal of narcissistic self-love is to project yourself onto another. Perfect.

Rose reached puberty early and was well-developed for her age. After years of being timid and bullied at school, she had learnt to assert herself and fight back. She found school difficult and did not engage academically. This included truanting when she could.

From the Wests' family home in Tobyfield Road, Bishop's Cleeve, Bill Letts spent a lot of time after work in the Smiths Club, drinking. Rose's mother, Daisy had obtained work as a cleaner, earning some money each afternoon through until mid- to late-evening. While she felt a sense of independence and empowerment through this, it also meant that she left Rose to look after Graham and Gordon. Rose and her younger brothers were known to have gone feral and wander around the streets of Bishop's Cleeve. By this stage Rose, big for her age, had toughened up; she was not frightened of other girls and had a reputation of being someone not to mess with as she could beat the living daylights out of any girl who crossed her.

Tobyfield Road was a half mile from the Lakeside Caravan site off Stoke Orchard Road, where Fred had been living since October 1967. Fred's habitual routine, very probably at some time every single day, was to cruise around ogling and fantasising about seducing or abducting impressionable young women. There is anecdotal evidence that young women truanting from Bishop's Cleeve Comprehensive often went to Fred's caravan. Some accounts point to him taking intimate pictures of some of these girls. By this stage, it is doubtful that there would have been a girl less engaged with the school, more peripheral to the activities, more susceptible to the allurement and excitement of meeting an older man than Rose. It is likely that Fred and Rose's reciprocating toxic chemistry flagged each to the other like the light from firefly.

Rose would have been available for Fred and already primed and groomed by her abusive father to comply with Fred's perverted repertoire. Rena was out and about on the town with other men a lot of the time. Fred was working the night shift at Oldacres Grain Factory.

Barbara White, a neighbour of the Wests, who became Barbara Letts told me several years ago, quietly in an off the cuff and unprompted conversation that, Fred West first made himself known to Rose when they were playing in the street outside their houses in Tobyfield Road. When Rose was bored with school she knew how to find her way to the nearby Lakeside Caravan Park.

Fred was known to visit the Pop In Cafe on Southgate Street, Gloucester. He would drive over there in his green Vauxhall Viva. Mary Bastholm was a waitress at the Pop In Cafe.

In 1995, I took a statement from a biker who remembered Fred West at the Pop In. He also remembered Anne McFall and

Mary Bastholm. He was vague about whether Rose West might on occasion have visited there.

When Fred was remanded in custody at Winson Green, he told his son Stephen that he had killed Mary Bastholm.

In so telling this to his son, he said that he would tell the police about the details and location of the body when he was good and ready. He then needed to expressly state, "There's only one person who'll ever tell them and that's me." The signification here is Fred's need to emphasise what, if he was telling the truth, was blatantly obvious. Why did he need to exclaim what should have been superfluous comment? Was it to reinforce the false narrative that hid the truth? This might be viewed as a faux pas, a subtle slip. What he is really communicating is that there was someone else who knew about what happened.

When I mentioned Mary Bastholm to Rose, she was at first taken aback, surprised that I should ever mention that part of the inquiry. I view her words when she eventually responded as guarded. She turned head away from me and quietly said, "No, I wouldn't know, would I? That was before I was on the scene." Yet there is evidence she and Fred were already acquainted.

The bonding and commitment that Fred made to Rose, without also killing Rose, meant that at some very early stage there was something that secured in her a very special and privileged position in his sick world, their warped 'love' was founded and depended on some deeply secret shared experience. This must have occurred long before the death of Charmaine and Rena, before they married and Rose became pregnant with Heather.

It is conceivable that Charmaine, who at the time of Mary Basthholm's death was a bright little five-year-old, was capable of repeating what she had seen or been told. Likewise, between punters, Rena may have inadvertently found out more than was good for her.

Rose herself admitted to her parents when she returned home at the age of sixteen that 'there wasn't anything that Fred wouldn't do, even murder'. That utterance was made in the autumn of 1972, by which time both Charmaine and Rena had been killed. At first glance, this makes the statement rather hollow, because Rose was eventually found by a court of law to have murdered Charmaine, while Rena's murder was attributed to Fred. However, in the garbled machinations and warped mindset of the pair of them, the word 'murder' may not have been the label they would have used for such unfortunate accidents and the removal of a problematic ex-wife.

Actually, the record of that incident and dialogue which occurred when Fred went to Tobyfield Road to retrieve his absconding young wife is even stranger because Fred recalled telling Rose that she had a minute to get in his car or otherwise another young woman would take her place in his bed that night. The reality is, each knew the other to be a killer, except Rose was intimating some extension possessed by Fred to the effect that he was a murderer over and beyond her own culpability and yet it held no real fear for her.

No one, apart from Fred and possibly his mother and father in Much Marcle, knew that Anne McFall was dead. The authorities certainly did not find out until 1994. There was nothing in the news. Whereas when Mary disappeared, there was a huge inquiry and extensive media coverage.

Rose could only know about Anne if Fred told her; she could only know Fred was involved with the disappearance of Mary Bastholm if Fred had volunteered that information to her or if she had been a party to the abduction, even as it remained firmly in the public mind and there was not the slightest finger of suspicion pointed at him by the police. Why at that early time in their relationship would he risk everything by telling a fourteen-year-old girl he hoped to woo that he was a killer?

It was not a credible proposition and yet I believe Rose knew. She knew; she could not help but know because she was party to what happened to Mary Bastholm. She was an accomplice, albeit a junior accomplice, who may not have been present at the time of dismemberment, but in all probability was present at the time of death.

She knew he was a killer, yet her bond with him overcame the knowledge that he had murdered young women; and the stark fact is she did not thereby become another expendable young victim. As they say, turkeys do not vote for Christmas. Something put her beyond fear of being killed by Fred. They were bonded to each other by an irreversible event that irredeemably captured both of them in a union that necessitated concealment and a warped trust in each other. As the evidence points to Charmaine and Rena being independently executed killings, the only possible combined venture is that relating to Mary Bastholm. This corrupted dove-tailing was the cement they translated as love. It was not Fred's poetry that won Rose over. She gave her heart to him because she was a young woman who had for many years been groomed to submit to a vicious father for fear of being beaten, as her siblings were. She chose to understand the sexual abuse she endured as a display of affection. She was safe and special in this privileged place, submitting to the will of a violent and perverted man. And at some point together, she had passed with him the point of no return, the initiation in blood by the murder of the tragic young Mary Bastholm.

The number of reports of a man trying to abduct young women were turning up the heat. Fred's methods were not working. He realised that having a young woman in the car with him would facilitate his illicit intent.

A possible scenario for Mary Bastholm's abduction and murder is as follows:

On the cold winter evening of Saturday January 6th 1968, fifteen-year-old Mary Bastholm was waiting at a bus stop on Bristol Road near to the junction with Tuffley Avenue. As you head out of Gloucester, this would be about half a mile further out of town from the Pop In Cafe. She would have finished her shift as a waitress at the Pop In Café and then gone home, got dressed and ready to go out. She was waiting for a bus to visit her boyfriend, who lived in the village of Hardwicke about five miles away.

At the Lakeside Caravan Park, while Rena had gone out on the town, the young Rose West called round to look after Charmaine and Anne Marie, who were then aged three and four years old. It was Fred's night off from his night shift at Oldacres in Bishop's Cleeve. He was restless. He had time on his hands. The girls were put to bed, possibly constrained in some way as Fred had boarded up beds to imprison Charmaine in her bed in Glasgow. Fred the coarse, rustic charmer would have flattered Rose, as was his custom and then forced himself upon her, which she would have been fully compliant with. With the night ahead, his fantasies would have been in overdrive and Rose was there to share his weird musings. He might have told Rose that he liked threesomes and he liked to tie girls up and whether she would be interested in participating, but first he would need to find another girl to complete the *ménage à trois*. He suggested that they go for a drive in his green Vauxhall Viva, most probably leaving the young girls asleep in the caravan.

They drove to Gloucester. They were cruising. They drove up the Bristol Road and past the bus stop where Mary was waiting. A witness confirmed seeing her waiting there at 8:15pm. That was the last time she was seen alive. There would have been a few people about. There was a large pub called the Bristol on the corner of Tuffley Avenue. It later became one of Rose's favourite venues for country and western nights. Locals would have been wandering in and out. Fred may have driven up Bristol Road and then turned around and come back down before turning around and again driving past Mary as she waited. When the coast was clear, Fred pulled up and told Rose to ask where the girl was going and then to say that as it was cold, they could give her a lift. Even with Rose in the car, Mary most likely declined the offer. When she did, with Fred behind the wheel and the engine ticking over, Fred told Rose to get out the car, grab her and tell her to do as she was told. In less than a minute, the hapless young woman had been forcefully wrenched into the back seat of the car, with Rose holding her to stop her struggling. In so doing, some of the Monopoly pieces from the set in her bag spilled out into the snow, where they were later recovered during the subsequent police inquiry.

Fred would have promptly accelerated away and after a while may have pulled in to turn around and punch their captive to subdue her. He would have been heading in the direction of Bristol. To indulge his warped lust would have required a place to go, certainly not in the middle of the countryside in the cold icy snow. He would have veered back towards Cheltenham, probably choosing not to exactly retrace his steps by driving back past the bus stop and then through the centre of Gloucester. More likely, he would have turned onto Cole Avenue and then followed Eastern Avenue back to Barnwood roundabout, returning to Bishop's Cleeve either via Churchdown and Swindon Village or otherwise through the centre of Cheltenham. Either way, it would have taken less than an hour. They would have returned to the Lakeside caravan. There was nowhere else to go. No other party could have been made privy to what was taking place.

The earliest they could have arrived back at the caravan would have been about 9pm. It would have been essential for Mary to have been bound and gagged. The Vauxhall Viva would have pulled up close to the door and Mary quickly and unceremoniously bundled inside. After being bound, gagged and sexually abused with Rose participating, Mary would have to have been quickly dispatched of and her body disposed of. This had to be before either the children woke up or Rena returned from her partying and sexual shenanigans in the early hours, probably at about 5am, as was her custom.

It has to be postulated that dismemberment may have taken place in the caravan or more likely in the work shed next door. After all, it cannot be ruled out that Anne McFall was dismembered in the caravan at Sandhurst. It was known that Fred would make himself useful as a handyman on the caravan park and had access to a works hut near his caravan. This hut stored sand, building materials and tools. It is possible he carried Mary's trussed-up body to that shed to carry out the dismemberment. Fred West would, as a practical labourer, have had sheets and bags available, as well as sacks that he would have obtained from Oldacres. He also had an array of knives and tools as the self-appointed site handyman.

What would have happened to the remains?

Habit, the desire for possession beyond death and the sense of enduring power in the conquest would have pointed to a burial at Much Marcle, his home turf; his stomping ground for trapping rabbits and culling squirrels; the place that was part of him. It was, after all, where in the preceding year he had buried Anne McFall. The modus operandi was established. Pattern would lend credence to this scenario. But this was the middle of winter and the ground was frozen, as was well testified by Superintendent Bennett, who as young police officer was involved in the search up on Painswick Beacon and beyond and, in his then capacity as a police frogman, he was deployed to scour the nearby waterways.

While it is true that if you can break frozen surface ground for no more than several inches, the underlying soil becomes increasingly pliable, even in the midst of winter and actually, if you dig down two or three feet, the ambient temperature of the soil remains fairly constant throughout the year, irrespective of hot summer days or freezing winter nights. Nevertheless, there were no soft boggy patches in the fields of Much Marcle in the middle of winter. In my view, taking into account also Fred's hideous proclivities, the overall prospect of such a scenario is untenable.

And it would have meant Fred would have had to leave the caravan probably in the very early hours of Sunday 7th January, driven over thirty-five miles to Much Marcle, chosen his spot, dug the hole, buried the remains and then driven back to Bishop's Cleeve. Given Fred's need to not only dismember but to also take body parts – even allowing for the skills he had acquired in his youth and later working at an abattoir – the whole process, including the round trip, would have taken about four hours. He would have barely been back at the caravan and cleaned up before Rena returned from her night on the town, although it is just as likely that Rena did not return for several days.

On balance it is more likely that dismemberment took place at the caravan park.

If Fred had buried Mary Bastholm at Much Marcle, it is surprising that he did not admit to her murder at the time of the excavations relating to Anne McFall and Rena Costello, as he must have weighed where an extra set of remains might have emerged, as they had done in the more confined space of the garden at 25 Cromwell Street. In addition, Fred had a blind deference to the miracles of modern science and high tech. When the police were excavating at Cromwell Street, they told Fred that they would employ ground detection equipment that would survey the soil. This would have related to geological equipment to detect any disturbance or disruption in the sub-soil. Fred would have assumed there was a kind of X-ray eye that would see skeletal remains under the ground. This points to the fact that Mary was not buried at Much Marcle, either at Finger Post or Letterbox Fields.

Fred occasionally fished in the small lake at the caravan park. It has to be another possibility that he weighted the bags containing dismembered limbs with sand and stones, and dropped them from a little rowing boat into the lake. From the account given by Superintendent Bennett while the weather was snowy and icy, waterways had not frozen over, making it feasible for Fred to have rowed into the centre of the little lake. A Google Maps search confirms the lake is still there, surrounded by a new development. It measures roughly sixty metres by twenty-five metres. It would not be a big task just to check it out.

One other piece of speculative evidence that points to Mary Bastholm being brought to Bishop's Cleeve that appeared in the reports was that of a watch found on Tobyfield Road which may have belonged to her.

CHARMAINE WEST

Of all the unravelling investigators had to painstakingly do to establish the facts, the case of little Charmaine West probably created the most divergence of perception.

In a way, the job of police investigator, when done properly, is a purer pursuit than that of the criminal lawyer, who will assess the evidence and either prosecute with a view to obtaining a conviction or, if acting for the defence, apply the evidence to cast doubt and convince the jury that the requisite standard of proof beyond reasonable doubt has not been met.

It is a high standard of proof. It means the jury must be sure. If there is any doubt, then the defendant must be given the benefit of that doubt. The criminal standard of proof is much higher than the civil standard of the 'balance of probabilities'.

In the adversarial system lauded as the bastion of British justice, the prosecution assesses the facts in relation to the strict legal requirements they must prove so as to get home with their case and secure a prosecution. This has to be cohesive and intelligible to the jury of laymen and women. The vehicle to achieve this is the story that the Crown maps out at the outset. The defence will also have prepared its story. Ultimately, whoever tells the best, most credible story – a story that most accurately utilises and dovetails with the established facts – is most likely to get a result in their favour. The use of the word 'story' is poignant. Implicit in it is the realm of mythmaking, yet facts once determined by deliberation in a court of law attain a solemnity and solidity as the truth.

While hard evidence in the form of official documents confirming a date of release from prison – or dated letters, where their provenance can be verified – are able to stand the test of time, witness testimony made twenty or thirty years after the event will inevitably carry a risk of innocent unreliability. Recent research has shown that the human brain does not operate like a library filing system, where all experiential data is neatly stored unless or until recollection is demanded. It has been shown that the brain has to completely reconfigure the memory anew in a process mediated by experience imported during the intervening years. This often results in the precise sequence of facts being altered in some way, which in a serious criminal case will have significant consequences. The law compensates for this risk within the general scope of abuse of process applications, as presented to Mr Justice Mantell in May 1995 before Rose West went to trial. The application, which also dealt with other abuse matters arising from press intrusion, did not find favour with the learned judge.

In Charmaine's case, the Crown conspicuously changed its story before the matter went to trial. Before Fred West hanged himself, the prosecution case was that he alone murdered Charmaine West. After he hanged himself, the prosecution case was that Rose West alone murdered Charmaine. That speaks volumes in illustrating the nebulous moveable reality of a storyline.

The initial charge against Fred West had the validity of being based on a voluntary admission made by him in which Charmaine's name was on a list made by Fred of a further nine victims. And even though he was to change his tune several times, Fred West did correctly specify where the remains would be found under the kitchen extension of 25 Midland Road.

During 1969 and 1970, Fred West had been convicted of a string of petty thefts, ranging from displaying a false car tax disc on his car to stealing five tyres from his employer. This all eventually caught up with him when the reoffending triggered activation of an earlier suspended sentence and in December 1970, Gloucester Magistrates' Court imposed ten months of imprisonment, which was served at HMP Leyhill, a category D open prison near Bristol. He served about seven months and was released on June 24th 1971.

The dates became crucial. If Fred was still in prison when Charmaine 'disappeared', then Fred could not be guilty of killing her. Not so according to the novel account devised by Richard Ferguson QC, whereby it was proffered that Fred may have absconded from the open prison, carried out the killing and then got the bus from Gloucester back to Leyhill and checked back into his cell. Category D prisons have a relaxed regime. Inmates have their own key to their cells and often go outside the prison boundaries to work in the horticulture in surrounding fields. Some long-term prisoners get overnight passes as a means to readjust to society after a long stretch. Some prisoners get assigned to do work in the surrounding community. There is no suggestion or documentary evidence that any of these options applied to a short-term prisoner like Fred West. The strategy was to raise a scintilla of doubt which could not be entirely ruled out by the prosecution. It was a line that I could not endorse with any enthusiasm. But Dick Ferguson was streetwise and when he first proposed the idea at a conference in his chambers in London, he had a certain gleefulness about the idea. I felt it was rather risible and dared to tell him as much, but it was how he felt the case should be put and I did not wish to raise his hackles. I was dealing with a deservedly big reputation and he believed it could serve the defence case well as it avoided critical dates based upon the state of growth of Charmaine's new set of front teeth, as evidenced in the dentition in her little skull recovered with her remains. Sasha Wass was quite chilled out about the idea, so who was I to argue?

Dr Whittaker, the Crown's expert odontologist, gave evidence based on an assessment of her dentition. Dr Whittaker compared the teeth recovered with her remains as a freeze-frame with dated photographic evidence of the little girl smiling. The original photograph was not of high fidelity and required more than a little extrapolation and estimation. Then *The Sun* published on its daily front page a high-quality colour picture of Anne Marie and Charmaine in their best outfits, smiling at the camera. This photograph could be precisely dated and revealed an accurate representation of the extent of eruption and growth of Charmaine's second set of front teeth. This enabled Dr Whittaker to calculate the expected rate of growth. It made it probable, but not certain, that Fred was still a prisoner at HMP Leyhill when Charmaine met her death. The uncertainty was increased by an expert odontologist, Dr Graham Richie, whom I had instructed to prepare a report on the state of Charmaine's dentition. Dr Richie's experience was in identifying the deceased from aircraft crashes. His view differed from Dr Whittaker and made it much more likely that Fred West would indeed have been released from HMP Leyhill by the time of Charmaine's demise. Dick Ferguson made it clear that he had no desire to call Mr Richie because it would embroil him in cross-examination of dental experts, which he felt was unnecessary and would muddy the waters.

The tragic, spirited little girl born in Glasgow on March 6th 1963 found herself in the charge of Fred and Rose West. Rena Costello had already been pregnant with Charmaine as a result of a brief affair with a Pakistani bus driver in Glasgow when she met up with Fred West. At the time Rena was working on the buses as conductress. It appears she shared her favours freely with the other members of staff. The sex trade was never far from Rena's life. She was young, sexually charged, a libertine. This suited Fred when he and Rena met. He may have been turned on by the idea of having sex with a woman carrying another man's child. Rena was sexually experienced and not at all phased by some of the weirder stuff Fred wanted between the sheets. She may actually have introduced him to playful bondage and sadomasochism.

So, there remain the interminable questions: did Fred really murder Charmaine on his own, did Rose murder Charmaine on her own or did the two of them together murder Charmaine?

I think there would be a consensus that the burial had all the hallmarks of Fred West: the neat rectangular hole about a metre and a half deep, the forty-seven missing bones from the little girl's hands and feet, the missing kneecaps, as well as part of the breastbone. There was coal dust with the remains, on account of the area of burial being originally located in the ground of a basement coal store which was, after some years, built over with a kitchen extension. This had encased the remains under two feet of concrete.

Rose, the seventeen-year-old mother from a dysfunctional background, who had given birth to her own child a month before her husband to be was sent to prison, was caring for Charmaine and Anne Marie in cold, inadequate accommodation without money to properly feed and clothe her young charges. Rose was struggling. She found Charmaine difficult. Where Anne Marie was quiet and obedient, Charmaine would resist, be defiant and fight back. She wanted to be with her real mum, Rena. Rose was not coping. It mattered to her for the children to be well turned out. She had skills of sewing and cooking, but when her parents, Daisy and Bill, made an impromptu visit, they were appalled at the state of the place. It was a mess: dirty nappies strewn across the floor and clothes piled up. She had already adopted the only manner of control she had known: harsh physical discipline. There was cruelty and meanness in her excessive admonition of Charmaine.

A young mum called Shirley Ann Giles lived upstairs with her daughter, Tracey, who was seven years old and the same age as Charmaine. They became good pals and would play together on the hallway stairs.

One morning, Shirley sent Tracey down to borrow some milk for breakfast. As she rushed into the kitchen, she was surprised to see Charmaine standing on a chair with her hands tied behind her back and Rose in the batting position with a wooden spoon in her hand. Charmaine kept still and silent. She did not seem intimidated by Rose's threatening stance. Shirley Giles moved with her daughter to Cinderford in early 1971 but remembers visiting in April 1971 so that Tracey could play with Charmaine, only to be told by Rose that Charmaine had gone to live with her mother, Rena, in Scotland. This date did not tally with correspondence between Fred and Rose that appeared to indicate Rose taking Anne Marie and Charmaine to visit Fred as late as May and even June of 1971.

Despite the 'no comment' response to all allegations of murder – which was in line with what I had strongly advised her to do – when she was belatedly confronted with the accusation of having murdered Charmaine, she was decidedly more flaky, taken aback, discernibly trying to control her emotions, almost needing someone to lean on. Her private protestations about Fred West were not convincing. I have no doubt that the reminder of Charmaine's demise struck a chord with Rose that was absent in the cold, blank denial for most of the victims. Admittedly, there was shock and despondency following her arrest in relation to Heather.

Charmaine was one of the resisters. She did not allow the oppression and abuse to destroy her will. Eventually, at the tender age of seven she would pay with her life; another future cruelly snuffed out.

Could Rose have been suffering from post-natal depression or post-natal post-traumatic stress disorder during 1971? As someone who had herself been in care and pregnant at sixteen, she should have been under the radar of social services, but she was not. This in itself would not make her more susceptible; her medical records indicate that Heather's birth was normal and her angst was with Charmaine, not her new baby. The evidence from the correspondence with Fred while he was in Leyhill was that the baby bonding process was sound, although she confirmed to me that she did not breastfeed any of her babies. She said that, "Tits were for fucking, not breast feeding."

What was unusual from Professor Knight's pathology report was that from the position of the bones and the lack of cut marks, the indication was that the body may only have been cut in half. This could mean that Fred was able to get the small body into the hole without cutting off each limb and decapitating it, or could mean that by the time he undertook the task, rigor mortis had already set in. If this was so, then it strongly suggests that Rose was the solitary killer.

It is likely that Rose did kill Charmaine in a fit of uncontrollable anger. In March 1971, hospital records show that Charmain had been admitted to A&E with a puncture wound to her foot. The die was cast; Rose was losing control.

Anne Marie West, in her evidence, had no doubt that Fred was still in prison when Charmaine, all of a sudden, disappeared. She described returning from school one day and Charmaine had gone. When she naturally asked where Charmain was, Rose told her Rena had collected her and taken her away.

RENA COSTELLO

For Rena, we do not just have to rely on what Fred West had to say. DC Hazel Savage had been acquainted with Rena from decades earlier during her early days in Gloucestershire Constabulary back in the late 1960s. As a rookie police constable, she had been sent to collect Rena on a warrant for absconding while on bail and bring her back from Scotland. On the long train journey back, DC Savage was able to probe and learn much of Rena and her lifestyle with Fred West.

Rena knew her own mind; she was independent and headstrong. She was not by nature a needy person and emotionally would not have been browbeaten by Fred West. Although physically she knew how to put up a fight, Fred was capable of inflicting serious harm on her, which he had on a number of occasions done.

Rena and Fred had married in Glasgow in 1963. Fred was twenty-one years old and Rena, although a couple of years younger, was at the time more street wise than he was. Rena was pregnant, carrying the child of a Pakistani bus driver with whom she had an affair whilst working as a bus conductress. While Rena was a Catholic, she very much subscribed to the view that the church was for sinners, not the saved. This is not to suggest that she regularly, if ever, attended mass. She was by nature a libertine – promiscuous and up for whatever fun the nightlife might bring. In the dour drudgery of 1960s working class Glasgow, sex, drink and late-night partying made life worth living. Rena was adventurous with sex and this no doubt turned Fred on. She also worked as a prostitute, which again ticked Fred's boxes for finding the ideal wife. Rena was attracted to the raffish country yokel, who shared her libertine values and varied sexual repertoire. Eighteen months later, Fred got Rena pregnant with Anne Marie and the family moved to Gloucestershire.

Rena, while energetic and having a reasonable work ethic, was not a natural homemaker, and her fondness for her two girls did not translate into sacrificing her libidinous pursuits to devotedly look after them each day. Her relationship with Fred was volatile and unstable and Rena frequently upped and left the squalid nest. The girls found themselves bouncing in and out of care homes. They were on the radar of social services for several years.

By 1971, Rena had long been off the scene. She was elsewhere plying her trade, first back in Scotland and then more recently in Reading. She did have an association with a pimp called Rolf, who was also known to Fred. In retracing events to try and build up a chronology, it is necessary not to import an assumed organisation into people's lives. Rena's life was pretty chaotic. She was rootless and one day merged into another. She may well have briefly arrived back in Gloucestershire as much by chance as by design. If she had been in the pub or partying and met a fella, she might wake up in any chance bed and not necessarily immediately know where she was. She would not have had a place to stay in Gloucester and more likely than not, she would have just been passing through, having cadged a ride with her pimp. But she was capable of composing herself and for brief intervals, adjusting her moral compass and acting on the nagging concerns for her children that may have clouded her hedonism.

Although she did not own a car herself, it is likely that Rena had been taught to drive while on the buses in Glasgow. Apart from Charmaine's biological father, several of the crew would have availed themselves of Rena's charms in the back room of the depot canteen. They would have been all too willing to show her how to fire up the ignition and work through the gears.

Back in Gloucester in August 1971, she first called at 25 Midland Road, but got no reply. Fred may have been out on a maintenance job for his boss and landlord Frank Zygmund. If Rose was home with the kids, she did not answer the door.

She had, either by agreement or otherwise, the use of her pimp's car. She drove out to Much Marcle to visit Moorcroft Cottage and speak to Walter West, whom she had always got on well with. Fred's brother Doug and his wife remember her visiting and then driving away after walking down to the field in the early evening where Walter was helping with the harvest. This was the last time they ever saw Rena. She may have been assured that Fred and Rose and the girls were still residing at 25 Midland Road. She drove back round to make contact with her two little girls.

At the time when she turned up, out of natural affection for her daughters, she stopped off at a corner sweet shop and bought a sixpenny lucky dip bag of the type young children would often buy on the way back from school. In these there might be a stick of liquorice, some love hearts and forget me nots, a sherbet, perhaps a card to collect and a little toy, which in this case included a little red plastic boomerang.

Charmaine never received that little token of maternal love because she was already dead. The boomerang ended up in the hole at Letterbox Field along with Rena's remains. The sweets may well have been given to Anne Marie as a gift from her doting daddy.

There is no record of that fateful visit to 25 Midland Road. As Rose never acknowledged knowing Rena at all, that is hardly surprising. Anne Marie, who was six years old at the time, has no recollection of her real mummy visiting. The account given by Fred in 1994 takes up the narrative.

He says he arranged to meet Rena in a pub in Barton Street at 9:30pm and when he got there, she was drunk with a load of Irish blokes.

How, when and why would he have made such an arrangement? Had he seen her earlier in the day? Had they had a telephone conversation, each from a different telephone kiosk? Of course not. Fred may have come to the door on that fateful evening and told Rena that Rose did not want her in the house. After all, Rena was still married to Fred and Rose was desperate to marry him. Her resentment turned to hatred every time she was intimate with Fred and had to view in bold letters 'RENA' inked on Fred's upper arm, which Rena had inked while Fred had slept all those years earlier in Glasgow. So, Fred said they would go to the pub to talk about matters. Rena was drinking as usual and got drunk.

Fred's interview account then predictably returns to the default waffle of some suddenly conjured romantic interlude where he drives her out, presumably in the pimp's car, to Much Marcle; they sit out on that summer's night, gaze at the stars and make wonderful, idyllic love twice before he suddenly 'loses it' and smashes her head against a gatepost before kicking her to death.

The element of kicking is curious. Kicking was a hallmark of Rose's when she lost her temper and became vile. It was not typical of Fred, who had a lifelong limp from his motorcycle accident. Furious kicking would be painful and probably make him lose his balance.

In his police interview Fred said as follows:

"I woke her up and we got out [of the car] and we made love against… by the tree there, just on the edge of the field."

Here, he actually changes his story midstream. At first, he is about to say they were making love against something and then after a pause says 'by' the tree. If sexual intercourse took place standing up in a field, it would be more feasible if they were against the tree, but he changes his mind. Was he saying that they 'made love' lying down on the rock-hard, bumpy summer ground? They almost certainly did not, as it would be excruciatingly uncomfortable for the person whose back was resting on the parched hard soil; unless, that is, Rena was already dead and naked and her body lying in the field when Fred had sex with her corpse. The initial allusion of having to wake her up in the car strongly betrays the truth that Rena was dead in the car. Fred's true recollection was having to carry her from the car into the field.

The question then is, why was the little red plastic boomerang and piece of chrome pipe eventually recovered with the remains? It raises the possibility that death had taken place several hours earlier, maybe in the basement of 25 Midland Road, which had been tidied up and the coal dust swept away after Fred had buried Charmaine. Fred was aware that Frank Zygmund had told him he had plans sometime in the future to excavate and refurbish the kitchen area of 25 Midland Road. This would have deterred Fred from burying Rena in that location. It is more likely that Fred killed Rena in the car and then drove to Much Marcle. As rigor mortis was setting in, Fred, to fulfil his fantasy of necrophilia, then needed to prise open the vagina and for this he first used the boomerang, because he liked it tight, and then found he needed slightly more aperture, so he used the chrome pipe.

It would have been well into the late summer night when Fred would have commenced the dismemberment at a selected area of soft ground at Letter Box field, a field he knew well from his childhood. There must also have been a considerable degree of planning if the car that was used was the one Rena had borrowed from her pimp. It would have meant that Fred would have needed to have collected and had with him a suitable knife and or saw for disarticulating the limbs and decapitating Rena. He may even have called back at 25 Midland Road after he left the pub with Rena and told her to wait in the car while he collected a bag. By that time she would have been too drunk to know what he was doing anyway. It should be pointed out that Fred West rarely, if ever imbibed alcohol himself, even though he has happy to encourage any young woman he might be with to indulge to her hearts content. Fred would have had his wits about him and would have had no difficulty driving.

What is not in doubt is that Rena's remains were buried at Letterbox Field and were excavated in May 1994 from where Fred told the interviewing officers they would be. The body had been dismembered with the legs disarticulated at the hip as well as decapitation having taken place. Forty-one small bones from the hands and feet were missing along with a kneecap.

LYNDA GOUGH

Lynda Gough had struggled at school, leaving at sixteen years of age to work as a seamstress at the Co-op. She was from Gloucester and from a cohesive family with loving and caring parents. In that respect, she was not typical of the girls who voluntarily found their way to 25 Cromwell Street. In 1973, Lynda was in her late teenage years and felt a need to rebel against her parents and wanted more freedom to do her own thing and not have to be back home by a certain time in the evening. She was a sociable young woman who was carving her own identity with a preference for the hippie subculture, with adventurous ingredients such as alternative belief systems, or perhaps from a visual fashion accessory perspective linking ideas of the occult and paganism. These might have involved flowery clothes, unusual nail varnish; she was the type of girl who might have preferred tarot cards or a Ouija board to playing Monopoly.

She had met a couple of the boys lodging at 25 Cromwell Street and had brief sexual dalliances with them. During this time, Lynda became friendly with Fred and Rose, who were always kind and supportive of her and understood that she wished to be more independent than was permissible living at home. When Caroline Owens returned to Cinderford, Fred and Rose asked Lynda if she would babysit for the children and shortly after, invited her to reside with them as the live-in childminder.

In April 1973, Lynda told her parents she was getting her own lodgings and moved out. Her parents were not happy at the prospect but felt that it was better to let their headstrong daughter get an idea of what the world was really like. To fight her rebelliousness would only serve to risk alienating their beloved daughter. Lynda left home on April 19th, taking all her things and leaving a message saying:

"Dear Mum and Dad,
    Please don't worry about me. I have got a flat and I will come and see you sometime.
                                                    Love Lin."

It is likely that Fred drove round and collected Lynda and her possessions. She was slim, with a nubile figure, long brown hair and she wore heavy-rimmed glasses, an appearance type not vastly different to Rose West at that time, who was two years older. As Fred was keen to point out, Lynda had a large bust for a slim girl. Even though Rose had a decent-sized chest, Lynda's bosoms were certainly larger. But what did that matter between friends?

At some stage shortly after moving in, Lynda got involved with Fred and Rose sexually. There is nothing to suggest that this was not initially consensual, but what is not in doubt was that within three weeks of moving to Cromwell Street, Lynda had been murdered, dismembered and buried in what had been a garage inspection pit in the back garden. It was the site where Fred would shortly build a downstairs bathroom.

The condition of the remains and the items recovered with them provided trace evidence for the fate that probably befell this young woman. Fred West also gave some indication of this scenario when he was interviewed by the police.

She had been gagged and bound with brown adhesive tape and white surgical tape extensively applied around her head to form a mask, with very little scope to breathe other than through a slit in the tape into which a tube was inserted. She may also have been bound with her own clothes that had been torn into strips for the purpose. West suggested that events were really an enactment of Lynda's own fantasies. He mentions the basement and the young women trussed and hanging. As John Bennett ruefully pointed out to me when I visited the wretched Cromwell Street basement in 1994, there were holes drilled in the beams for the purposes of suspending bound and gagged young women while Fred and Rose did to them whatever they wished. I have no doubt he was entirely correct in his assumption.

In Lynda's case the roughness, brutality and intensity of the sadomasochism went beyond any imaginable spectrum. The tragic young woman was the helpless prey in the feeding frenzy of wild beasts, toxically manic, hysterically fuelled by a mix of unchecked and uncontrollable abuse of power over another person. Lynda had become the helpless quarry of deficient, damaged, otherwise simpering, servile, anonymous human beings who happened to possess within them a vile capacity for psychopathic excess. I am reluctant to even go as far and say that such a disgusting episode was in essence borne of extreme sexual urges. I suspect it had more to do with repressed feelings of insecurity, inadequacy and a need for revenge.

The dismemberment was very extensive; it was a deliberate, painstaking mutilation of the corpse. Her legs had been disarticulated at the hip, her hands and feet had been cut off, her breastbone had been removed, seven of her ribs and twenty-five wrist and ankle bones were missing and she had probably been decapitated. Five cervical vertebrae bones, many fingers, toes, both kneecaps and parts of the wrists were also absent. Such significant parts of the victim's skeleton had not just been overlooked on excavation or somehow withered and evaporated in the intervening years. Both Fred and Rose West were asked by the police about what happened to these missing bones. Neither volunteered a satisfactory reply.

The consensus among police, psychologists and criminologists is that the taking of bodily mementos is an extension of the psychopath's repertoire, either a fascination with some aspect of the body, which could also include an internal organ or in the desire for absolute domination to retain possession of parts of the body.

The removal of the breastbone raises the spectre of a concentration on Lynda's breasts, which might have been anticipated. It is possible that her breasts had been cut off during torture, probably by Rose.

These were souvenirs stolen from the victims as much as the little hippie bangles and rings they wore on their wrists or fingers or the clothing they were wearing. I recall Rose West being asked whether Fred made the bones into a necklace for her. She, of course, remained no comment.

Some observers have suggested that burial at Much Marcle, Midland Road and then at Cromwell Street fitted this pattern of desire to retain possession of the human quarry. It is instructive that in Fred West's later police interviews when his mind was at times decidedly unsteady; in an almost dreamlike state he would claim that he could still feel these young women to be still with him, that he could feel their presence drifting up from the basement.

I recall two pieces of information in the preparation of the case for trial. One was an informal comment by Professor Knight into an inquiry by the police as to whether fingers and toes could have been cut off while the victims were still alive. He thoughtfully and quietly reflected that it was possible without killing the victims. The other piece of information came from a gynaecologist who had been instructed to prepare a report for the benefit of the defence. I was prompted to explore this area by the evidence of a number of dildos, some of which were of huge magnitude, that were recovered from 25 Cromwell Street and were used during sex by Rose. The question I needed answering was whether the rough application of an oversized dildo to the vaginas of the victims could have been a cause of death? The considered opinion I received was that such an occurrence would be unusual and unlikely; the vagina is, after all, designed to be sufficiently flexible to enable the delivery of a baby. Nevertheless, such an eventuality was possible where an object might result in rupturing of the vaginal wall and death could then conceivably result from the loss of blood through haemorrhaging. There is no evidence that there was such an eventuality and in any event, it was not a scenario proffered by the prosecution at Rose West's trial.

During the second week of May 1973, Lynda's mother, Mrs June Gough, was concerned that she had not heard from her daughter and made enquiries at her work and with one or two acquaintances. This led her around to Cromwell Street and eventually to the correct address at number 25. Mrs Gough, many years later at the trial, recalled a plump-ish lady coming to the door (in fact Rose was pregnant at the time); she believed this to be the same woman who had called around several weeks earlier to go for a drink with her daughter shortly before she moved out. She asked if her daughter was staying at 25 Cromwell Street and was curtly told that she had left and moved on. At this point, Mrs Gough recognised that the woman was wearing Lynda's slippers and then, peering through to the back of the house, noticed some of her daughter's clothes on the washing line. Rose then abruptly explained that Lynda had not been good at looking after the children and had gone to Devon to work at a holiday camp. Puzzled and unsettled, Mrs Gough left it there. She never saw her daughter again.

CAROL ANN COOPER

In November 1973, Carol Ann Cooper was fifteen years old. She had been in care at the Pines Children's Home, Worcester since the age of thirteen. Her father had placed her there following the breakdown of his second marriage. Carol's natural mother had died when she was four years old. Her father had been in the RAF and then worked as an insurance salesman. Her early years were not happy. The domestic turbulence and emotional deficit made her rebellious as a teenager; she kicked out against authority while also longing for a secure home life. She wanted to be loved. People close to her said that she was an attention seeker and that if someone showed interest and affection towards her, she would be theirs.

She was five foot six, physically strong and fit with bright blue eyes. She had her nickname, 'Caz', tattooed on her arm. She did it herself. On a fateful November evening, Carol had earned a privileged pass from the Pines and was going to stay at her grandmother's after an evening out with her boyfriend, Andrew, and other friends. Her relationship with Andrew had been strained, but they fancied each other and wanted to see each other again. They arranged a date for the following evening. Andrew gave her eighteen pence to catch the bus. He saw her get on the No. 5 bus from the centre of Worcester travelling to the Warndon suburb.

No one knows how Caz ended up snared by Fred and Rose West. She was seen getting on the bus. She should have been safe. The inference is that she must have encountered Fred and or Rose driving past her after she alighted at her destination. Speculation that she was already known to the Wests and had even been to Cromwell Street is fanciful. Worcester has and had then its own centre of gravity, its own cafes and bars, its own generation of restless young people, its own motorcycle gangs and young predatory males, its own waifs and strays, and vulnerable young girls. To imagine that there is some fringe underclass, some nexus revolving in a coordinated social network between disparate urban centres, where everybody knows everybody between Gloucester, Tewkesbury and Worcester is, of course, an oversimplification. The most probable scenario is that Fred and Rose were on the prowl in their Ford Popular and had seen the need to trawl far from their own locality. They would have pulled up on the kerb as Carol walked to her grandmother's and were able to offer this bored, bold, brazen, adventurous and needy young woman a lift, maybe to a party, to the pub or for a drink. Whatever it was, the young woman did not need much persuading. She was never seen again.

"Rose told me it was kinky love sessions that went wrong. That's how the girls came to get killed." This was what Fred told the police during his extensive interviews.

The truth is Rose did not need to tell Fred anything; he was present with her when these diabolical outrages were committed. Fred was outwardly a snivelling, grovelling little gnome of a man who could soft soap inexperienced young women. The sexually perverse, sadistic killer lurked within this pathetic exterior. In Rose he created another monster. Her stuff was that of a sexually abused, timid, downtrodden young woman with a deep-rooted attachment disorder. This was the clay from which he moulded a partner who could, with his encouragement, whip herself up in into a searing, screeching, wild, hysterical frenzy of unmitigated anger and violence, all directed at some helpless, trussed-up young victim for whom there was no mercy and no hope.

Theories have been put forward that their killing of Carol was a calculation to avoid the mishaps and intrusions of the law that had occurred with Caroline Owens. I suspect that this was not really the only or a major consideration. They already knew how to avoid detection. Caroline was a mistake that they had, in any event, got away with. It is more correct to say that the act of killing simply did not matter to them. After all, they had both killed before. In these one-sided sadistic orgies, primitive unconscious drives reigned freely; they were not mediated by any kind of rational thought. The logic kicked in after the event, when Fred would 'sort it out' by embarking on his extended pleasure-seeking modus operandi of body disposal.

With Carol Ann Cooper's remains was an elasticated cloth wound around her jaw. She was tightly and inescapably gagged. There was clearly a need to stop her shouting out. Her plight would have been desperately under protest and by no stretch of imagination consensual. The routine would have been for her to have been bundled, bound and gagged, from the car to the basement at 25 Cromwell Street, where she would have been trussed up and her breathing further restricted by tape around her head, allowing for some nasal air intake. She was then suspended from a beam and sadistically sexually abused by Fred and Rose. She may have had dildos used on her. She may have been beaten with a metal buckled leather belt. It is possible that Fred had sexual intercourse, but this would have preceded any severing of fingers and toes, whether before or after death. The indications are that Fred was turned off by bodily fluids of women, at least while they were alive. His preoccupation with the menstrual cycles of his wife and daughters and other girls lodging at Cromwell Street was because of his innate repulsion. He nevertheless bizarrely had no reservation in dismembering bodies with all the blood and gore that entailed.

Fifty of Carol's bones were missing from the remains recovered. These included wrist bones and thirty-five finger and toe bones. Her legs had been disarticulated at the hip. Part of her breastbone was missing, and it appeared as though her head had been ceremoniously and neatly placed in the makeshift grave over the remains.

The philosopher George Berkeley once asked whether if a tree fell in forest and no one was there to perceive it, would it make a noise? The saddest aspect of Carol Ann Cooper's case was that, apart from her boyfriend of the moment, there was no one really to mourn her or miss her, no grieving loved ones. And soon her grandmother would die, then Carol's lonely, tortured passing would, at least for twenty years, be erased from memory.

LUCY PARTINGTON

The indiscriminate nature of Fred and Rose's reign of terror is highlighted by the abduction and murder of Lucy Partington. Waifs and strays may have been their staple diet, but their opportunistic lust spared no unsuspecting young woman. By unsuspecting, I mean a belief that in a modern, civilised society with strong institutions of law and order and a benevolent liberal democratic state, it should be possible, without a second thought, to walk freely down the street and to wait to catch a bus without fear of threat or intimidation, let alone abduction.

Lucy Partington was a conscientious and intellectual university student. She was thoughtful and religious. She had recently converted to Roman Catholicism. She did not have a boyfriend. She was in her final year at University of Exeter studying English Literature. It was the Christmas vacation of 1973 and she was staying with her mother at the family home in the quaint Cotswold village of Gretton, not far from Winchcombe, about ten miles north of Cheltenham, as you head towards Tewkesbury.

She very much had in mind that her finals were on the horizon. It was her hope after Exeter to study for a postgraduate degree at the Courtauld Institute in London. She was from a high-achieving middle-class family. Her father, who was separated from her mother, was an industrial chemist and her mother was an architect. Her uncle was the writer Kingsley Amis, and as a child Lucy played with her cousin Martin Amis, who also became a novelist. Lucy was close to her siblings: an elder sister, Marian and younger brothers, David and Mark.

On December 27th, Lucy was visiting an old school friend, Helen Render, from her Pate's Grammar school days. Helen had a disability and Lucy was a close and caring friend. While at Helen's, she completed her Courtauld application and, upon saying farewell to Helen at about 10:15pm after supper, set off to post the letter on the way to catch the bus back to Gretton. The bus stop was three minutes away on Evesham Road heading out to Cheltenham, just before the racecourse. Lucy's brother, David, had said that if the bus did not turn up on time, he would be happy to give her a lift. Lucy was never seen again.

It is evident that Fred and Rose West drove past Lucy while she was waiting for a bus and she ended up in their vehicle. A friend of Lucy's had, some months earlier, had an alarming experience when a scruffy man on his own fitting Fred West's description had been persistent in offering a lift and had to be strenuously declined. The prospect of Lucy willingly accepting a lift is doubtful. It has been suggested that the Wests would have driven along that road from Gloucester to Bishop's Cleeve and at Christmas-time, that would have been a destination.

This scenario needs to be analysed. If Fred and Rose had been visiting the Letts's home in Tobyfield Road, they would have had Anne Marie, aged nine years; Heather, aged three years; Mae, aged two years and Stephen, who was a baby of five months old. This would have been a full car. There was no room for Lucy to get in and she would have declined the absurdity of being offered a lift in such circumstances. In addition, in order to be heading in the right direction to offer a lift, the Wests would have needed to travelling towards Bishop's Cleeve; but there is no way a family would arrange a visit with the children after ten in the evening. If they had been returning to Gloucester, they would have been on the wrong side of the road, heading in the wrong direction. If Anne Marie had been in the car, she would have been old enough to know if some stranger was being abducted, beaten and gagged.

Marian Partington, Lucy's sister, in her book *If You Sit Very Still* mentions a discussion that Lucy had had at a party she had attended just a few weeks before her abduction. She was at a get-together at her tutor's house in Exeter when a friend said they intended to hitchhike. Lucy responded to strongly disapprove, but her tutor said, "Well, I suppose it would be all right if there was a woman as well as a man in the car."

It is possible that one of the young women lodging at Cromwell Street was babysitting while Fred and Rose went out cruising around on the prowl. But in that eventuality Fred and Rose would have, on their return to Cromwell Street, had some dialogue with the babysitter about the children. By December 1973, there was limited access into the cellar either from a narrow gap in from the rear garden or otherwise through the inside of the house. What is absolutely certain is that Lucy would not have gone there willingly.

Lucy's remains were recovered from an excavation of the cellar in March 1994. When interviewed about Lucy, Fred came up with a crude and demonstrably fictitious story about being in a relationship with her and that she wanted him to meet her parents, but when he said he did not want to meet them, she then told him that she was pregnant with his child and demanded a thousand pounds for an abortion or otherwise she would tell Rose. So then Fred 'lost it' and strangled her. The truth is that, as with the other victims, after abduction, Lucy would have been beaten, bound and gagged, and sexually abused. She would have been strung up in the basement. She would have been raped and tormented as a plaything for the sick sadistic pleasure of both Fred and Rose. The duration of her suffering at the hands of the Wests may well have been about seven days because as the Crown pointed out, accident and emergency medical notes confirm that late in the evening of January 3rd, Fred West attended at Gloucester General Hospital with a deep gash to his left hand, consistent with an inadvertently self-inflicted wound. Such a wound could well have been caused in the subdued light of the cellar as Fred West, sweating in some manically perverse heightened mental state, wielded a sharp blade as he frantically cut and hacked, dismembering the body.

It cannot be known whether both Fred and Rose were present at the time of her killing, but the knowledge that her life would have to end was, without doubt, common to the pair of them. From what we know of Fred West's proclivity to enjoy the process of dismemberment, it is likely that he went back down to the basement, probably after a cup of tea and a cheese sandwich, to check on the state of the victim. Rose had, by now, already sated her sadistic lust and had other things to get on with; maybe she was getting the children's school uniforms ready for the new term, maybe she had punters to entertain, maybe she just went to bed.

If Lucy was exhausted, limp and unconscious, with her expression hidden by bound tape and gagging, it may have been unclear whether she was still alive. West may have strangled her to make sure, because he enjoyed strangling. He could have dispatched his quarry speedily with a strategically placed knife wound. He may have strangled and stabbed her. Whatever it was, at this stage it was a prerequisite to a sick, ritualistic process of dismemberment.

Lucy had had her legs disarticulated at the hip. She had been decapitated; heavy binding tape was around her skull; and her right shoulder blade, three ribs and left kneecap were missing. Fifty-two foot and toe bones, eleven ankle and three wrist bones were also missing, as were bones from her fingers and toes. A knife dropped into the hole with the dismembered body lends credence to the theory that Fred injured himself in the process of dismemberment.

Like the next victim, Thérèse Siegenthaler, who followed a few months after Lucy, she had no connection whatsoever with the Wests or 25 Cromwell Street. Both were students and both wore glasses (as did Lynda Gough). It is possible that the approximate build and the wearing of glasses may have had a fascination for Rose West in arbitrarily selecting victims that had some passing resemblance to herself?

When opportunity is given to warped sadistic feelings, similarity prompts a prurient curiosity in the features and body of the chosen victim; control enables passing impulses to morph from attraction into hatred and rage. The simultaneous invasion of personal effects, the quality and cleanliness of clothing, the scent of the fabric cleaner, the contents of handbags, diaries, jewellery; all would excite comparisons and give rise to invidious assumptions about the lives of these women. Fred and Rose West would reinforce each other's warped, irrational utterings that first belittled and ridiculed and then contrived to justify treating them as less than human, so as rapidly to progress to a sense of justification in doing with them as they pleased and then taking their lives.

I recall with some regret when Lucy's mother telephoned me at my office in May 1994, requesting that I consent to the release of her daughter's remains so that the funeral could be arranged. She had obtained my number from the police and sounded calm and dignified in having to discuss matters with me, the solicitor for one of the alleged perpetrators of Lucy's murder. I had to explain that it was normal practice in murder cases for the solicitors of suspects to arrange a second opinion on the pathology report. I acknowledged that from the information that was being made public, it might be reasonable to wonder why a second opinion might be necessary. I expressed my condolences and stated that I well understood why she would wish to progress arrangements for a dignified burial after so many years. I apologised for the fact that I was the one who, in discharging my duties, was the person holding things up. Mrs Partington sincerely and magnanimously said that she understood that I had my job to do and that she hoped the remains could be released as soon as possible. I stated that I would do my best to expedite matters. I was also aware that Howard Ogden would likewise need to consent to the release. Lucy's remains were only finally released when Fred West committed suicide on 1st January 1995, many months after I had consented to their release. By that stage, Bobbetts MCann were acting for Fred.

THÉRÈSE SIEGENTHALER

Thérèse Siegenthaler was a twenty-one-year-old Swiss sociology undergraduate studying at Woolwich College of Further Education in South East London. It was the Easter vacation and she was hitching to catch a ferry to Ireland for a pre-arranged meeting with a Catholic priest, who shared an interest in South African politics. She was one of five children of divorced Swiss parents. She was, however, sufficiently fluent in English to study in London. She was petite, but with a slim, strong physique; brown hair; large-rimmed glasses and did not wear make-up. Her family described her as confident; she had trained in judo and would have had some belief in her ability for basic self-defence. She had had boyfriends and was sexually aware. She was also someone of high principles.

The probability is that Fred West did pick her up, as she was hitchhiking. Precisely where is not clear. West claimed that it was near to Evesham. This does appear to be consistent with his stomping ground as it was north of Gloucestershire. It could also have been broadly in the direction of Holyhead, which may have been the destination port to catch the ferry to Dublin. It goes with the territory of hitchhiking to allow for slight detours and inconveniences. It may also have meant she was allowing some flexibility as to the departure time of the ferry she intended to board. Whatever happened, once she climbed into Fred West's Austin 35, her fate was sealed. She was never seen alive again, except by Fred and Rose.

It is likely that he started talking dirty before stopping the vehicle and asking her for sex. She would have resisted before being repeatedly punched until he knocked her out. He may then have raped her in the back of the van, which according to Anne Marie, had a mattress in the back, so that he could also use his works vehicle as his 'shagging wagon'. It was about this time that Fred had started taking the eleven-year-old Anne Marie on building jobs with him and forcing her to have sex in the rear compartment. He would have bound her hands and later her legs, gagged her and taken her back to 25 Cromwell Street, where for Thérèse, the nightmare would only become markedly worse. She would have been unceremoniously dumped into the cellar, probably via the back garden basement vent. She would then have been Fred and Rose's plaything before dying from the sadistic treatment or killed to ensure her silence. The routine was by now tried and tested. The Wests were, they believed, killing with impunity.

In interviews, Fred admitted that they had bound and gagged the young woman. Heavy packing tape had repeatedly been wrapped around her head and a small scarf binding gagged her mouth, all making breathing laboured and difficult. The young woman would have been in enormous discomfort even before being hoisted up on one of the basement beams.

West admitted that there had been 'kinky' sex and sadomasochism, because, as was his typical reply, that was what the girl wanted. She then got all lovey-dovey and wanted a relationship with Fred rather than just sex, so rather than upsetting Rose, he 'lost it' and strangled the young woman. It is not difficult to unpick the truth from the nonsense in this narrative.

An alternative scenario, which is just about plausible, is that Fred, after picking up Miss Siegenthaler as she was hitchhiking, through chat found out a little bit about her, in particular the fact that all her family were in Switzerland and that she was essentially alone in the UK. He may well have put on the charm and suggested that she come back to Cromwell Street, possibly even to stay the night as a lodger before continuing on her travels the following day.

Such a scenario would have more immediately involved Rose in initiating the physical and sexual abuse, leading ultimately to the young Swiss woman's awful incarceration in the basement.

Thérèse was in close contact with her family. They knew she was only going to Ireland for a week and she had already bought a ticket to a theatre production in London for when she returned. She had also told her father that she would be flying to Zurich to see her family later in the year. Her disappearance was reported to the Metropolitan Police. It was clear that she had not made some rash decision to run away. She had 3,600 Swiss francs in her bank account, a sum that remained untouched as the months passed by. It was evident that she had met with some serious mishap.

When her remains were recovered from the basement of 25 Cromwell Street, apart from the tape bound round her skull and the cloth gag, there were rope bindings. Her collarbone was missing, as were five ankle bones, nine wrist bones, and twenty-four finger and toe bones.

SHIRLEY HUBBARD

In November 1974, Shirley Hubbard was a fifteen-and-a-half-year-old schoolgirl. She was originally from Birmingham, where her birth name was Shirley Lloyd, but her parents separated when she was two years old. After a time in a care home, she was fostered to James and Linda Hubbard and when she was twelve, assumed their surname.

She was an attractive, flirtatious young woman who resided with her foster parents on Ombersley Road in Droitwich. She was known to slope off from school or sneak out of her ground floor bedroom window at home to meet with boyfriends. In October 1974, she had run away from home, taking a duffle bag with her possessions and left a note for her foster parents saying that she had run away and that she would be in touch. A week later, she was found camping in a field with a soldier.

On Thursday November 14th, she again packed a duffle bag with her possessions and left home. It is known that on that day she went to her work placement at the make-up section of Debenhams in Worcester. She then met her boyfriend, Daniel Davis. They bought some food and sat along the riverbank before visiting Daniel's family. At about 8:30pm, Daniel saw Shirley onto a bus heading from Worcester to Droitwich. She was never seen again. Daniel had arranged to see her the following evening at 7pm. He waited for her, but she never turned up. He was disappointed but guessed that she had met someone else. Shirley was never seen alive again.

While there are many similarities with Carol Ann Cooper's disappearance, it is nevertheless evident that Shirley already had some plan not to return home, although she did not apparently confide her plans with her boyfriend. It is not clear whether Shirley was carrying her duffle bag with her possessions during her sociable afternoon with Daniel and then later with his family and if it was why someone did not ask her where she was going.

Whatever the whys and wherefores, the tragic outcome was that Shirley Hubbard came into the clutches of Fred and Rose West. With mechanical certainty, she was abducted, bound, gagged and trussed up, subjected to violent, depraved, sadomasochistic physical and sexual abuse before eventually dying from the physical trauma to her body or otherwise killed to ensure she did not have a chance to report the perpetrators of the outrage committed against her.

The forensic and pathology reports on the remains of Shirley Hubbard indicated that heavy adhesive tape had been wound around her head at least twelve times, thereby making a complete mask from the top to her mouth, which was then gagged with tape. To enable her to just about breathe, two pieces of a thin, transparent tube had been forced up through the tape mask and pushed deep into her nostrils. This would imitate the rubber suits which covered faces in the pornographic videos that Fred and Rose collected with such enthusiasm. Missing from the remains were forty of her bones, including seven wrist bones, thirteen finger and toe bones and the third thoracic vertebrae. She had been decapitated and her legs were disarticulated at the hip.

The idea is that the restriction of the airways is supposed to heighten the sexual experience of the person so bound and impeded. The curious aspect of this is the suggestion that this appalling spectacle somehow was about the sensual experience of the victim, which is of course absurd. This was no carefully negotiated contract between someone with a predisposition to sexual subservience and someone with a preference for domination with the essential ingredient of mutual consent and respect for safety and welfare. Apart from anything else, as psychopaths the Wests were devoid of empathy and cared not a jot about the enjoyment or the pain and suffering of the captive young woman.

The compulsive, increasingly degenerate repertoire of Fred and Rose West was marginally about sex. Fred would have his momentary dabble, forcing his grubby little tool into the body of a completely traumatised, hyperventilating, barely able to breathe, trussed-up young victim, as she bled in unimaginable discomfort and pain. Rose would gratuitously and vengefully dish out a beating, with wet buckle belts, hands, fists, stabbing and abusing with vibrators and outrageously sized dildos. Yet the orgy of wickedly trapping and breaking the bodies of innocent young women was because they discovered they could, so they did, because this dysfunctional, inadequate couple was getting one over on the rest of humanity. This serves to emphasise how despicable their actions were. It provided some kind of horribly distorted mutual affirmation. For Rose, it was a grotesque valve for the seething rage within her. For Fred, it was a good day at the office, doing what he did with treacherous guile, satisfying his enduring fascination with killing and dismembering.

The occasional comments of lodgers complaining of wild banging, thumping and loud, strange, eerie noises coming from the cellar of 25 Cromwell Street some nights during the 1970s is documented in the statements of evidence obtained by the police during the investigation. It bears a contemporaneous audible trace to the horror of those events.

JUANITA MOTT

Juanita Mott's parents split up when she was a child. Her father was a US serviceman and her mother an English woman, who remarried and lived in Coney Hill, Gloucester, where she subsequently had two further daughters. In 1972, Juanita left school to work in a bottling factory before finding herself unemployed. During this time, she became familiar with the cheap lodgings in Cromwell Street and visited friends and acquaintances there frequently. She knew Fred West. She had been in trouble with the law in 1974. She was an attractive girl who, though headstrong and independent, was not regarded as the brightest spark on the block. She did briefly reside at 25 Cromwell Street, but then moved out.

In 1975, when Juanita was eighteen, to save money she gladly accepted the offer from her friend, Jennifer Baldwin, to reside with her family at their bungalow in Newent, a picturesque little town about ten miles west of Gloucester. Geographically, it is regarded as part of the Forest of Dean, although in terms of its architecture and its market gardening and wine growing, has more in common with the neighbouring county of Herefordshire. It was a town Fred West had visited to try his luck with the local wenches in his teenage years as he motorcycled around the nearby countryside near to Much Marcle.

At about 8pm on Friday April 11th 1975, Juanita was hitchhiking from Newent to Gloucester on a weekend night out as she often did. Jennifer was getting married the following day and as Juanita had arranged to look after Jennifer's children during the ceremony, she would not have intended a late evening. As Juanita's social and travel habits were predictable and known by Fred and Rose West, the fact that they happened to be driving along the route from Newent at that time is not that surprising. And it is possible that she was interested in a relationship with Fred West.

What is not so clear, and this applies to a number of the West's victims, is why this young woman who had freely and without incident been coming and going from the lion's den for a couple of years should then be singled out as the next target? What might trigger the arbitrary bloodlust of a psychopath? Could it be some innocent comment by one of her friends within earshot of Fred or Rose? Might it have been some item of clothing or the way she was sitting inadvertently showing too much leg, or a glimpse of her knickers? Was it a perfume or a body odour or the way she wore her hair? Was it purely indiscriminate opportunism? Maybe she was not targeted as the next victim but was picked up by Fred West for a casual dalliance.

Whatever it was, Juanita Mott was picked up on that early springtime evening and she was never seen alive again.

With the remains there were two white knee-length socks wrapped around the skull; also around the skull as a gag were two nylon stockings, a pair of knickers and brassiere. The two square and one-metre deep grave also had a seven-foot length of nylon-covered rope with various knots in it. In an interview, Fred West had described 'making love' to Juanita Mott on a mattress in the basement. She may have been bound and incapacitated prostrate rather than suspended from a beam. At some stage, Rose would have joined in to sexually abuse and humiliate the young victim before she was murdered.

It is possible that Fred was having a sneaky impromptu shag when Rose joined in, armed with whips, knives and dildos and upped the ante. She may have been particularly angry with Juanita for rebuffing earlier sexual overtures, which was the reason Juanita had moved out the year before. At some stage, something caused a violent departure from the usual course of mechanical destruction of the captured young woman. It may have been Rose who delivered the killer blow with a heavy hammer belonging to Fred that happened to be with building tools belonging to Fred that were nearby on the basement floor. Whatever happened, this constituted an additional unusual feature as to the violence of her demise. The base of her skull was badly fractured in a way that would have required such a very heavy blunt force, the kind of damage that might result from being aggressively and purposefully smashed over the head with a lump hammer.

The condition of Juanita's remains when excavated from the cellar at 25 Cromwell street bore all the hallmarks of her slayers' brutal handiwork. She had been decapitated; her legs had been disarticulated at the hip. Bones missing from the remains included three neck vertebrae, her eleventh thoracic vertebrae, both of her kneecaps, a rib, parts of her hands and a number of her toes. A total of eighty bones were absent.

According to police investigatory records, Juanita Mott's disappearance was never reported to the police. This is another great regret in the rotten West saga. If there had been a contemporaneous missing persons file opened, it would almost certainly have led the police to Fred and Rose West's door. It would have been an opportunity for the police to search 25 Cromwell Street and consider the accumulating plethora of sadomasochistic paraphernalia, pornographic home movies, photographs of female genitalia and possibly send some sniffer dogs into the basement. Alas, it would be another twenty years and several more victims later before that happened.

SHIRLEY ROBINSON

Shirley Robinson was born in October 1959 in Rutland. Her father, Roy, was in the RAF and so the family often moved. In

1961, her father was posted to Singapore and then the family returned to Darlington. Her parents split up. First she stayed with her mother and then with her father and then with her mother again. When her mother remarried, Shirley's relationship with her broke down and she was sent to board at a special school in Wolverhampton, as she had specific learning needs. She was then moved to a school in Bristol. At fourteen, she ran away from the school and took various temporary jobs. At this time, she realised that she was bisexual. She also started working as a prostitute. By the time she was sixteen, she had started working as a waitress in a gay club in Bristol.

Bill Letts met up with Shirley Robinson in Bristol. Maybe he was visiting the gay club at the time. In any event, he offered her a job as a live-in waitress at the Green Lantern Cafe on Bristol Road, Gloucester that he had set up with Fred West. One morning in April 1977, Fred stopped off at the cafe and saw Shirley. Eventually, she got into a conversation with Fred West, who was in his benign wise older man mode. Shirley found him easy to talk to and told him that she was bisexual, a fact that would have prompted West to encourage a meeting with Rose and the prospect of a new sexual adventure at Shirley's expense. After a few days, Shirley told Fred that Bill Letts was trying to mess about with her sexually and that she found this a big turn-off. Full of tea and sympathy, without hesitation Fred offered the young woman a room as a lodger at 25 Cromwell Street, where she would remain for the next fifteen months becoming, for a time an integral part of the weird extended family set up.

Very soon Shirley was nurtured into a *ménage à trois*, which apparently she acceded to in a full and consensual way. In addition to an initial blossoming of a lesbian friendship with Rose, Shirley would also help Fred with small building jobs in the evening, including at 24 and 25 Midland Road and addresses of other properties in Cromwell Street. These were opportunities for Fred and Shirley to get close and there seems little doubt that she was smitten with him and readily offered herself to him behind Rose's back.

Everyone in the house knew she was in an ongoing sexual relationship with Fred. She was pregnant, although Fred and Rose proffered some shambolic pretence that Fred was covering for some businessman who had made Shirley pregnant. This may have suited a phoney self-image Fred liked to portray as a noble savage, replicating the supposedly magnanimous gesture when he married Rena Costello when she was pregnant with another man's child. And at the same time, ostensibly it saved Rose's blushes. After all, it would be intolerable for anyone to seriously imagine that any young pretender in the West household could have designs of stepping into the shoes of the now-dominant matriarch.

Fred enjoyed the tension this created with Rose, who for some months was on edge but trying to control her rage. It could only be a matter of time before the valve would blow. Fred would fan the flames by announcing Shirley as the next Mrs West. The naïve and foolish girl believed she was secure and a viable competitor with Rose for Fred's affection. It was all an illusion, part of some hideous game that Fred was cultivating. It demonstrates another dimension to Fred West's psychopathy. The charade he created played a cruel game with the intensely felt emotions of a young woman pregnant with his child, falsely leading her to believe there was some prospect of a future together. Those delicate emotions were as pliable and disposable as the limbs of her body that would soon be dismembered and thrown into a hole dug in the rear garden of 25 Cromwell Street.

At this time, Rose was pregnant with the child of one of her black lovers. The baby, Tara, was born on December 9th 1978. Shirley's pregnancy had been confirmed by a doctor at the

Rikinal Clinic in the Park, Gloucester in October 1977. She had just turned eighteen years old. Her baby was due in June 1978. Rose found herself pregnant again very quickly, this time with a child belonging to Fred. It is reasonable to believe that the emotional tension and competition between Fred and Rose at this time was intense. While Fred had encouraged his wife to have a baby with one of their Jamaican friends, this now affected him; he was conflicted, it hurt him and he felt he needed revenge and it suited him to hurt Rose with the prospect of Shirley having his child. He even went as far as to dress up in his best suit and pose with Shirley for a professional photograph as though they were newly engaged. Rose turned on Shirley with venom.

Shirley's remains were the second set to be recovered during the weekend of February 26th 1994. Her left femur had come out of the ground during the excavation of the garden in search of Heather West. It led to Fred promptly admitting to killing Shirley Robinson and Alison Chambers in addition to Heather.

Her remains were located in a hole two feet by two feet and about three feet deep outside and to the side of the downstairs kitchen extension in the part of the rear garden nearest to the house. There was no tape or bindings with her bones, thus bearing evidence that the motive here was to get rid of a young woman, an interloper who had incurred Rose's wrath by aspiring to be her successor in Fred's life as the next Mrs Fred West. Nevertheless, her body had been dismembered, with her legs crudely hacked off at the hip, both her kneecaps were missing, as was the upper part of her breastbone, two of her ribs, many wrist and ankle bones, as well as many bones from her fingers and toes. None of Shirley's hair was present. This is unusual and indicates that West may have scalped her. The baby had also been cut out of her and the remains located next to Shirley's. A few tiny bones of the baby were also missing.

The likelihood is that Shirley would have been summarily dispatched by strangulation, probably after a confrontation with Fred. Liz Brewer recalls that Shirley was tired and depressed and had decided to return to 25 Cromwell Street to rest rather than go out with her.

When first interviewed in 1994, Rose denied even knowing who Shirley Robinson was. The evidence from Anne Marie, who remembered Shirley fondly as a lodger who would play with her; Liz Brewer, who knew her well as a long-term lodger and Shirley's medical records that confirmed her address and Fred's admissions, made it impossible that Rose could not have known who she was. Nearer the trial, Rose suddenly remembered precisely who Shirley was. Such inconsistencies did not help her cause.

Fred and Rose told people that Shirley had decided to go to Germany to see her father, which was plausible. They cancelled her supplementary benefits and for a time fraudulently claimed unemployment benefits for her, prompting an official from the DHS, Peter Gregson, to call at 25 Cromwell Street. Rose answered the door to confirm Shirley had gone abroad.

ALISON CHAMBERS

Alison Chambers, or Ali as she was known, had been born in Hanover, Germany in 1963 while her father was serving with RAF. Her parents split up when she was thirteen and she went to live with her mother, who remarried and moved in Pontypridd, South Wales. Alison did not settle and was sent to a boarding school nearby. After running away from the school that West Glamorgan Social Services had placed her in, now aged sixteen, she was sent to Jordan's Brook House on the outskirts of Gloucester. Alison did not like staying in the home, which she shared with twenty-one other young women, who similarly came from unsettled home environments.

It is easy to describe these young women as wayward, headstrong, difficult or even delinquent, but to do so does them all a great disservice. Their insecurities and consequent reactions in absconding, withdrawing and generally not fitting in are really predictable symptoms. What they all craved was a cohesive, loving family environment, independence and some excitement in what for most of them were dreary lives that appeared to offer little hope. And the illusion and trickery of satisfying those needs was offered in spades by Fred and Rose West at their Shangri-La, 25 Cromwell Street.

Social services' records indicate that from her arrival in December 1978 to the discontinuation of her record in September 1979, Alison Chambers absconded eight times in nine months from Jordan's Brook. It is evident from her roommate, Sharon Compton, that like many other girls from the home, Alison became a regular visitor to Cromwell Street, where Rose would offer orange squash, biscuits and a sympathetic ear to listen to their various tales of woe. Rose was the agony aunt.

Alison was not a popular girl at the home and is remembered as a fantasist who would imagine her life as rather different to the way it was. She loved to write poetry and dreamed of living an idyllic life on a farm. It is evident, however, that she was articulate and had a work placement at a firm of solicitors in Westgate Street, Gloucester as a junior clerk/receptionist. She was remembered as smartly turned out and presentable.

I find the recurring narrative about 'the farm' interesting. It permeated the dreams and aspirations of not only Alison, but also Heather. It is fair to speculate that in spinning a yarn, Fred could safely wax lyrical in talking about farms on account of his own rural background. It may provide a valuable starting point for unpicking some of Fred's lies. It was clearly fertile ground used by Rose in her storytelling as a pretext to allure young women to the spider's web.

Mention was made of a farm in Stoke Valley. The caravan park near Stoke Orchard was where Fred was living when he first came into contact with Rose. In 1980, when Fred was arrested for receiving stolen goods, some of the tapes stolen disclosed what Fred described as him making love to Rose at a farm out at Stoke Orchard. The possibility of Mary Bastholm's body being disposed of at Stoke Orchard has already been considered. I believe that when Fred and Rose used the word 'farm', he was using it as a collective term for a burial site other than 25 Cromwell Street or 25 Midland Road. Fred's earliest victims were buried in farmer's fields at Much Marcle. I also believe that the word 'farm' referred ominously to Hempsted waste tip in Gloucester. Fred, in his later police interviews, mentioned bodies buried at a farm. When Rose showed Alison a picture of a farm, what she was really saying to her was that they were going to sexually abuse her and then kill her.

Immersion in rural life normally inculcates an acute sense of the seasons, of life's cycles, of birth, growth, summer and autumnal harvest, of winter's fading and hibernation, of tilling and ploughing and making ready for the renewal of the following spring. For Fred, there seems to have been a fixation on the perverted abuse of sheep, the slaughter of spring lambs and pigs, the trapping of rabbits and squirrels, and the farm turf rich, amidst the soil and scrub, with multifarious bones of all the creatures that for a passing moment thrived with young, beating hearts before being snared and butchered to feed the family's needs. For Fred West more than anything, 'farm' meant death and burial. He saw himself as the grim reaper. Maybe he was.

It is quite possible that Alison consensually entered into a sexual relationship with both Fred and Rose. She was also acting as the nanny to the five young West children. She moved in with the Wests in early August 1979. Sharon Compton recalls arranging to meet her on August 6th to hand over a few of her possessions that she had omitted to take when she packed her things to leave Jordan's Brook the preceding day. Alison did not turn up. However, in September, Alison wrote a letter to her mother and stepfather in South Wales, explaining that she had found support and friendship with a caring family and was helping to look after the children. She told them not to worry or try to find her and that in due course she would contact them. That was the last that was ever heard of her.

It is inevitable that in some outrageous frenzy of violent, sadomasochistic sex, Alison was bound and battered before eventually being killed, the latest human sacrifice at the altar of these depraved psychopaths. Her fashionable, purple, shiny buckle belt was tightly strapped around her jaw and secured at the top of her head. Pieces of hair remained trapped in the buckle.

Alison's remains were found under a garden pond made of blue bricks that Fred had stolen from a building site. This was located a metre back from the downstairs bathroom extension. She had been dismembered, legs removed at the hip and she had been decapitated, although the bones were cleanly severed without the usual hack marks. Even though her fingernails were found, twenty-seven of her thirty wrist and ankle bones and sixty-three of her finger and toe bones were missing. Also absent were both of her kneecaps and the upper part of her breastbone.

The first bone recovered in the House of Horrors inquiry, even before Heather's remains were located, was Alison Chamber's left femur.

HEATHER WEST

On a summer's day, the setting would have had a rustic charm, with the green rolling fields in the silt plane of the meandering river Wye. And there, nestled close to the river, was the unassuming parish church of St Michael's in the village of Tintern, on the Gwent border with Gloucestershire in the Forest of Dean.

But this was the bleak mid-winter; the air was cold, the uncut grass amidst the old leaning gravestones of the church cemetery was windswept and the little chapel too exposed to avoid the winter chill whistling through the nooks and crannies of the old, wooden doors and crumbling, leaded windows.

The officiating priest, the Rev Julian White, was a towering man with long hair and a swarthy, black beard and an appropriately solemn face. He was clad in a long, black priestly gown and a dog collar. He greeted the handful of attendees, including three of the West siblings – Mae, Stephen and Tara – who had covertly been advised where and when the funeral was to take place. The secrecy was necessary to avoid the risk of an undignified media scrum.

There had been a disagreement between Mae and Stephen of the one part and their half-sister, Anne Marie, on account of her agreeing to give evidence for the prosecution at her stepmother's trial. The situation appeared to have been mediated by the respective parties' publishers, one of whom was present. Whatever happened, Anne Marie was not in attendance and neither was Rose West, who, fresh from her conviction for ten murders, including Heather, had applied to the governor at Durham for attendance on compassionate grounds. Her request, perhaps not unexpectedly, had been turned down. As her solicitor, I was present, along with my wife, Katherine. Also present at the back of

117

the tiny chapel, stood a couple of police officers in civilian clothes, who had been involved in the investigation.

It was a strange gathering. The setting had a gothic foreboding, Kafkaesque in a way, below grey skies, amidst the old tombstones, a new grave was neatly dug and yet yards away, on the same level the wild wintry current swept the river fast by the edge. And this was Heather's sanctuary, her place of rest, yet even now there was a vulnerability as nature growled across the fields and whistled and rattled in the belfry.

It was Wednesday December 20th 1995 when Heather West came home to a place she had never lived. The service was dignified, but there could be no joy in remembering a life lived, a life that had expired so many years earlier. There was no music, no favourite pop song, no personal anthem recalling the good times, just simple words and a little prayer.

Stephen made a statement:

"After laying her to rest, we can now resume our lives."

This statement, though sounding abrupt, was a sincere wish for closure for his sister. Mae and Stephen as young children had missed their older sister terribly. Their parents were dismissive of their enquiries about Heather. They had made their own efforts to find her, contacting children's television programmes asking for help. All to no avail.

Anne Marie's last message to her half-sister had been left on the gate at 25 Cromwell Street nearly a year earlier. She had written:

"To my sister Heather, I've searched and sought, I've wept and prayed we'd meet again some sunny day. Missing you so very much. Will always love and remember you. All my fondest love, Big Sis, Anna Marie."

FODIWIL was the cryptic acronym that Heather had needed to use when she wrote down her humble, unambitious dream of a life away from 25 Cromwell Street, away from the sinister, oppressive clutches of her parents. 'Forest of Dean I will live'. That such a statement should be so subversive, create such anxiety in the mind of the author, provides some measure of the underlying fears she had of the regime she had grown up in.

Tintern was the place she returned to. This reminded me of William Wordsworth's poem of idyllic beauty upon his own revisiting of the picturesque Wye Valley. No doubt they were sentiments also felt by Heather.

Tintern Abbey:

"The day is come when I again repose
Here, under this dark sycamore, and view
These plots of cottage-ground, these orchard-tufts,
Which, at this season, with their unripe fruits,
Are clad in one green hue, and lose themselves."

All the other victims had had their funerals and were reburied earlier at private family services. She was the last victim, but the first full set of remains to be recovered; she was the gateway to the gruelling unravelling, discovery and recovery of the other victims. She was the last to be reburied with the sanctity of a Christian burial in consecrated ground. Her funeral had been postponed in what proved to be the false hope that Rose would be able to attend as a free woman.

On February 24th 1994, the police commenced their planned and co-ordinated exercise to methodically excavate the rear garden of 25 Cromwell Street. Fred and Rose had been arrested on suspicion of her murder before the digging commenced. They were actively looking for the site that Fred had buried Heather. He had admitted as much in an interview.

In June 1987, Heather had left Hucclecote Secondary School, having recently completed her school certificate exams. She was actively looking for work and desperately wanted to leave home. Her heart was set on a job at a holiday camp in Devon. It had been an upsetting blow for her when she was telephoned to say that her application had been unsuccessful.

Her desperation was on account of becoming the principal focus of Fred's attention after Anne Marie had left home. Heather, as a result became withdrawn and unhappy. It was also clear that she had grown to dislike men. She was self-conscious and avoided playing sports. Her reasons included fear of the numerous bruises on her body being seen by other girls. Her closest friend at school was Denise Harrison, whose parents, Ronalzo and Gloria, were unfortunately close friends of Fred and Rose. In their estimation, Fred would never harm his children. Heather confided in Denise about the physical and sexual abuse she was enduring and told her that her father had raped her. Her sympathetic friend, upon relaying this distressing information to her mum and dad, was told by her parents not to repeat such allegations.

By this time Fred, would routinely barge into the bathroom when Heather was washing. He would pull the clothes off her bed. He would tell her that it was a father's right to take his daughter's virginity. He would grab her, push her around, invade her space, make it plain to her that he could do what he wanted with her. Around this time there is little doubt that the sexual harassment and abuse escalated to full sexual intercourse, which Heather would have detested with all her being and frantically resisted. It is also evident from what Mae and Stephen have said on the subject that Rose encouraged Fred; she did nothing to protect her eldest daughter and was, if anything, more likely to dish out physical abuse.

When Mae had had a boyfriend stay overnight on one occasion, he had awoken in the night upon hearing the terrified wailing and screaming of a young woman. At breakfast the following day, he asked what the noise had been and was told by Rose not to worry, it was just Heather in one of her moods.

On that rainy early summer's day, Friday June 19th 1987, when the other kids were at school and Fred and Rose were both at home alone with Heather, something precipitated the terrifying events that unfolded and resulted in Heather's murder. There would have been a build-up of tension: Heather's lack of co-operation; being withdrawn and morose; not doing her chores; being moody and disagreeable when the holiday camp job did not materialise; refusing Fred's abusive overtures, possibly kicking out at him to keep him at bay.

Rose had been becoming increasingly angry at her eldest daughter's stubbornness. There was also concern that she had been talking outside the family about her parents sexually interfering with the children. Had Mr Harrison reported back to Fred what his daughter had been told?

Fred was first interviewed by attending the police station voluntarily – that is, not under arrest – at the request of the police on February 25th 1994, following execution of the search warrant. The police had requested his attendance at 2pm in the afternoon. At the time, Fred was on a building job less than half an hour away in Frampton Mansell near to Gloucester. It is known that he left that job promptly but did not turn up at the police station until 7:30pm. There is ongoing speculation about what tracks he covered and secrets he concealed during those lost hours. At that stage, he told the interviewing police that Heather had gone off with a woman in a red miniskirt and that she was into all sorts of drugs and illegal stuff. He had actually seen her about from time to time, including while he was resident at the bail hostel in Birmingham in 1992.

After the interview, Fred returned to 25 Cromwell Street for the last time. The following morning, the police called to arrest him on suspicion of the murder of Heather West. As he got into the police car with DC Hazel Savage, he told her that he had killed his daughter. In interview, under caution and with a legal representative and appropriate adult present, Fred said that he had strangled Heather when she threatened to give drugs to the younger children that would make them jump off the church roof next door. He said this enraged him and he grabbed his daughter by throat and accidently strangled her.

As the excavation of the garden continued, there was initially a problem finding any remains and when Fred became aware of this, he decided to backtrack and change his story and try and assure the officers that Heather was really alive and well.

Although not part of the evidence, Stephen West later wrote that he had witnessed around the time of Heather's disappearance his mother kicking the living daylights out of her until she stopped moving. In their book *Inside 25 Cromwell St*, both Mae and Stephen describe the kind of extreme punishment they were both routinely subjected to by Rose.

Two short pieces of rope were found with Heather's remains. They would have been used to bind her hands. There were no items of clothing in her makeshift grave, which means she was nude when the body was dismembered. It is certain that Heather's last minutes on this earth would have included being held, bound and raped, such an event being preceded and succeeded by a vicious beating, most likely from Fred and Rose in concert.

Thirty-eight of Heathers bones were missing, including twenty-two finger and toe bones, fifteen of her wrist and ankle bones as well as her right kneecap. She had been decapitated and her legs disarticulated at the hip. Professor Knight also noted that the pelvis had been smashed in two, he believed with an implement such as a meat cleaver.

OTHER VICTIMS?

There is a general consensus among experts – including Superintendent John Bennett and Paul Britton, the forensic psychologist who advised the police during the investigation, as well as a number of criminologists and crime writers – that it is more than likely that there were other unknown victims of the Wests' reign of terror.

There are known incidents of Fred West being closely involved in documented fatalities in the 1960s. The first such incident was the death of a three-year-old boy on November 4th 1965 in Glasgow, when the Mr Whippy ice cream van that West was driving reversed over the child. With hindsight, could this 'accident' have been easily avoided or is there not a lingering doubt as to whether it was a deliberate and callous act?

In Gloucestershire, there was then the perplexing circumstances of a young man, by the name of Robin Holt, in his mid-teens whom Fred had befriended and was doubtless influencing with his preoccupation with deviant sex. The young man disappeared from his home in Gloucester in February 1967. He had, later that month, been sighted in Much Marcle and then on March 1st 1967, his body was found hanging in a disused cowshed near to the Sandhurst Lane Caravan Park where Fred was then living with Anne McFall. On the shed floor were a number of pornographic magazines, all open on explicit pages and someone had drawn in pen nooses around the necks of the models posing on the pages. The coroner returned a verdict of suicide, but Fred West's fingerprints may well have been all over those pages.

An assessment based on the forensic profiling of serial killers confirms that they do not stop until they are caught. In many cases, such killers like to play games with the police to show how clever they are. In Fred West's case, while he covered his tracks with methodical thoroughness, he was also incredibly indiscrete, whether to workmates, neighbours, shopkeepers, people he met in the street or anyone who could be bothered to listen to his nauseating drivel. The irony was that because the indiscretion was uttered by an affable, diminutive, petty thief, whom people dismissed as a rather exploitable clown with a dirty mind, his frequent references to torture chambers, underage sex, bondage and abuse fell on deaf ears. Besides, he was always working to support his large family. He would return each evening to a house full of kids and lodgers. He appeared to be an open book, yet his pathetic exterior was the vehicle that enabled a monster to hide in plain sight.

When attention is paid to the dates of abduction and killing of the known victims – i.e. July 1967 (Anne McFall), January 1968 (Mary Bastholm), May 1971 (Charmaine West), June 1971 (Rena Costello), April 1973 (Lynda Gough), November 1973 (Carol Ann Cooper), December 1973 (Lucy Partington), April 1974 (Thérèse Siegenthaler), November 1974 (Shirley Hubbard), April 1975 (Juanita Mott), May 1978 (Shirley Robinson), August 1979 (Alison Chambers), June 1987 (Heather West) – the implication is that any significant gaps indicate incidents of abduction and killing that have not been discovered.

That young women could disappear and not be reported missing may seem absurd but is all too familiar to the police. In the West case, Juanita Mott, Carol Ann Cooper and Alison Chambers were not reported as missing persons, and neither were Charmaine and Heather West, nor Rena Costello.

Nationwide, there is a register of missing persons that has thousands of names on it. Even where people are reported missing, finding out where they are or what fate may have befallen them may take decades and sometimes never be established.

Fred West, although an inveterate liar, completely unreliable, and someone who repeatedly changed his story and reinvented his version of the truth, nevertheless, at various stages stated in police interviews, to his solicitor, appropriate adult or to his son Stephen that there were many more victims over the years. He told his appropriate adult, Janet Leach, that there were another twenty victims.

On no occasion did he give any precise details of the location of other remains, other than to vaguely talk of a 'farm' where he would take his captives.

There are other pointers as well. Brian Leveson QC emphasised the notable relevance in relation to the sequence of events in the abduction, torture, killing and dismemberment of Lucy Partington when Fred West turned up at the casualty department of Gloucester General Hospital on January 3rd 1973 with a deep knife wound to his hand. This incident should be compared with Rose West likewise turning up late at night at the said casualty department with a nasty gash to her hand in 1976. The only problem is that no victim whose abuse, killing or dismemberment might be attributed as the cause has been identified. Yet there is the ominous, lurking suspicion that that precisely was the cause.

Fred West, in attempting to assist the police in identifying which victims the recovered remains belonged to, kept mentioning a Dutch girl whom he obviously recalled killing, yet her remains were not among those at Cromwell Street. There is supporting evidence from lodgers who recall a Dutch girl staying at Cromwell Street. There could have been no confusion with Thérèse Siegenthaler, who was never a lodger.

Recently, I was sitting in the hot tub after a workout at DW Sports Gym. A stocky old builder with a bad hip by the name of Derek Myatt climbed in. He was a lively man and clearly he wanted to talk. He recognised me as the solicitor who had acted in the West case. He had much that he wanted to get off his chest.

"They don't know how many victims there were, do they? They'll never find out now. They're under fifty feet of soil."

When Derek Myatt was a young man, Hempsted Tip was a pit ten feet deep with a layer of sand at the base. Hempsted Tip is now called Hempsted Hill and is forty feet high with years of accumulated waste. The Ash lorries had to observe protocol in going to the tip. The dustbin lorries would line up where designated and each in turn throughout the day unload their waste and as soon as they had done so, a tractor with a large bucket would first tip sand and soil on top and then spread the material evenly, covering the waste before the next dustcart tipped its load. As of 2019, the authorities regard Hempsted Tip as at capacity and future waste will be disposed of at a new state-of-the-art incinerator, Javelin Park, at the side of the M5 motorway just south of Gloucester. If human remains were deposited at Hempsted off the back of dustcarts, there could never by any possibility of recovering them now.

He then explained to me how his brother, Rob Myatt, for many years from the 1970s onwards worked on the bins with Fred West's brother John. Rob was in the Scorpion Motorcycle Club that used to hang out at the Pop In Cafe on Southgate Street. He mentioned Jasper Davis, a friend of Rob's who also worked on the bins on the same crew as John West and was also in the Scorpions. It was their routine to stop off at John's brother's place at 25 Cromwell Street most days for coffee or lunch. During these breaks, if Fred was about, he would, in an impromptu way suddenly chuck random full bin bags on the back of the dustcart. They never thought anything about this, except on one occasion something did catch their attention and it was something Rob and Jasper remembered and discussed afterwards. They had been outside the house standing by the lorry when Fred came out with a large bin bag which he threw into the rubbish compartment on the back, but as he did so, both Rob and Jasper noticed that within the bin bag was another container, a full cloth sack. It puzzled them why anyone would need to put a sack inside another bag just to dispose of rubbish?

He also intimated that Rob was rather coy about discussing all that went on when 25 Cromwell Street was visited, but the indication is that a number of Scorpions stayed at the address for a while and engaged in gang bangs with Rose. This has been corroborated by a separate witness.

In the late 1960s, Derek worked as a labourer for EG Bartlet, who had the maintenance contract at Brockworth Caravan Park and also the sewage works nearby. He remembers Fred West being evicted and when the manager went to his caravan to get him out, he found him in situ with a young girl tied up on a bed.

He also had a clear memory of the way things were with the girls at Jordan's Brook House. It was a Reform School for Girls in those days. It remains a social services establishment but is now an administrative centre. It had opened in 1969 following the closure of the Bowden Hall which had hitherto served a similar function. Bowden Hall is about a mile away from Jordan's Brook House, located in what was then rural land on the outskirts of Gloucester. Residential development at Abbeydale has brought the site much more into the urban sprawl. Bowden Hall is now run as a successful hotel.

All the girls at Jordan's Brook had come from difficult backgrounds and had, for one reason or another, ended up in care. Some had run away from home; some had already strayed into prostitution. Derek remembers that it was fair game each Sunday afternoon for many randy young Gloucester men to cruise the surrounding lanes with some fags and a bottle of booze, and pip the horn and wave at the teenage girls walking around, who in many cases were waiting for the boys to drive past. The boys invariably would stop and have a brief conversation with the girls, who delighted in the prospect of some amorous reprieve from the boredom of their humdrum day-to-day existence in the home. Derek reckoned that by all accounts on most occasions, when they stopped and spoke to the girls, the boys would get lucky.

This was the milieu in which Fred West could cruise and prowl with impunity. We know that many young women from Jordan's Brook House found their way to 25 Cromwell Street. Regrettably, no one is able to say how many others became the lost tragic victims of the House of Horrors.

As Geoffrey Wansell points out in his work *An Evil Love*: "No fewer than twenty-two young women were to go missing, their 'whereabouts unknown', after they left the children's home between 1970 and 1994. The whereabouts of another forty-two young people who left its care, including Alison Chambers, were not recorded."

I have no doubt about the truth of everything Derek Myatt told me. He is a salt of the earth sort of bloke; for many years in his capacity as a gamekeeper he worked for Conrad Sheward, the solicitor who had acted for Fred and Rose West in a magistrates' court case in 1972 involving the abduction and sexual assault of Caroline Owens. He also acted in Fred West's numerous petty theft matters which eventually led to a suspended sentence being activated and Fred serving a prison sentence.

While it is informative, how much further does such anecdotal testimony take an investigation? It reinforces what is already known and illustrates how almost everyone who lived in Gloucester at that time either had some direct story relating to the Wests, or a victim, or someone who worked with Fred or went to school with the children or knew someone who did.

It is my belief that when Fred talked of other victims who were buried at a 'farm' near Gloucester, this was his cryptic way of intimating that victims who were killed at Cromwell Street were then dismembered, put in sacks and bin liner bags, thrown on the back of a dustcart and unwittingly taken to Hempsted Tip. To the Wests, Hempsted Tip was a farm.

6.

THE TRIAL

INTRO

The media scrum is jostling for a view, arms speculatively reaching as they grasp valuable photographic kit, furiously clicking in the hope that the lens will magic a million-dollar image of Rose West inside the prison wagon as it arrives at the Crown Court building. It is October 3rd 1995, a mild autumn day. There is a macabre festive feel as the burgeoning throng oscillates in unsteady lines along the pavements and streets around the large Winchester court complex. The citizens of Winchester inevitably drawn to the spectacle by that curious prurience that possesses all human kind.

Public interest has many facets. While it is vested with gravitas and duty, it is also the realm of intrigue, fascination, emotion, titillation and participation by proxy. It is the people's justice, so to say, and twelve good and true citizens of the town drawn from the electoral register will be randomly called to discharge their onerous duty by listening to the harrowing evidence, and then, attentive to the speeches of counsel and judge's summing, will eventually retire to deliberate on whether the case has in all or in part been made.

I can tell you now from the perspective of the defence, to a large degree the tactics, strategy and trajectory of this case were dependent on Rose West's attendance at one interview in August 1992 relating to the preceding child abuse allegation which had resulted in her arrest as being complicit with Fred. That case, which although a precursor, was entirely separate and independent of the murder trial, an investigation where the remit was completely removed from any suggestion of murder.

The Police and Criminal Evidence Act of 1984 and the Codes of Practice ancillary to it provide a safeguard guaranteeing the integrity of the process of arrest and investigation of someone suspected of committing an offence. This includes all manner of matters, ranging from the right to legal representation, procedures for taking fingerprints, intimate samples, periods of detention, charging and bailing. It also prescribes strict rules for the interviewing of suspects. The necessity for such an elaborate piece of legislation arose from a number of appalling miscarriages of justice involving forced confessions written by investigating officers in the good old, bad old days when suspects were handed blank pages or fabricated statements to sign, whether they had read and understood the content or not. In some cases, the suspects had been held indefinitely and badly treated through beatings and isolation. British justice had to be better than that.

Before interview, the arresting officer has to restate the police caution. In 1992, it was worded thus:

"You have been arrested on suspicion of... you do not have to say anything but anything you do say may be taken down and used in evidence against you."

This statement expressly reminds the suspect of their fundamental right against self-incrimination. It gives the suspect an absolute right to remain silent should they choose not to answer any questions whatsoever, essentially a 'no comment' interview.

The Criminal Justice and Public Order Act 1994, which was given the Royal Assent on November 3rd 1994, amended Code C of the Codes of Practice as follows:

"You do not have to say anything, but it may harm your defence if you do not mention when questioned something which you later rely on in Court. Anything you do say may be given in evidence."

"...for an inference to be drawn when a suspect fails or refuses to answer a question about one of these matters or to answer it satisfactorily, the suspect must first be told in ordinary language: (a) what offence is being investigated; (b) what fact they are being asked to account for; (c) this fact may be due to them taking part in the commission of the offence; (d) a court may draw a proper inference if they fail or refuse to account for this fact; and (e) a record is being made of the interview and it may be given in evidence if they are brought to trial."

A suspect who chose to remain silent during interview and then decides to give evidence at court may find her evidence tainted by a formal adverse inference being drawn from the earlier silence. In other words, she may be less likely to be believed.

In Rose's interviews on August 11th 1992, in accord with standard procedure for police in a serious inquiry, particularly involving children or domestic abuse, there is initial questioning to find out something of the background. This goes beyond confirming name and address but still asks what on the face of it are innocuous, unproblematic questions, like: how may children are there in the family? What are their ages? Are they at school or are they working? Do they still live at home or have they moved out?

Rose was vehemently protesting her innocence and visibly annoyed that anyone should even suspect her, the mother of eight children, and stepmother to Anne Marie, of such abuse. In relation to those questions, I could have advised Rose to go 'no comment'. But why would I do that? Why should she not simply give a reply when asked about Heather and what she was doing and where she was? Had some mystic voice told me that I was dealing with the tip of the iceberg? What impression would it make when the client wished to stress that the allegation was no more than malicious talk originating from kids in the street?

There could be no reason not to answer such questions. If anything, not answering such simple questions would have immediately set alarm bells ringing and may actually have resulted in an accelerated murder investigation.

The great irony in all this is that in 1992, the question of Heather's whereabouts was not only relatively innocuous, it was also irrelevant in establishing any fact relevant to the commission of the offence of child sex abuse against a younger daughter of the family. In view of the witness statement made by Anne Marie, the police may have wondered whether Heather had likewise been abused, but by that stage they already had all the evidence they needed to pass the charging threshold and Fred had already been remanded in custody. As Rose had not been arrested for the murder of Heather (at that stage) even if she had been subject to the later statutory amendment (which in August 1992 she was not) still no adverse inference could have been drawn had she opted to remain silent.

Rose and Fred independently did answer questions about Heather. Rose was evasive about Heather's age and whether she had ever been reported missing. Rose had returned home from shopping and Heather had gone. She said she did not know where Heather was when first asked if she had had any contact, since Rose said, "No." She further stated that she could not remember whether either her or Fred had reported Heather missing.

Rose was asked if Heather had any money when she left home, to which she replied, "I don't know."

It was then put to her that it must have been distressing, losing touch with her firstborn, to which she made the inconsistent reply, "It's been awful."

She then said, "I can remember now why I didn't pursue Heather – because things pointed to her being a lesbian… She had taken whatever she had in her room, her personal things, clothing… She refused to know about all the normal things of living and went off to Devon with a lady. I didn't want her to stay here, not in those circumstances, not if she was going to practise what she was doing. She was a lesbian and that was why she wanted to leave; it wasn't good for the rest of the children."

Rose was then asked, "Are you a lesbian?" to which she replied, "No," that she had never been a lesbian.

Rose then blatantly contradicted her earlier reply by saying that because she did not want Heather upsetting the other children, she had given her six hundred pounds to set her up on her way. Then Rose told Hazel Savage that one of Heather's friends had told her she was fine, 'getting on with her life'. Rose had spoken to Heather on the telephone and her daughter had said that she was all right, even though sometimes Heather had been drinking or whatever. Rose explained that it was only her who spoke to her, as Heather would have nothing to do with Fred. She kept the telephone calls secret from the children as well, so as not to upset them.

The interviewing officers also asked about Charmaine West, to which Rose explained that Char had wanted to be with her mother, so Rena called to collect her when they lived at Midland

Road and took her back to Scotland with her.

The interviewing officer was Hazel Savage, who was already smelling a very nasty rat. The police made enquiries about Heather's medical and national insurance record in the intervening years, both of which drew a blank. Hazel told Rose directly that she was far from satisfied and would not let the matter drop, whatever else was to be decided. Hazel also at this early stage flagged up the Caroline Owens assault matter from 1972.

And so, Rose had chosen to give an account to get herself off the hook of the child abuse allegation, which for other reasons ultimately did not proceed. In so doing, both Fred and Rose had snookered themselves when, in February 1994, the police recovered Heather's remains from the bottom of the back garden at 25 Cromwell Street.

At the outset of the trial Dick Ferguson had sought unsuccessfully severance of the counts relating to Heather, Charmaine and Shirley Robinson on the basis that the so called 'strikingly similar system' that the Crown sought to establish in relation to the other victims had no relevance to these deaths. Severance would mean a separate indictment, separate trials, separate juries, which would clearly have benefited the defence. As it was, all counts remained on the same bill of indictment and provided the glaring spectre that Rose, as much as Fred, was entirely familiar with the act of killing and then concealment.

Without giving a clarifying account and live evidence at her trial in 1995, the reality was overwhelmingly that Rose had been complicit to concealing the murder, dismemberment and burial of her firstborn daughter.

Such complicity in the light of the similar fact evidence would have made a convincing case as to Rose's treachery and culpability in the killing of the other victims. Indeed, sections of these tapes were played at Winchester as part of the prosecution case. The Crown's task would have been made markedly more difficult had Rose West remained silent and had had no reason to step into the witness box to give an account of herself. And in choosing to give evidence, she would now have to run the gauntlet of Brian Leveson's cross-examination. Either way, the 1992 interviews were grist for the prosecution's mill.

First and foremost, though, it was for the prosecution to prove its case beyond reasonable doubt. That is a high standard of proof required in all criminal trials. It really means that the jury must be sure of the guilt of the accused. It is a much higher standard of proof than the civil 'balance of probabilities'. And, as has been emphasised, the case against Rose was circumstantial. As Brian Leveson pointed out in his opening, no one could point their finger directly at the accused and say that they had seen Rose West kill any one of the victims. So heavy reliance was placed on binding together the evidence of those witnesses who had been abused but survived, so as to convince the jury that there was indeed such striking similarity that the only plausible conclusion was that the victims had been killed by whoever had assaulted the survivors.

PROSECUTION CASE

There was a lengthy opening where the Crown set out its stall in depth and told its story, a story the veracity of which it would seek to demonstrate by credible witness testimony supported by precise forensic detail confirming the identity of the victims and the condition of their remains.

On October 8th, the prosecution called its first witnesses, starting with Rose's mother, Daisy. She remembered Rose briefly being placed in care at the age of fifteen to try and keep her away from Fred West. She remembered Rose as no more than a child, very babyish for her age. She also recalled Rose returning home with a baby when she was sixteen and telling her that 'there was nothing he [Fred] wouldn't do' and her mother believed that she said 'even murder'.

Rose's sister Glenys then gave evidence, clearly feeling disgusted and let down by Rose. She remembered Fred telling her that Shirley Robinson was pregnant with his child. She too remembered Rose as very childish for her age. She also remembered that Heather had always said she would leave home at sixteen, so it was no surprise when she was no longer at 25 Cromwell Street. Then followed Shirley Ann Giles, who lived upstairs from the Wests when they resided at 25 Midland Road. Her recollection of dates was relevant to the Crown's case against Rose in relation to the murder of Charmaine. The Giles' had left to live in Cinderford in January of 1971 but returned because Shirley's daughter, Tracey wanted to see Charmaine. They recall visiting in Midland Road in April 1971 to be told then that Charmaine had gone to stay with her real mum in Scotland: "And bloody good riddance." She told the court the words that Rose had used. This date actually precedes the preferred date which the Crown believed Charmaine was killed based on visits by Rose to see Fred in HMP Leyhill and their letters to each other at that time.

A Mr Whitcomb was called to confirm the record of Fred West's incarceration at Leyhill. Under cross-examination he conceded that it was possible for prisoners to abscond overnight and return the following day without being detected.

Elizabeth Agius was a neighbour when Fred and Rose moved into 25 Midland Road. She resided in a next-door flat with her baby. She was Maltese. Her husband was abroad at the time. She became a friend and would often socialise in the Wests' flat, babysitting for them if they went out in the evening. On one occasion, Fred said to her that they had been out looking for girls and with Rose in the car it was easier to pick them up. He told her that Rose was a prostitute. Fred made it very clear that he fancied Mrs Agius and was also trying to interest her in a tryst with Rose. She assured the court that it was all talk and nothing happened. She said she had visited the Wests when they had moved to Cromwell Street and Fred had shown her a trap door to the cellar, which he said he was going to turn into a playroom for the kids as well as a torture chamber.

It came out in evidence that Elizabeth Agius had actually had sex with Fred but was not prepared to admit it because it would destroy her marriage. By 1994, she had long since been residing in Malta with her husband. It also came out that she had been paid to give television interviews and had contacted *The Sun* newspaper even before contacting the police. These two features damaged her credibility.

The first key 'similar fact' witness for the crown was Caroline Owens, the lodger and childminder for the West children in 1972, a woman whom the Crown would say experienced a succession of abominations, namely an abduction, beating, binding with rope and duct tape, and rape and sexual assault that was strikingly similar to the evidence discernible from the associated paraphernalia found with the remains of the murder victims. Crucially and unquestionably, her ordeal was a matter of court record from Gloucester Magistrates' Court in 1972. Even though she had sold her story for the sum of £20,000 to a tabloid, her credibility could not and would not be shaken notwithstanding rigorous cross-examination by Richard Ferguson.

The mother of Lynda Gough then gave evidence. Her daughter, the seamstress, had been befriended by the Wests in April 1973. As a rebellious teen, she had left a comfortable home to live as a lodger and childminder at 25 Cromwell Street. She was sexually abused, tortured and murdered within three weeks of moving there. Mrs Gough described how she called round to visit her daughter only to be told by a young woman who answered the door and fitted the description of Rose, that Lynda had moved on. Mrs Gough noticed that Rose was wearing her daughter's slippers.

A number of lodgers from the early 1970s then gave evidence testifying to the unbounded libertine atmosphere at 25 Cromwell Street. Many young men and women came and went, often having casual sex with each other. This was confirmed by Ben Stanniland and David Evans, who were invited by Fred to have sex with Rose. Liz Brewer confirmed how Rose was preoccupied with sex but in many ways had a favourable impression of her time lodging with the Wests. She was able to provide evidence of the relationship between Fred West and Shirley Robinson. In cross-examination she admitted to being paid £10,000 by a tabloid.

The following Monday, October 16th, Miss A commenced her evidence. A lonely, dejected young woman, unhappy to be in local authority care through no fault of her own, Miss A had repeatedly absconded from Jordan's Brook House and made her way to Cromwell Street. She had visited on several occasions and received reassuring tea and sympathy from Rose.

Miss A was given anonymity because at the time of the West case she was also the principal witness in a rape trial that was sub judice and pending in Southampton. When that matter eventually came to trial, it resulted in a conviction. The Crown was particularly sensitive for two other reasons. Firstly, since her days visiting 25 Cromwell Street, she had made a previous allegation of rape, which whatever its merits, she had decided to withdraw before the case came to trial. Secondly, the *Daily Express* had interviewed her about her ordeal at the hands of Fred and Rose West and by selling her story, Miss A inevitably compromised her credibility. Had she embellished her story to make it more saleable? Had she varied the version that she then gave to the police? Was what she said contaminated by what she had read? Did what she say contaminate other prosecution witnesses?

For a woman who had struggled in life after a difficult start and abusive encounters, the £30,000 she was paid was a lot of money. It was no wonder the leading prosecution counsel's demeanour was more of grim determination than upbeat optimism.

She gave her evidence of the cajoling and abusive, touchy-feely, sexualised girls' talk from Rose and then being bundled into a room, bound and intimately assaulted by Rose and then raped by Fred.

In cross-examination, Richard Ferguson asked her about a relationship she had had prior to her alleged abuse with Rose West's brother Graham Letts when she was fourteen years old and he was nineteen. They had for a time lived together. She admitted this had occurred and that at that time she had also been blackmailed and raped by a neighbour, but she said she did not know Graham Letts was Rose's brother.

He then questioned her about her medical records, indicating that she had spent time in a psychiatric hospital, that she was schizophrenic and had hallucinations of a headless man. Miss A denied she had been detained at a psychiatric hospital but that she had a vision of a man dressed in black which she thought was Fred West. He asked her why, if her allegations were true, she had not reported the matter all those years ago?

She admitted she had received a significant payment of £30,000 to sell her story to a tabloid.

Evidence was then heard from a neighbour, Margareta Dix, who while making favourable comments about the Wests' neighbourliness when her husband died, also remembered Rose with a black eye and broken lenses in her glasses after Fred had beaten her up. Rose said, "And after all I have done for that man." An old client of Rose West's called Arthur Dobbs then gave evidence confirming that Rose did work as a prostitute.

Next into the witness box was Kathryn Halliday, who's distracted and underwhelming evidence must have triggered a moment of despondency for the prosecution. She had been subjected to incrementally increasingly extremes of domination and rough sex by Rose with Fred as the ever present voyeur and ring master. The only problem was Halliday was an experienced woman and consensual participant who repreatedlby returned for more. She described this as a moth drawn to a flame, words put in there mouth, no doubt, by the tabloid she had sold her tawdry tale to for £8000, as Richard Ferguson QC was quick to put to her in a cross-examination that pretty well shredded her evidential worth.

Anne Marie's evidence followed and was listened to by all present with a stirring sense of pathos and outrage. Anne Marie had since 1992 made twenty-one lengthy and consistent statements to the police. Between tears and displays of emotion, she quietly told of her life and the abuse and rape that she had endured during her childhood years at the hands of her father and stepmother. Given Anne Marie's known delicate state of mind and the enormity of the task in hand, the timetabling of the court business proved at this juncture to be woeful as the court had to adjourn her testimony midstream so that the jury could, as pre-arranged, visit 25 Cromwell Street and view the cellar for themselves. This meant she would have to wait a day and night before resuming her evidence with cross-examination by Richard Ferguson. The stress was too much, and she inadvertently took an overdose, but was sufficiently revived in time to be able to continue her testimony after being passed fit by a psychiatrist. Like Caroline Owens, she felt a duty to those victims who did not make it, in particular her mother, Rena, and sister, Charmaine.

Dick Ferguson put it to her that Rose had never bound or gagged her, that Rose had never sexually abused her or been present when she had been abused and that the incident in the cellar when she was bound to a metal frame and had a vibrator inserted into her vagina at the age of eight years old never happened. To all of these questions, Anne Marie quietly affirmed that it had all happened and was true. Rose's later admission to me that everything Anne Marie had said was indeed true speaks volumes about the truth of everything else Rose denied during the trial and in many cases continues to deny.

Taped recorders were then set up in the courtroom to enable the prosecution to play four tapes of police interviews with Rose West. These included sections of the 1992 interviews and the initial 1994 interviews where Rose clumsily tried to cover her tracks on the comments she had earlier made. The sections played emphasised for the jury Rose's capacity for belligerence, aggression and use of foul language. The tape recordings demonstrated the pattern of transference where Rose accused Heather of being nasty and vindictive, of deliberately hurting the younger children. She explained how she knew Heather was a lesbian because Heather knew what knickers her teachers were wearing. She also repeatedly put forward an alibi of being sent out by Fred to spend a night with another man when Heather disappeared.

Professor Bernard Knight then gave the pathology evidence, detailing the location and state of each set of remains and the number of bones missing.

Dr David Whittaker, the expert odontologist, provided evidence of his methods in dovetailing dentition with photographs of the victims as a means to verify identity. In the case of Charmaine, his demonstration in the witness box was compelling. The question arose of what period of time would have elapsed between the photograph being taken in April

1971 and the condition of the little girl's erupting second set of front teeth as freeze-framed in time at the date of her death? Dr Whittaker indicated there was a margin of error of a couple of months.

The forensic expertise of Professor Knight and Dr Whittaker in enabling particular sets of remains to be precisely matched to specific names in a long list of, in some cases, random names of missing persons and to do so expeditiously and under pressure was, by any objective standard, an exceptional accomplishment.

The final witness for the prosecution was Superintendent John Bennett, a duty it was apparent he had been dreading, but he quietly moved into the witness box and took the oath. It must have been with regret that he was obliged, on behalf of Gloucestershire Constabulary, to disown DC Hazel Savage MBE, the heroic mover and shaker of the West case, for her error in making it known that she had been offered a book deal.

Brian Leveson then formally confirmed to the judge that that concluded the case for the prosecution.

DEFENCE CASE

At midday on October 30th, Rose West went into the witness box.

Examination in chief should be relatively straightforward, with questions presented to the defendant that can be answered briefly, preferably as a yes or no. The defence counsel asked her about her early life and initially she followed the script of her proof of evidence. She described how, as an impressionable young woman, Fred had wooed her and then wanted her to sleep with other men.

Her description of feeling 'shock and horror' when Fred

persisted on successive days in trying to chat her up at a bus stop appeared plainly contrived. She was tearful in responding to questions about Charmaine, and then explained how she was routinely pregnant. She described 25 Cromwell Street and the damp basement. She admitted her preference for women and was contrite about her involvement in the 1972 sexual assault on Caroline Owens. She said she wanted to leave Fred, but he was the breadwinner. She became clearly upset when asked about Heather and then used a rhetorical question when asked about Miss A. At the end of the examination in chief she still had credibility, but she was not a good witness and her testimony did not go well.

From a personal perspective, I felt for the first time that Rose actually had her own agenda; she was bold enough to tell an unscripted story and to do it as it suited her. This was a woman who had been hoodwinking men, ad-libbing little dalliances and false romances, a seasoned whore, brazen and proficient in the art of lying. Were all those voluminous moans and groans of sexual ecstasy just a pretence? Of course they were. Rose was telling the truth when she had told a prison psychiatrist she had never had an orgasm. So there was some part of her that felt she could outwit the system, play by her own rules and not worry about what the experts had told her. She was going to give whatever answer she believed fitted the moment; she was going to reconfigure her persona as she thought might best impress the jury. She was definitely an instinctive reactor. She did not stick to the advice that had been given to give short brief answers.

On a rudimentary level, she was clear and adamant in refuting the counts on the indictment when put to her by the defence counsel, but beyond that, in the cold, clinical scrutiny of the courtroom, what little she had offered her defence in compiling her proof of evidence, she appeared now to abandon as just another exercise in whitewash. She had been repeatedly reminded that she did not have to be a squeaky-clean nice person to be not guilty of murder. She chose to go off track and improvise her own spin on her life in response to the allegations and criticise others who had made incriminating statements against her; chief among those was Anne Marie.

The result was that she came across as rather insincere and two-dimensional. If her evidence in chief did not help her cause, she was systematically shredded by Brian Leveson QC in cross-examination.

The rule given to all students of advocacy is to proceed with great care in the questions you put in cross-examination. You need to know what the witness is going to tell you. You need to be brief; like marine commandos, you go in smartly and get out quickly. You do not risk eliciting answers that blow the case away. With those caveats being second nature to an experienced advocate, there was, nevertheless, fertile territory on offer when Brian Leveson commenced his relentless and lengthy cross-examination. As a softening-up process, he launched a series of mocking negative assertions to the effect that while Rose West had resided at 25 Cromwell Street for over twenty years with her murderous husband Fred, she had never seen blood on his clothes, or his hands or in the bathroom; she had never seen a body or remains. He knew the replies would always be a flustered catalogue of denials.

Demeanour of the accused can be critical. It goes beyond mere appearance and evolves with the time spent in the witness box. There is no place to run to. The jury will form an impression. A defendant may be emotional or calm or angry depending on the questions that are put to them and those responses may be understandable and gain sympathy, but inconsistency – where a defendant wavers between a combative stance and deference, where memory is demonstrably selective, and worst of all, where a question posed in cross-examination is answered with a rhetorical question – is really quite damaging. Rose, in trying to 'dance pretty' fell into every trap. She was reminded of how she had told her parents there was nothing Fred West would not do, even murder. She was asked about Charmaine and the letter she sent to Fred in prison saying that Charmaine liked to be treated rough. She was combative and assertive and angry in her denial of involvement in the abuse of Anne Marie. She denied all and any wrongdoing and when questions were too taxing, she did not remember; she claimed not to remember Shirley Robinson, who was pregnant with Fred's child when she was murdered in 1978, yet she could remember details of Lynda Gough, a victim from 1973. At lunchtime on November 3rd, Rose was released from the witness box.

Rose West had been in the witness box for nearly three days; prosecuting leading counsel confidently prolonged her agony as her unchoreographed improvisation lurched incongruously one way and then another, demonstrating there was something fictitious and unreliable in what she had to say.

If there had not been that particular Houdini's box to try and climb out of – of Rose's early claims relating to Heather's leaving home, being given money and later telephoning her – the trial may have been quite different and certainly much shorter. The prosecution case had always been one of building a compelling circumstantial case based on the similar fact evidence from live witnesses, namely Caroline Owens, Miss A, Kathryn Halliday and Anne Marie Davis, identifying the similarities in the modus operandi of abduction, restraints with cords and tape, sadism and rape and asking the jury to accept that this blueprint was clearly discernible from the bindings found on the victims.

The prosecution always knew that there was a serious credibility issue with much of the trial evidence, not least because witnesses had received large sums of money from the press to tell their stories; there was a risk of contamination of content because of the publicity, even a risk of the jury forming preconceived ideas. It was also impossible to know in advance how a witness was going to perform under pressure. The witnesses were damaged people struggling to cope with the ordinary, mundane difficulties of their lives. The prosecution always knew that Richard Ferguson QC would exploit this deficiency with skill and precision, which he indeed did. The reality was that the high point of the defence was the impact of Ferguson's exemplary cross-examination. Objectively, if things had been different, he might, by half-time, have done enough to cast a doubt. And that was all that was required of the defence. A half-time submission at the close of the Crown's case might have been justified. If there had been a ruling by the judge against such a submission, then the defence would have briefly only called the number of women who testified that they remembered in the 1970s being accosted by a man very much fitting the description of Fred West.

This evidence of several women who believed they had had close encounters with Fred West trying to pick them up in a green car on his own many years earlier was heard by the jury. These were Janette Clarke, Mrs C and Alison Clinton.

As it was Judge Mantell, dealt with this evidence in a cursory, perhaps slightly dismissive way. He gave the impression that he did not regard it as valuable and did point out that it was not in dispute that Fred West had, in his early days in the 1960s, tried to pick women up in his car on his own. He might at that juncture have provided balance by reminding the jury that Fred had admitted to murdering Anne McFall on his own in July 1967, whose remains were found at Letterbox Field in Much Marcle, dismembered and with bindings, together with her nearly full-term infant.

The court also heard from Terry Crick, who had visited Fred West's caravan in Bishop's Cleeve in the late 1960s and Fred had shown him some particularly unpleasant-looking contraptions, which he claimed were his kit for carrying out abortions. Being called as a witness to revisit those distant memories was deeply disturbing to Crick, who was in any event a troubled man. Shortly after the trial, he committed suicide.

On November 3rd the defence then played, for the benefit of the jury, sections of Fred West's self-incriminatory tapes, the evidence from the grave. Four out of 145 tapes were selected to be played. This unusual scenario resulted from Fred's pre-trial suicide, whereby a statutory exception to the best evidence rule came into play. The best evidence is live oral evidence where the witness is in attendance at court and can be cross-examined on his testimony. In relation to first-hand hearsay, section 23 of the Criminal Justice Act 1988 provides that documentary evidence of any statement that could have been made by a witness as direct oral evidence had he been available can be admitted if the witness has died and the statement had been made to a police officer.

In the first recording (tape 3, from February 25th 1994) Fred described in a perfunctory, unemotional manner, killing and dismembering Heather, whom he remembered becoming incontinent as he strangled her. In the other tapes, Fred was heard explaining that he killed all of the victims, because instead of just wanting sex from him, they wanted a relationship and threatened to tell Rose.

Tapes were also played in which Fred gave an account of killing Rena and then Charmaine as an afterthought because he had forgotten that he had left her in the car when he went with Rena to Letterbox Field and killed her.

The account given relating to Lucy Partington was particularly scurrilous, suggesting that they were in a relationship and that at first, she wanted him to meet her parents and then demanded *£1,000* off him so that she could have an abortion to get rid of his baby. The account was such complete and utter rubbish and demonstrably showed Fred West to be an inveterate liar that I was surprised that the defence counsel had determined that it would somehow advance the defence case. Such close details of evidence were a matter for counsel. It remains my view that it was misguided and unnecessary to highlight that section of taped interview and it would only serve to underline to the jury that Fred West was not worth listening to.

The prosecution then made and was granted an application to present further evidence. This was evidence in rebuttal to the exculpatory statements contained in the Fred West taped interviews admitted as evidence on behalf of the defence. Such evidence would thereby enable the jury to hear evidence of how Fred West changed his tune and placed all the blame for the killings on Rose.

Evidence was heard from a Mr Guest who many years earlier had filed a mislaid social inquiry report relating to the Wests' abuse of Caroline Owens. There was evidence from Lucy Partington's mother based on family diaries conclusively showing that Fred West's assertions were impossible and entirely false. Then the prison doctor at Winson Green – Dr MacMaster, who had attended to Fred West between August and December 1994 – gave evidence. He stated that Fred had told him that Rose was running a brothel, that Heather helped dig her own grave, that Rose was preparing her for prostitution and that Rose was burying young women in the garden.

And then finally, Fred West's appropriate adult, Janet Leach, was called to testify to what Fred West had confided in her over dozens of hours of private consultation. Appropriate adults are an additional tier of safeguards where detainees may be vulnerable on account of mental instability or where there are concerns because of the seriousness of the allegations the suspect is being questioned about. It is seen as beneficial to the well-being of the detainee to have present a disinterested volunteer, who is not a lawyer and has no vested interest in any outcome, other than to ensure the suitable emotional safeguarding of the person they are assigned to. Janet Leach had only just joined the local scheme in Cheltenham, which was run by the Young Homeless Project.

Mrs Leach had five children of her own and was juggling the role of mother with studying, as she had recently gone back into education with hope of obtaining a social work qualification. She was from a socially minded household. Her husband, who around that time she became separated from, was the Labour Parliamentary Candidate for Cheltenham, which I guess must have been another unenviable position to be in. I recall Janet Leach telling me at an early stage in the 1994 investigation that Fred West had been her first police station call-out on the appropriate adult scheme. She was still working out which doors to go through and which buzzers to push.

Her evidence was that Fred had told her on February 27th that he had made a pact with Rose whereby he would take the blame for everything and that way she would be free to get on with her life. Janet Leach said that in the ensuing months Fred maintained that stance without wavering. Then later he claimed he was always at work when Rose killed. He would help with dismemberment and burial. Fingers were cut off to make identification difficult. He told her that all the deaths were because of sex that had gone wrong. They were all accidental. She said that Fred West would change his tune about whether it was Rose or himself who had killed Heather.

Janet Leach stated that she had kept in touch with Fred West and visited him regularly at Winson Green. She had last spoken to him on December 23rd.

Dick Ferguson then had the opportunity to cross-examine Mrs Leach, which he did with customary incisiveness. He challenged her on her selective commentary and asked her about Fred saying other people were also involved in the killings. He asked Janet Leach why she did not disclose these inconsistencies to the police and yet chose to make statements undermining his defence solicitor? He asked Janet Leach whether Fred West was stringing her along and manipulating her.

At the commencement of the afternoon session, the court was told that during the lunch adjournment that Janet Leach had collapsed and had been taken to hospital; she was suspected of suffering a minor stroke. Dick Ferguson emphasised to the judge that it was essential to the defence case for him to be able to complete his cross-examination of the witness. A week later he got his opportunity. On November 13th, Mrs Leach was brought back to court.

Defence leading counsel asked her why she had maintained contact with Fred West after the formal interviews had concluded and he had been charged and remanded into custody – her role, after all, had long since concluded? Ferguson added that the police expressly disapproved of her actions, so what was she doing?

She said she wanted him to say where the other bodies were buried. Ferguson disputed this and suggested she maintained contact for other reasons. He then told her and the court that overtures had been made on behalf of a woman who wanted to write a book. A letter was then produced and shown to her. It was from the *Daily Mirror*, offering her a first option fee of £7,500 and the sum of £100,000 upon publication of a book. Janet Leach had been lying. She clearly had a vested interest. Finally, Dick Ferguson finished the onslaught that had wiped out any credibility Mrs Leach could have had and further reduced her to a nervous wreck. Before she left the witness box, upon re-examination by Brian Leveson, she told the court that Fred West had told her there were another twenty victims buried in fields.

At this stage, if things had been different, for example, the court, having heard no testimony from Rose, may possibly have heard the Fred West incriminatory tapes, the evidence from the grave and then would have heard the evidence in rebuttal, which was itself tarnished by Janet Leach lying on oath about selling her story and entering into a book deal. It is a moot point whether the defence would even have presented this startling confessional evidence.

I recall Dick Ferguson discussing this issue at length. While he had reminded Rose several times that she did not need to get into the witness box if she did not want to, he felt that the tapes needed to be played and he pointed out that without them, there was actually very little else the defence could put forward. The point is, the defence do not have to prove anything at all and the Crown case was, in some crucial respects, problematic.

These were recurring themes and were still being pondered and mulled over by the defence team even in the moments before going into court on the days they were timetabled to be dealt with.

On November 13th, the court heard closing speeches.

As an artist, I was impressed with the judge's metaphor to describe the styles of presentation of the respective leading counsel for the prosecution and defence as comparing a Canaletto with a Van Gogh.

In his closing speech, Brian Leveson, in going through the evidence, emphasised that Rose West was a demonstrable liar, whose persistent denials lacked credibility and in relation to specific victims, her accounts were palpably risible. He portrayed her as tough and resilient, by no means without intelligence, a woman in control, a strategist. And yet, he pointed out to the jury, she insisted that all the torture and killing that went on did so without her knowledge and behind her back.

Yet the idea of Rose West as in control and strategic was lost on me. She had spent three days in the witness box where her lies did find her out. She had been ceremoniously taken to task and destroyed. Was this picture really consistent with her court performance? Would the jury not see through this? I could see nothing clever or strategic in her desperation to utter some sticking plaster words to support her scrambled recollection of her years at 25 Cromwell Street and earlier.

Richard Ferguson reminded the jury that there was not one shred of direct evidence of Rosemary West ever having killed anyone. She was not on trial for cruelty to her children, or of being a rapist, but rather for murder. Ferguson reminded the jury of how the murderous career of Fred West had commenced long before he met Rose and how numerous witnesses had testified to a man fitting his description trying to force them into his car. Finally, he sought to try and explain why Rose West might have told untruths for reasons that had nothing to do with avoiding her involvement in murder. He compared Mr Leveson to a mountain guide who, on finding a gap in the path, jumped that void and then invited those following him to do the same. Was that really something that it would be proper for the jury to do?

The judge's summing up was lengthy and meticulous. It lasted over three days and picked apart the evidence that had been heard in the preceding weeks. Summing up is an exercise in objectivity. It is not for the judge to tell the jury whether to convict or not and a judge has to be scrupulous in avoiding slipping in his own opinions or prejudices, whether by dismissive intonation, omission of comment on parts of the evidence or overemphasis of other testimony. In other words, it is a balancing act that a judge of Mr Justice Mantell's calibre would be very well-versed in.

DELIBERATION AND VERDICT

The jury was sent out at 11:45am on Monday November 20th. The court was adjourned while the jury went about the onerous task of deliberating on the ten counts of murder on the indictment. After the gravitas, drama and unremitting solemnity of Court 3, I felt a curious respite as the disparate cohort of journalists, writers, photographers, police, CPS lawyers, defence and prosecuting counsel assembled in the comfortable seating along the carpeted and spacious corridors and waiting areas of the court complex. I had been aware, over the weeks, of friendly pressmen using sociability as a pretext to see whether they might elicit some indiscrete nugget of information. What I might say now was not going to change the outcome; it was not going to result in a dubious, gap-filling little soundbite. And there had, in any event, been a cautious camaraderie between the various participating agents. This appears to be the case where people are, for whatever reason, drawn into the moment and drama of some national or international event. At stake was the robustness of the justice system in one of the most high-profile criminal trials in the history of English law. At stake was whether my client would be spending the rest of her life in prison. At stake was whether for the families of the victims there was some sense of closure and resolution.

At 4:30pm, the judge called the jury back into court to enquire of the foreman if there was any decision. On receiving a negative reply, he sent the jury to a hotel for the night and required their attendance for continued deliberation the following day. At 3pm on November 21st, the court announced that parties were to return to Court 3. Once the court was reconvened and the jury in place, the judge again asked the foreman if there was yet a decision. The court clerk was asked to read count 1 of the indictment relating to Charmaine West. The foreman declared the jury's finding of guilt. The court clerk then went through the other counts which were undecided, until count 10 of the indictment relating to Heather West was read. The foreman declared the jury's finding of guilt. The judge then sent the jury out to continue its deliberations.

At 4:30pm, the jury filed back into court and the foreman stood as count 7 relating to Shirley Robinson was read and he declared a further finding of guilt.

The following day, November 22nd, at noon the jury returned with two questions for the judge to clarify.

The first question was whether the total lack of direct evidence other than the presence of the victims' remains at 25 Cromwell Street would prevent a finding of guilt? The second question was whether the jury was allowed to find guilt based on the victims' remains combined with what happened to the witnesses who gave similar fact evidence as evidence of the victims contained in the counts?

In reply to both questions, Judge Mantell affirmed that provided the jury could satisfy itself as to the necessary inferences that the prosecution had invited them to draw, then they were entitled to arrive at such conclusions. The judge then reminded them also of the items found with the remains.

Within an hour, the jury returned to court with verdicts on the remaining seven counts, all of which were findings of guilt. Rose West had been convicted of ten counts of murder.

Judge Mantell then said as follows:

"Stand up. Rosemary Pauline West, on each of ten counts of murder of which you have been unanimously convicted by the jury, the sentence is one of life imprisonment. If attention is paid to what I think, you will never be released. Take her down."

The judge ordered that four other charges on the indictment, two of rape and two of indecent assault should remain on the file.

Rose West was taken down to the cells. I promptly, along with Sasha Wass, went to the holding cells to speak to Rose. Sasha put her arm around her to try and console her, but she was inconsolable, shocked and weeping like I had never seen her before. The ground had been taken away from under her feet. In her misery, through the panting, breathless tears, in broken whispers she cursed 'that flippin' Fred West'.

At that precise point in time, I did not think it realistic to try and engage Rose in a meaningful dialogue about the way forward, other than to say that we would, of course, be lodging an appeal. Nevertheless, what was absent in her distress and desolation was a desperate plea: "Look, I am innocent. I did not do this and yet I have been convicted. This cannot happen to me. I am an innocent person."

Would you not expect someone so condemned to such a dreadful catalogue of killing to at least want to utter a plaintiff statement of their innocence?

Not Rose West. Not then and not later when she was calmer and I visited her at HMP Durham in December 1995. By then she had obviously done a lot of thinking. She was calm and matter-of-fact. She expressed a resignation at her situation. Nowhere, even then, was that sense of panic that I felt would be a natural response when an innocent person finds themselves wrongly convicted. Instead, she was content to acquiesce in the appeal. I felt she was almost a bystander to her own legal process. "Let's see how it goes."

I recall in the weeks leading to Rose's appeal she said that she had to plan for making a life for herself in prison. Her priority had been to reconcile herself to her children, and while some headway was made, that ambition vanished over time. In the weeks leading up to Rose's appeal, I recall if there was any frisson of excitement or expectation, it related more to her short-lived dalliance with Myra Hindley.

Richard Ferguson was convinced that she had had a raw deal, that the judge should have balanced his reply to the foreman of the jury's questions by reminding him of the defence contentions. As he had said on earlier occasions, this was not the end of the matter. There would be an appeal and, if needs be, a public campaign to rectify the injustice of her trial by media. His sense of strict and courageous unbiased adherence to justice for all, no matter how disdainful or demonised the client might be, was decidedly out of synchronisation with the nation's sense that there had been some kind of resolution to one of the most awful episodes in the country's criminal history.

When Rose was send back to HMP Durham, her status had changed. She was now a lifer as opposed to a remand prisoner. Her admission back into the prison required an extended period on the hospital wing for assessment. On her return to the Female Wing, I visited her to discuss her appeal. Already she was conceding facts that she had hitherto vehemently denied. Her relationship with her children was in a state of flux. The realisation of the convictions for serial murder changed the family dynamic. Rose West the mother was also a sadistic multiple murderer. How did she now wear that culturally treasured and safe label of mother? The incongruity was as stressful for her as it was for her children. It is one thing to be accused and another to be convicted.

She was now admitting that her somewhat romanticised version of her childhood was untrue (as if we did not already know). She had been sexually abused by her father over a very long period of time and her sexual relationship with her father had continued even after she was with Fred West. Significantly, she also finally admitted that everything Anne Marie had said was true.

APPEAL

In March 1996, I travelled up to the Royal Courts of Justice on the Strand for the hearing of application for leave to appeal the conviction and sentence of Rose West. The central theme of the application was the prejudicial effect of press coverage and evidence tainted by payments to witnesses. The arguments were heard in the Lord Chief Justice's court. It was the last case that Lord Taylor CJ heard before retiring and dying shortly thereafter from brain cancer, a condition he was already aware of and, indeed, the reason for his premature retirement. The appeal courtrooms are imbued with Victorian Gothic splendour with tall ceilings, neat panelling and fine wood comprising the elevated bench of the Lord Justices of Appeal.

Brian Masters, the writer looked very at home, busily writing away at a desk he had manged to secure just beneath the judicial bench. I was slightly unnerved when at the commencement of hearing Lord Taylor glanced sternly in my direction and made a caustic comment about an unhelpful article that had appeared in *The Guardian* that very morning. I was aware of Duncan Campbell, the journalist visiting my office at his request, not mine, for an interview in the preceding week. I viewed what I said to him as innocuous. After all, the jury had reached its verdict and nothing I could say to a journalist could possibly have the slightest sway on the impartiality of appeal court judges when weighing the arguments presented to them by leading counsel. Furthermore, it is precisely in the nature and territory of appeals to campaign to promote public awareness where it is felt a case should be given further condition by the justice system. While that had not been my aim, as the case was already listed to be heard, I nevertheless felt it was an observation Lord Taylor did not need to make.

The grounds for an appeal to the Criminal Division of the Appeal Court have to be precisely stated based on points of law. Unlike appeals from the magistrates' court to a crown court, it is not possible to gratuitously say, "I do not like the result, therefore I want a rehearing on facts as well as law." In the West case, the grounds largely, though not exclusively, related to matters that had been raised well before the trial, firstly at the committal hearing in February 1995 and then at a preliminary application in July 1995. They were set out as follows:

- The trial judge wrongly exercised his discretion in refusing to stay the indictment. The issue here was abuse of process involving effect of the passing of time on the ability of witness to properly recall precise events. It also dealt with media intrusion, adverse publicity and the non-availability of corroborating documentations, such as the statement made in 1972 by Caroline Owens.
- The second ground of appeal dealt at length with press payments to witnesses and the effect this had on the validity of their testimony.
- The trial judge erred in law in admitting similar fact evidence. Alternatively, he wrongly exercised his discretion in allowing this evidence to go before a jury. That having admitted the similar fact evidence, the trial judge wrongly exercised his discretion in refusing to sever the murders of Charmaine West, Shirley Robinson and Heather West. That the verdicts in respect of Lynda Gough, Carol Ann Cooper, Lucy Partington, Thérèse Siegenthaler, Shirley Hubbard, Juanita Mott and Alison Chambers were unsafe and unsatisfactory in that the similar fact evidence

was tainted by the interference of the media.
- That the trial judge erred in law in failing to remind the jury of the defence case both in his summing up and on November 22nd when they sought further direction on the similar fact evidence.

Mr Justice Mantell, as an immensely experienced judge, had a very clear idea of the boundaries. Any ground for appeal challenging the way he exercised his discretion was always going to be difficult, as indeed proved to be the case. His response to the foreman of the jury on November 22nd arguably lacked a modicum of balance. The question of media intrusion in the trial process involving payments to witnesses was a stronger contention.

After the arguments had been presented, case law referenced and incisive questions raised by the appeal court judges for clarification by counsel, the Lord Chief Justice stated the appeal was dismissed and that a written decision would be available in seven days' time.

I recall then taking the tube to Pimlico and spending a few hours at the Tate Britain before setting off back to Gloucester.

The ninety-page decision was duly served about a week later setting out the appeal court's reasons. In relation to the press, the judgment in summary said as follows:

REGINA V WEST (ROSEMARY): CACD 3 APR 1996

References: Times 03-Apr-1996, 95/7813/S2, [1996] 2 Cr App R 374

Lord Taylor CJ

Ratio: Payments to witnesses in criminal trials by media need investigation and control. Nevertheless, the fact that a number of witnesses had sold their stories to the media before the trial, which was disclosed to the defence before or during the trial, was not considered to give rise to even an arguable ground of appeal. Lord Taylor CJ said, "But, however lurid the reporting, there can scarcely ever have been a case more calculated to shock the public, who were entitled to know the facts. The question raised on behalf of the defence is whether a fair trial could be held after such intensive publicity adverse to the accused. In our view, it could. To hold otherwise would mean that if allegations of murder are sufficiently horrendous so as to inevitably to shock the nation, the accused cannot be tried. That would be absurd. Moreover, as providing the judge effectively warns the jury to act only on the evidence given in court, there is no reason to suppose that they would do otherwise."

Jurisdiction: England and Wales

7.

LAMELLA

I.

Why did Fred and Rose West do what they did? What made them serial killers? Could what happened have been avoided? These questions are not within the remit of criminal proceedings. In the concise logic of the law such questions are not relevant in the establishment of guilt. Despite the occasional performance of some practitioners, courts of criminal law are not places for endless exotic debate and discourse. The rules of relevance and admissibility are strict. In the West case perhaps ten per cent of the evidence gathered during the investigation was used at the trial and yet the officers in the case executed their duties with economy and efficiency. There was no wild goose chase, despite Fred West's best efforts to deceive them. And the ninety per cent of material that was not used was intimately connected with the inquiry.

It can be glibly stated that Fred and Rose West did what they did because they were both sadistic, psychopathic killers, who, through a turn of fate, found each other and thereafter reinforced, combined and covered for each other's appalling proclivities. Is it really sufficient to just park the matter there? To conclude that in the general span of humankind, some people will become serial killers?

Should not allowances be made for the fact that when Daisy Letts was pregnant with Rose, she was suffering from mental instability which made her obsessive, anxious and depressed? For this, she had been prescribed electroconvulsive therapy, which continued throughout the pregnancy, right up to the week before Rose was born.

It might be thought that such a seemingly incompatible combination could never be entertained because of obvious concerns about harming the baby. Surprisingly, clinical research indicates ECT as an available treatment during pregnancy in severe cases of neonatal anxiety, depression or psychosis. NICE recommends alternative therapies as preferable, although this does not exclude ECT. Epidemiological studies suggest some risk to the foetus, with possible reduction in amniotic fluid or bradyarrhythmia (reduced heartbeat) but with statistically tolerable teratogenic outcomes. In a limited number of cases the statistics indicate foetal death. But miscarriage may have resulted in those cases anyway. There is no statistical data to indicate increased risk of brain damage or neonatal emotional distress.

Should consideration be given to the theory of psychopathic development as a result of front temporal lobe damage arising from accident trauma, as has been indicated as a likely consequence of Fred West's motorcycle accident when he was eighteen years old and/or the serious fall he had from a first-floor balcony at a club in Ledbury three years later?

There is an abundance of clinical evidence supporting personality change, aggression, disinhibition, slowness and sexualised behaviour. The symptoms can vary greatly but significantly identify patients as socially disarmed, in that they become inept, socially indiscrete, slow and obvious. Fred, while he could never be accused of being intelligent in a conventional sense of the word, was a man possessed of savvy and guile who knew how, with sleight of hand, to pull the wool over people's eyes and cover his tracks with the charm of a rustic psychopath. Maybe the accident did cause personality changes as a result of brain injury. His family in Much Marcle thought Fred changed after the motorcycle crash, which had left him in a coma for a week.

Some analysts chart certain patterns of nascent behaviour in fledgling serial killers which tend to be present in the formative childhood years. These include demonstrable acts of cruelty to animals, such as a family pet. A predisposition to acts of arson is also so recognised. On the evidence, Fred West did not conspicuously display these behaviours; although in a practical, hands-on, brass tack, do-it-yourself rustic environment, a propensity for such cruelty could be hidden. It was commonplace to hunt and kill rabbits for food, to catch squirrels and sell their furry tails as charms, for all the family to assist in slaughtering the domestic pig, which would then be hung upside down to let it bleed out so as to have meat for the winter.

Who is to say that when Fred was left alone, he did not incorporate his own sadistic little rituals? He certainly displayed symptoms and was encouraged in his nurturing to be a psychopath. The scruffy little urchin was a mummy's boy, who was mischievous and smug; he took advantage of people and knew he could get away with whatever he wanted, because his mother would protect him, so he pleased himself and did not care about the consequences.

Can it ever be a plausible exercise to consider Fred and Rose West's respective psychological developments in order to try and unpick the monsters they became?

Thus far, no one can say with any certainty what goes on in another person's mind. Neuroscience is making great strides in mapping neurological functions, but it is still very much in its infancy. Interestingly, Stephen West told me that after Fred's post-mortem, slices of his father's brain had been retained for study. One wonders what, if any, research value such cold, dead grey matter might have possessed and is, of course, a very different proposition to the electrical plotting of regions of vital, fully functioning brains. But even if patterns of electrical impulses could one day flag someone up as a psychopath, what value is such information? It does not prove the commission of an offence. There are plenty of captains of industry out there conquering the world of business who would profile very neatly as having psychopathic personalities. By the same token, if the criminal justice system had permitted lie detector tests to be used during the West investigation, what good would they have done? If they worked properly, they would have established that both Fred and Rose were inveterate liars. Surprise, surprise; where would that have taken the case? John Bennett and his team of officers had already demonstrated that contention during the PACE interviews. In the context of an investigation into such a murky, torrid catalogue of depravity, what semblance of truth capable of being elicited was so obtained through physical, sensorially validated, empirical real evidence? At the level of a serious criminal investigation, the vast majority of what Fred and Rose did say was either demonstrably untrue or entirely flaky and unreliable.

On another level though, in the case of Fred, what he did say – and in the case of Rose, what she did not say – may have been highly beneficial to analyse.

Fred's digressions make an interesting starting point. During interviews, the police were right to let him wander off into some place where fantasy and reality became blurred in his consciousness. A trained analyst may well have viewed a subject in such a state as a plum ripe for picking. It is true that the more outlandish discursion occurred after he changed solicitor. It must be assumed that Tony Miles rigorously underlined that he was there to defend Fred, that he was innocent until proven guilty and that if what he stated in earlier interviews was untrue and just to protect Rose, then he would need to restate the facts. By this time, Fred was aware that Rose had blanked him at court, refused to respond to any indirect overtures via visits of the children and had made it clear that she wanted nothing more to do with him. Initially, whether it was posturing borne out of a strange love, whether it was a curious truth singularly immanent in a psychopath, devoid of human empathy, who by some convoluted play of reason could absolve Rose of blame precisely because, like all women, she was ultimately a pliable doll, a sophisticated vehicle of fetish, a plaything whom he was only ever capable of completely objectifying and in his mind, her free will was necessarily negated.

And then there is the residual possibility that in the actual scheme of murder, Rose was innocent.

As defence junior counsel, Sasha Wass, stressed to Rose on more than one occasion, while Rose might have done some awful things – she might have abused Anne Marie; she might have, in moments of anger, beaten Stephen and Mae; she might have prostituted herself; she might have participated in rough sex – but none of that made her a murderer. However, by denying everything, she risked becoming two-dimensional and demonstrably unreliable.

It is not such an outlandish proposition if consideration is given to the new phenomena of AI dolls in Japan and the USA, where some men have bizarrely asserted a growing sexual and emotional attachment to them. You need to imagine one of these men deciding one day for whatever reason to chop a doll into bits. This might be, for example, because his wife has become pregnant and is concerned, irritated or possibly even jealous of his preoccupation with the doll. It might be that the wife herself decides to break the doll into bits to put an end to such obsessive distraction of his attention from where it should rightfully be. Such a scenario, it can be argued, might not be so dissimilar to the Wests.

Rose was often pregnant at the time that known victims were killed. And in the case of two of the victims, Anne McFall and Shirley Robinson, they were heavily pregnant at the time of death, as the remains of their unborn infants were found with their skeletal remains. It is accepted that Anne McFall's murder in 1967 preceded the time when Rose could ever have been involved. Shirley Robinson, however, was a lodger at 25 Cromwell Street in 1977 and her 'relationship' with Fred was subject of widespread gossip among the lodgers.

II.

Psychoanalysis is often challenged as a pseudoscience, where its findings cannot be rigorously tested by repeatable empirical methods, yet it has been with us for over a century and is thriving; in the realms of both psychology and psychiatry, it is often the best we have.

Could it have been used to help establish the truth as to what really happened to the victims and to ascertain the number of victims there really were? Possibly, if the process had triggered a cathartic response in the subject. The problem is, such outcomes can take years to arrive at, if ever. And there would have been ethical issues. Psychoanalysis is a therapy, not a prosecution evidence gathering tool. It would first require the consent of the subject submitting to it. Why would they? As a defence solicitor, my clear advice to the client would be not to go near it. Defence leading counsel, Richard Ferguson QC, made it his mantra not to let prying stray 'experts' get anywhere near to Rose West, irrespective of whether they were selling sociology, religion, psychology, probation, psychiatry, devil worship or even snake oil.

Assumptions about client confidentiality can be dangerously misplaced and particularly invidious when interviews are secured by cast-iron assurances of legal privilege. The law of legal professional privilege is a fundamental right of the client that has been recognised in common law for over 400 years. It is also, by virtue of article 6 of the European Convention on Human Rights, a human right so designed to protect a litigant client and thereby the integrity of the justice system. Litigation privilege applies in relation to confidential communications between legal advisers or their clients and any third party, if they are made for the sole or dominant purpose of conducting existing or reasonably contemplated litigation which is adversarial rather than investigative. It is this limb that should cover expert medical, psychiatric or psychology reports. It is evident that often the courts have ruled that it does not. By the same token it has also been recognised that admissions made to a priest, even in the sacrament of confession, are not so covered by professional confidentiality. At Rose West's trial, the Crown was permitted to call Fred's appropriate adult, Janet Leach, as well as a prison doctor who attended Fred on the pretext of assessing his well-being. This was evidence in rebuttal to exculpatory statements contained in the Fred West taped interviews that was admitted as evidence on behalf of the defence.

It is true that on a number of occasions during the trial process and in the preceding investigation, Fred and Rose had found themselves subject to psychological enquiry as well as interview by psychiatrists. This was for other purposes, e.g. assessment of the risk of self-harm on admission to prison and psychological profiling in relation to the child abuse allegations in 1992/93. Fred boasted proudly to his family that he had hoodwinked the psychologist and told him that he was physically unable to satisfy Rose's insatiable appetite for sex and had been impotent for many years with chronic erectile dysfunction. This, he said, was because of a serious accident when he was hit between the legs with a metal bar while at work.

I find it surprising that the clinical specialists did not on a rudimentary level challenge this explanation and request a physical examination in addition to checking his medical records, for example, admission to A&E, as what Fred was describing was a physical injury to his genitals, which would have caused severe trauma, with either laceration or heavy bruising and probably with injury to his testicles as well as his penis. There was no suggestion that Fred had a testicle missing and clearly had not been 'physically' castrated by the accident. He told the psychologist that the accident had happened nineteen years prior to the interview, which would have meant around 1973. Was Fred not thereby, in his mind anyway, laying down a marker, allaying suspicion, conjuring a possible defence for the monster that had rampaged all those years before and continued to hide in full view?

Impotency is a male problem that is more often associated with stress, anxiety or reduced levels of the hormone testosterone, recognising that such factors can operate in an integrated way. And as experts in the field will confirm for both men and women, the brain is the essential key in matters of sex and libido. While it is true that physical trauma can have a psychological impact, that is clearly not what Fred was intimating.

What is interesting is that it suited Fred's self-image, the figure he created to act out his sexual power play fantasy, for him to project a sexually diminished 'man'. Do not expect Fred to proffer such explanations out of candour or despair. He promoted that as part of his persona because he was comfortable in 'that' skin; it pleased him to do so. It may well also have been an entrenched strategy to deceive, another chameleon-like guise to deflect any possible suspicion that might fall upon him.

While there is evidence that Fred suffered from premature ejaculation and was more, in Rose's words, a 'wham, bam, thank you ma'am' sort of bloke, as might be gleaned from the evidence of Caroline Owens in which she describes Fred having a sheepish 'dabble' while Rose was out of earshot. There was also evidence in the form of a photograph recovered from Cromwell Street during the initial child abuse inquiry in which Fred was relaxing at home, stark naked in an easy chair. His penis was evidently erect. It is believed that this photograph was one of the pictures destroyed in 1993 after the abuse trial collapsed, when a whole bundle of material was apparently disposed of. It was one of many photographs that I had been served with on restricted terms.

It is worth just pausing here. The 1993 child abuse inquiry collapsed because the children refused to give evidence against their parents. In hindsight, this is very understandable. But it could not have been ruled out that they could change their minds sometime in the future. Would a responsible prosecutor kick such a serious case into oblivion by destroying real evidence? Did not that photograph alone gainsay a possible future defence by Fred that he could not have raped and buggered his thirteen-year-old daughter because he was impotent?

And many other photographs that were disclosed to me may equally have clarified issues in the nebulous circumstantial matrix upon which the subsequent serial murder case was based. In particular, a series of small Kodak Brownie black-and-white photographs of close-ups of vaginas. There were at least a dozen of these and in some, there appeared some anatomical trauma or disturbance that was deserving of assessment by a medical professional. While this series of photographs did form part of the evidence presented to magistrates sitting in childcare proceedings, as far as I am aware, no specific expert analysis was carried out on these pictures.

I recall another solicitor, a seasoned practitioner in childcare work, an unemotional man with an economy of words whom no one would accuse of a vivid imagination, who nevertheless felt moved to wander over to me in the small, office-like courtroom that was the upstairs courtroom No. 4 of Gloucester Magistrates' court. He said to me that he viewed the series of intimate pictures as disturbing and that the anatomical features upon which they were focussed appeared to display trauma in some way. Within two years, the full significance of his observation became apparent.

III.

Please excuse a brief digression while I deal with the matter of lost or destroyed evidence that troubled the defence in the preparation of the case.

In the early 1990s, a former police officer by the name of Harold Morgan (not to be confused or associated with any serving police officer by the name of Morgan who participated in the 1994/95 investigation), following retirement had obtained employment with Gloucestershire County Council at Shire Hall. From there, he had been given work within the social services department, in the nondescript square-glazed 1960s annexe across the car park from the Bearlands central police station.

171

His duties included collecting and filing material used in care proceedings. If he had still been in the constabulary, his role would probably be designated as exhibits officer. In this capacity, it was Mr Morgan in his infinite wisdom who destroyed a large amount of photographic material, which, in addition to polaroid snapshots of vaginas, included photographs of people in tight black rubber bondage outfits, together with an assortment of dildos of varying sizes and pictures of erect penises. Yet he preserved, whether by accident or otherwise, a set of half a dozen pornographic movies, some of them commercial and some of them homemade, featuring Rose with various men and on her own demonstrating her virtuosity in depraved party tricks, including blowing cigarette rings with her vagina, the wonders of water sports as she peed on a towel, or using her vagina as a vehicle for appearing and disappearing beer glasses, apples and oranges, which would miraculously emerge and roll towards the camera lens, all in glorious technicolour.

It is only in recent years through local contacts that I have learnt of Harold Morgan's role. Pre-trial, my repeated enquires via the CPS drew a frustrating blank. Morgan has been dead some years now, but the information I have about him is that while he, like many blokes, operated within a broad sweep of the law, he was well-known for susceptibilities that could, had his managers chosen, undermined his employment. In modern parlance, he would probably be described as a predatory male in the workplace, who sexually harassed female colleagues, making them feel uncomfortable by staring at their legs and making unwelcome sexualised comments. I have information that he belonged to a swinger's club.

The destruction and consequent non-disclosure of these photographs formed part of the reasoning that I used in the application to the Criminal Cases Review Commission made in 2001.

IV.

When Rose was first remanded into custody at Pucklechurch, near Bristol, she was seen by a psychiatrist. While I have not had sight of that report, when I visited, I routinely discussed with Rose who she had seen and what she had said with a view to pre-trial safeguarding to prevent risk of disclosures that could be exploited by the Crown as incriminating. Rose told me that she had been asked about her sexuality and it was evident that there had been probing questions about her psychosexual dynamic. She told the doctor that she had never in her life experienced an orgasm.

Could this have been a lie? If so, what purpose would it have served? As she made the comment to an expert, and for Rose to say anything at all that was not evasive, lends credibility. And it begs the question as to what on earth was she experiencing over all those years? If it really was the truth, it blew the lid on an ocean of sexual charade. I recalled ploughing through reams of statements that diametrically contradicted such a contention. There were the family holidays at caravan parks where adjoining holidaymakers had reason to complain about the excessive volume through the night from Rose as she was seemingly pleasured by nocturnal sexual antics. Then there was the testimony of the children, who would sit in a downstairs room to watch early evening television and yet had to endure the audible trace of sexual activity in 'Rose's room' upstairs as she entertained a steady stream of men. While the unplugged volume may have made microphones and amplifiers unnecessary, nevertheless Fred insisted on having sound electronically relayed to the downstairs room and when he came in from work and sat down next to his children in his grubby kit, he would insist on turning up the sound to ensure he did not miss one copulatory groan; likewise, he seemed to require the children to be on the receiving end.

It cannot be overstated how Rose chose to remain silent and in place of explanations would shrug and utter breathless exasperations at the absurdity of asking her anything at all. It was as though she was vexed and taxed to engage her mind to deal with enquiries into seemingly innocuous facts. She could, when it suited, be animated to tell superficial anecdotes about the children and life in the family, but she set the terms of reference for those conversations. Anything remotely challenging or potentially incriminating she would brush away and say that that was a question Fred West should answer. And yes, she usually referred to Fred as 'Fred West', in quite an impersonal way. I suspect this was a deliberate ploy to emphasise a distance from him. I suspect, particularly after his death, that she did not wish to betray residual feelings for him.

When I visited her on the afternoon of January 1st 1995 to tell her that Fred had hanged himself, her expression, her demeanour and her body language were a complex compendium of conflicting signs. When I first told her, she was momentarily silent save for quiet gasp. I sensed an excitement at the prospect that this was a major development that somehow had tilted the future very much in her favour (an impression that was to be short-lived). I detected also the welling of a lump in her throat and a tearful swell clouding her eyes that never became a stream on her cheek.

The ninety per cent of material unused in the case included hundreds of covert tapes from a bugging device that had been installed in the safe houses where Rose stayed with Mae in the hope that Rose would make revelations while unaware and off her guard.

When Rose West was bailed by the police on February 27th 1994 after being interviewed about her daughter Heather, she initially went back to 25 Cromwell Street, where it was arranged that her older children Mae and Stephen would also reside, to meet safeguarding concerns. Shortly thereafter the police realised that as it was a crime scene, it was inappropriate for a suspect to stay there. The property was to be taken apart brick by brick in the search for evidence. In addition, the horrendous media frenzy meant that she was at risk if her whereabouts became known. For these reasons, she was placed in a police safe house, initially in a 1970s three bedroom semi-detached at Kimberley Close, Longlevens, Gloucester, where she was able to reside, it was hoped, in anonymous seclusion until she answered her bail scheduled for April 24th.

She was staying there with Mae and Stephen, who was also staying some of the time at his girlfriend's parents' house. I visited Rose one evening in early March. Only a handful of people were told on a need-to-know basis where Rose was.

It was curious to sit in the modern nondescript lounge with Rose and her daughter, watching the television and chatting small talk. It provided an insight into how all the bad stuff could happen and, if she indeed did know, she could just bury it all away in her mind and carry on with family conversation, absorbed in the trivia of a soap opera or whether to have beans or spaghetti for lunch. We had no idea the entire house had been bugged. As Lacan might say, the symbolic big 'Other' was mediating the family communication. What was being said was what a family at home in an evening would be expected to talk about. The gross divergence with the enormity of what Rose was facing is symptomatic of a psychopath. Why wasn't she falling apart, totally distraught and distracted by the allegations against her?

If she was, it was well-hidden within her calm exterior as she enjoyed the peace and tranquillity of quality time with her daughter Mae. While the tapes, if on a factual level failed to betray any condemnatory dialogue, for a psychodynamic interpretation, they were most informative. But that is not the way the justice system works. It is no doubt the case that judges have confidence in medically trained psychiatrists but are wary of the subjectivity of psychology.

To emphasise just how closely Rose kept her cards to her chest, while there were hours of muffled scuffling as bodies shifted on the sofa, with the drone of soap operas on the telly, small talk and chit chat, giggles and groans, not one incriminating statement was uttered. Not that it would have helped the Crown's case if she had, because while the police insisted they had approval of the Home Secretary to set up the bugging operation, I for one never saw any confirmatory written authority for such an oppressive and unusual activity by or on behalf of the state. From a legal point of view, it is reasonable to speculate that had the Crown Prosecution Service sought to introduce any incriminating material so obtained, the defence would have had strong grounds for it to be excluded.

Rose's capacity for having a duplicitous persona, a double life, a mindset of stark contrasts, is further well illustrated by her friendship in the mid-1970s with an upstanding and decent young woman called Maxine Brown, a girl guide, who like Rose was also at this time in her late teens to early twenties. Maxine Brown met Rose at a dance. They started chatting and became friends; it was always entirely platonic with never any suggestion of sexual overtures. They would buy each other a drink and put their handbags nearby on the floor to have a dance, to wait and see if any blokes would come up to them and dance with them. What Maxine remembered about Rose was how she would have to go home early, because she was not allowed to stay out late and she also had to look after some kids. Maxine had no idea Rose was married with her own children, let alone the rest of horrendous luggage that she was carrying.

Maxine always felt slightly sorry for Rose. It felt as though she was slightly downtrodden, just trying to make a bit of space in her life for a little bit of girlie fun, some quality time away from the drudgery. Maxine noticed the strange, homemade, loose-fitting flowery dresses that Rose would wear that seemed very old-fashioned, not at all stylish, and with these she wore childish, knee-length white socks – so uncool – probably the reason that Rose never seemed to get off with any blokes at the discos. She thought Rose was just another meek and mild, wilting little wallflower hoping that Prince Charming would come along and sweep her off her feet.

Post-conviction and post-appeal I am aware that Rose went through a prolonged and thorough programme of psychological assessment at HMP Durham. She never disclosed to me what the precise findings of that were, other than to say that she found it helpful and that she was getting somewhere and wanted to move on with her life, albeit resigned to a future in prison. It was around this time that I had prepared an application to the Criminal Cases Review Commission, which Rose had co-operated with and was actually lodged, when she contacted me to say that she no longer wanted me to proceed with the review. When I asked her if she was intimating that she was guilty to the murders, she said that she was not. A strange state of mind to try and square. There were rumours that came back via sources from the prison that she had actually made admissions to a psychologist that she had become attached to, but I have no verification of this and Rose has never admitted her guilt to me or to anyone publicly.

V.

Fred and Rose both came from families where there was intergenerational abuse. Fred's mother had sex with him. Fred had sex with his younger sister, Daisy, and as a teenager was arrested and charged with incest after he got her pregnant. She refused to testify against him and intimated that another boy was responsible and so Fred was not convicted. Daisy had an abortion. She was only thirteen years old at the time. Rose's father, Bill Letts, had sex with her. After Bill Letts's wife, also called Daisy, moved out, only Rose, who was fifteen at the time, remained with Bill. During this time Bill Letts's father, Walter, would come and visit. It is believed he also had sex with Rose. Bill Letts continued to have sex with Rose after she was cohabiting with Fred. Fred acquiesced and probably encouraged this as he also encouraged Bill Letts to have sex with Fred's daughter, Anne Marie. Fred also regularly had sex with Anne Marie. As a teenager, Rose had shared a bed with her two younger brothers, Graham and Gordon. She had sex with both of them. Fred used to invite his younger brother John West around to 25 Cromwell Street. John would then take it in turns to rape Fred and Rose's daughters: Anne Marie, Heather and Mae. John committed suicide some months after Fred, while awaiting trial for rape.

Anne Marie describes leaving home, having two babies of her own and then having to undergo a hysterectomy because the anatomy of her reproductive system had been so badly damaged by years of sexual abuse. It was only then that she realised that she did not come from a 'normal family'. This may sound like stating the obvious, but childhood experience of the world is that which the parent – or parents – presents to the child. That is unavoidably their normality. What is normal becomes entirely flexible. In extreme circumstances, children survive because of their amazing psychological adaptability. Their minds have a plasticity. I have friends who were the only child, and that was normal to them; friends who were brought up by lesbians in a time of differing attitudes to today, and that was normal to them; I have ten children, and for them a household with ten children is completely normal.

What is also interesting is how Anne Marie stated that she still had affection and love for the father who abused her, although it is evident that any similar bond with Rose did not remain. Naturally, Anne Marie also expressed love and affection for all her siblings.

This does beg the question as to what part of the capacity to love is acquired by example and how much of it is innate within each of us? While hate is a negative internalised failing in human nature, it may be as the poets and metaphysicians might assert that love is out there, a cosmic force that transcends humanity, but which may capture our hearts in a pure, honest, uncorrupted way.

It is remarkable how, despite being abused and deceived by Fred, who she well knew seriously wronged her and used her for his corrupt and warped gratification, Anne Marie had been able to salvage something, find something worthy of retaining in a residual love and affection that Fred had for her as his daddy's girl. Akin to this, it should be kept in mind how her hard-wired coping mechanism erased all conscious memory of some significantly traumatic events, yet preserved others. The evidence of Miss A strongly suggested that one of the other girls in the room when she was raped was indeed Anne Marie, a fact Anne Marie concedes but just cannot recall.

While it is evident from statements, media accounts and Anne Marie's own testimony that she has had to confront many demons and at times struggled with the luggage from her past – and, on more occasions than she may wish to remember, be coaxed down from jumping off Westgate Bridge – she nevertheless has survived, has a responsible job, is independent, sociable and, most important, in her relationships, her concepts and capacity for love and affection are well-adjusted.

Antisocial Personality Disorder is listed in the *Diagnostic and Statistical Manual of Mental Disorders, Fifth Edition (DSM-*

5). This is the reference manual that defines the symptoms of mental disorders. Antisocial Personality Disorder encompasses both the psychopath and the sociopath. The terms are often used interchangeably, but there are differences. It is suggested that psychopaths are more likely to be born, whereas sociopaths may more likely be a product of nurture. Psychopaths have a greater capacity for planning, whereas sociopaths are often reckless. Psychopaths are more likely to totally lack empathy for other people and be indifferent to the suffering of others. Psychopaths and sociopaths are both dangerous, although it does not automatically mean that they will become killers. Most serial killers are psychopaths.

Fred's total lack of regard for natural marital boundaries suggests that he really had no feelings for Rose. Even if she really was enjoying her promiscuous freedom (which she always denied), does it not still demonstrate that he could not care less, that inside he was devoid of normal responses, that in his psychopathic universe, even the close family relationship that he appeared so committed to was a device created to deceive, manipulate, conceal and exploit?

Yet while psychopaths have no empathy with others, do they not still feel their own pain?

Even if love and marriage is a myth, it occupied an awful lot of his time and energy.

Perhaps Fred the monster did craft the alter ego of the semi-impotent Fred: garrulous, smutty, trivial, a petty crook, easily handled, a cheap and economically exploitable tradesman. Maybe somewhere, sometime, Fred did hurt as nature, as the circumstances might suppose?

Could Fred, in his perverted mental dominion, have conjured a system of self-placating compensatory justice wherein he fabricates a mortifying situation where he suffers constantly the indignation of witnessing in plain sight and sound every man off the street being free to ejaculate into his wife, the mother of his children, while he then has to go to work and earn the money to pay the bills? What man could bear such an intrusive invasion into the heart of what should be the centre of his reason for living?

Was the awfulness of this contrived situation the price paid to justify the abomination in taking whatever girl he wanted, and without compunction invading her rights, discretion, free will, binding and abusing her, ravishing her young, nubile body, torturing and tormenting her, taking her life and then further abusing her dead body before dismembering her like some inanimate piece of furniture?

Was one not a revenge for the other? If so, was this cycle of revenge born in the abuse of his childhood, which must be explored more fully?

VI.

On its own, this would place the motivation for the murders squarely on Fred's shoulders, yet he acted jointly with Rose. So together, what was it with Fred and Rose? In psychoanalytic terms, their combined symptom was the commission of a sadistic serial murder. How far is it possible to unravel what aberrant psychological history that would thereby reveal the causes?

The lawmakers in society do not like unconscious action. Apart from some minor offences of strict liability, to commit a crime there needs to be a guilty act – the actus reus – and a guilty mind – the mens rea. If conduct could be attributed as the fault of intervening events that change a person's nature or radically disrupt their nurture, if every one of us is driven by unconscious impulses and processes that we can do nothing about, in such a seemingly deterministic world, culpability would evaporate, free will no more than a figment of our collective imagination. In such a world, the courts of justice would be obsolete; it would be as farcical as determining guilt where a pride of lions killed a deer and a pack of hyenas then stole part of the carcass. Fred was aware of society's need for individual responsibility. His ploy whenever he took advantage of local girls in his teenage years was, after sexual assault or rape, to claim that he had had a blackout and life would then carry on as though the incident was airbrushed from history. This mind game was in the collective psyche of the family, who would never discuss in public the perverse eccentricities of what went on behind the closed doors in the squalor of rustic family life, up close and personal.

Fred's mantra from an early age was 'I want, I take'. In a moment of early awkward passion, inappropriately grabbing a girl can be understood, within reason. It seems this was something he did often and then, in accordance with his father's advice, if he could overpower the young women, he would have his way. His nurture took him beyond what was acceptable. If such conduct might accord with front temporal lobe brain damage, Fred's refined mantra of 'I want, I take, but in order to do so I will employ deceit, subterfuge and guile, and then once ensnared, I will do with the girl what I want' certainly is not consistent with the behaviours resultant from such injury. Such conduct is, however, in its sophistication, typical of a psychopath. The planning involved requires some anticipated timespan in order to achieve his goal and indicates that he was not acting in a moment of uncontrollable passion. In using verbal persuasion, he did not need physical restraint, either his arms or ropes, to capture the girl. The conclusion, if it needed to be stated, is that the artefacts of bindings were, first and foremost, pure fetish rather than physical necessities to achieve his goal. This emanated from Fred well in advance of his meeting Rose.

Freud's psychoanalysis, in seeking to understand psychosexual dynamics, theorised about how developmental history may create neuroses, psychoses and psychopathic disorders, and mapped the framework, subsequently revisited and reinterpreted by Jacques Lacan, where an integral facet was the domain of the seemingly unknowable unconscious.

Fred's introduction to sex in his mother's bed deeply impacted the rest of his life. As a mummy's boy, the obvious favouritism fed his innate narcissism. He was cheeky. He got away with misdemeanours at home and tested boundaries at school, where he did not engage in class; possibly today they would diagnose attention deficit hyperactivity disorder. But if he crossed a line and got into trouble, his mother would defend him and normalise unacceptable transgressions. He loved his mother and he also feared her in equal measure, as she had become the disciplinarian within the West household. She had taken to wearing a belt with which to beat the children when they challenged her.

In the cramped, primitive, farm labourer's dwelling that intimately housed a growing family of two adults and eight children, it is entirely comprehensible how mother and the chosen eldest son may have found themselves in slumber next to each other. And from there, as the pubescent Fred lay with an erection, Daisy took hold and masturbated him before inviting him to cheekily straddle her while she introduced his young tool into her vagina. By this time, the thirty-two-year old mother had a matronly body with a big belly. She had delivered eight babies. Her nether regions would have been large and flabby, the matronly cavity massive compared with that of the sheep whose hind legs Walter had taught Fred to stuff in his wellington boots before coupling.

The smell of manure and bodily odours would have been prevalent. Washing was challenging. Fred was always characterised as grubby and dishevelled. Daisy would have sweated at toil in the house and garden, her crevasses streamed with bacteria gathering in bodily fluids, as her hearty sexual urges disgorged hot flows into the lining of her vagina. The close scent of women remained essential in Fred's perverted enjoyment of enforced sexual encounters. As Caroline Owens candidly recalled in her witness statement, midstream in the sick repertoire of Fred and Rose's abuse of her, he needed to pause and have a sniff between the cheeks of her buttocks.

Attachment, when a child's essential emotional and physical needs are met by some significant other person, is a profound overarching mechanism in the formation of a human being. It is ever-present well before the formal language communication of 'Mummy, I want'. It starts in the womb; it is an ever-present requirement to secure the child's development. In a baby's earliest moments on this planet, predominantly, the person providing for those needs is the child's mother. At first, the signification for this attachment is on a sensory level. In addition to visual communication, where the mother adoringly showers loving attention with her eyes into the baby's eyes, there are the auditory senses, as well as touching and feeling and the sense of smell.

While much of Fred's upbringing was dysfunctional and went hideously wrong, it is possible that his early attachment was relatively normal. The attachment of smell, however, proved later to be integral in his rank depravity. The semen-stained knickers he would require Rose to give to him as a souvenir after he had sent her out for the night would ceremoniously be burnt and the scorched remnants placed in a jar on the sideboard, where Fred could relax by taking the lid off them and sniffing. He was acutely aware of when the young women at Cromwell Street were having their periods and would comment on the fact. In Anne Marie's case, he would mock her by saying, "Oh,

I see Harry Rags is running in the two-thirty." It is likely that he was attracted to the scents of stress hormones released by the severely distressed and traumatised girls that he and Rose abused. Over the hours or days, they would perspire profusely; they would have no opportunity to go to the toilet. All these odours were available for Fred's pleasure.

When the police searched 25 Cromwell Street in 1992, they seized a set of full-body black rubber suits. The officers commented that they had been worn because they could smell the human sweat. Fred would have been acutely aware of that and had no desire to wash them.

It is likely that there was some particular heightened event in Fred's childhood that is not documented and we may never find out about that consolidated this sensory perversion, which was integral to his psychopathy. After all, the source of the scent would be something material in the body. Who is to know whether the body parts he retained in some way satisfied this craving?

It is accepted that 'partialism' – that is, a particular fascination with certain parts of the body – is a separately recognised phenomenon in murderous psychopathy. In the sense that it is a fascination with some material thing makes it a form of fetish.

Fred's description of his father, Walter, was that he was a big, burly, bold countryman, who taught Fred much of the country craft. He also encouraged him in matters of sex to go and get and take what was on offer without qualms. There is anecdotal evidence of Fred watching his father during the summer bailing, taking his chances as he would force himself on a young maiden.

One wonders whether there was some particular event that, while outwardly not earth-shattering, was terrifying to Fred as a young child. Maybe something occurred on a late summer's evening, well past his bedtime, out in the fields, watching the hay stubble being burnt off while he held a trapped rabbit; maybe his father was next to him, sweatily wrestling some wench to the ground, and as he ripped her knickers off, they landed on the impressionable young boy's head, drenched as they were from the sweat and toil of the long day in the field. Perhaps she had already been frolicking with some other farm labourer. Perhaps his father and the wench teased and involved the young Fred. Perhaps as they rolled over, they landed on the young boy and squashed his rabbit, causing the animal's flesh to tear and bleed out across Fred's neck and arm. Perhaps, distracted in the sexual antics, they did not realise that the stubble was burning too close to where they were, and the wench's skirt and drawers caught alight; her buttocks were scorched and her hair singed. And all the while, there was Fred in close proximity, squashed and gasping for breath in the smoky air as the light faded and the atmosphere filled with all these overpowering, sexually charged, noxious odours.

Yet the evidence is that Fred avoided foreplay, was repulsed by cunnilingus and found menstruation unpleasant, despite his unhealthy interest in always knowing when and which of his daughters were having a period.

Fred's initiation in the matrimonial bed may have been preceded by him watching Walter giving Daisy a good, solid rustic shagging. He would have watched his father ploughing his chunky girth in and out of Mummy. Then Fred's turn came. Walter may or may not have been present and complicit.

Fred's young mind would have been a conflicted torrent of fear, combined with testosterone-fuelled excitement, anxiety at the unknown and taboo, and an awareness of stepping outside boundaries. He would also have felt a gripping sense of inferiority as his little plonker hardly touched the sides of the well-worn maternal fanny. Nevertheless, Fred's energetic young torso grinding vigorously on his mother's loins, pressing her clitoris to carnal pleasure would have filled the hot sweaty bed, imbuing the young Fred with her sexual electricity; the hapless young man thereby surfing on the wave of her plundering orgasm. This mad, surreal disconnect from normality would have empowered Fred and fed his narcissism. He may also have confused his ecstasy with that of his mother. In the height of sexual initiation, his mind may have unconsciously confused his being with that of his mother. The self that was him was crushed and subsumed in that of his mother; like a film show of his birth was being played back in reverse. At a most primitive level, psychologically, he was crippled, destroyed, powerless, as though his body was broken into bits and ceased to exist. As a coping mechanism, his conscious mind stepped outside of his body and he became the voyeuristic observer of the incestuous performance in which he was actively participating. The subject became reintegrated into the object, and for an instant, immortal. Fred was his mother and then what came out of her was the thing he felt destroyed in the very moment of separate existence; as a sexual being, he had fleetingly sensed immortality. He was in a surreal distortion of nature at its most delicate and elusive, revisiting, re-enacting the primal tragic drama of his own emerging individual consciousness and in ceasing to exist, he glimpsed the domain of the dreadful unknown torment that lurks habitually in the unconscious, what Lacan categorises as the domain of the 'Real'.

From the discourses of critical theory, Lacan imports a structure to the unconscious in that primitive drives have signification, they have symptoms. For Lacan, the structure was linguistic, in the sense of a signifier and a signified, so say the unconscious of the 'Real' subliminally 'talks' to the conscious, for example through dreams, but signification can also be manifest through symptoms, aberrant states that may present as neurosis, psychosis or sexual perversion.

Fred West was always scruffy and dishevelled. He rarely combed his hair. Although usually clad in work overalls, even when wearing a suit, it bothered him not to work in it, in case it got smudged with mud and oil. Was this some kind of look he cultivated, comparable today with designer stubble and distressed jeans? To be a psychopath and narcissistic, yet never look in a mirror needs some explaining. Could it be that he dreaded the sight of his mother whenever he glanced into a mirror?

It might be a hypothesis that after the sexual traumas of his childhood, some sense of the 'Real' was never entirely hidden for Fred, more precisely through his unconscious he was exposed to that thing, the terrible void beyond language that the subject can never know. This intrusion of rank, unbridled desire, the utterly amoral impulse of sexual urge was perpetually live streamed into his disinhibited consciousness and catastrophically, the psychodynamic disaster did not end there.

A number of writers have flagged up Fred's deficiency in sexual prowess and his inability to satisfy Rose, identifying his small manhood and premature ejaculation. This is modern culturally borne stereotyping and over-simplification. Firstly, the size of Fred's penis was not a determinate of whether he ejaculated prematurely. As has been stated, Fred perpetuated a myth about being damaged down below in an industrial accident, yet photographic evidence shows he was capable of sustained erection and while he may not have been King Kong, he was anatomically complete and functioning. In the narcissistic Fred West there was an insurmountable gulf between the nascent imaginary ego, that is, his overinflated self-image that occurs prior to the properly formed 'Subject' person, which evolves from the process of psychological 'castration' and acceptance of the name of the Father. That is in the socially and linguistically moderated 'Symbolic' realm, where the 'Subject' person is possessed of the 'lack', and thereby they see themselves as they really are.

There were a number of consequences of this failure of his development and integration in the 'Symbolic' register. It meant he demanded the agency of other men, in particular big Jamaican men, to be his surrogates, to perform with Rose as his ego would require of himself. The adverts placed in local swinger's magazines for 'West Indian W.E male' were Fred's idea, not Rose's. Rose told me repeatedly that Fred constantly kept on at her to engage in these extramarital liaisons with men he chose. She also said that the large, oversized dildos were Fred's idea. This nagging went beyond verbal haranguing and on more than one occasion, Fred would beat Rose into submission by punching her in the face if she resisted. The whole elaborate sexual enactment arose from Fred's choice to present as inadequate; it gave him control, curiously as a means to make anodyne the actual true unresolved inadequacy deeply seared within his psyche. It was not that Fred could not satisfy Rose any more than he could any other woman and it was not that Rose expressly or otherwise told Fred that he could not satisfy her, it was Fred that needed Rose not to be satisfied as a pretext for him to manipulate her as a sex object to be used by other men for Fred's proxy satisfaction.

This is more than theory. It is at odds with the perception of their relationship that was presented by the Crown and it is at odds with the simple stereotyping that has dovetailed so well the demonising of Rose West in the popular press. It is also based on many hours of discussion I had with Rose where she insisted to me that this dynamic was a constant that pervaded their relationship over the years they were together. She was as adamant in explaining this to me as she was in her admission that she preferred close, physical, sexual relationships with women rather than with men.

I remember asking Rose about a set of dildos that had been recovered from Cromwell Street in 1992. One or two of these contraptions were massive in length and girth. Again, she was quick to explain in her fast, breathless, chattery tone: "They ain't for my benefit. I don't flippin' want them. It's what Fred wants. He likes to see them used. That Fred West is a sick bastard. It's the kind of stuff he gets off on."

They were meeting his warped, perverted expectations about what a man physically should be. It had nothing whatsoever to do with the sexual pleasure of Rose or another woman. And Fred placed the blame for his terribly dislocated and broken self entirely with his mother, who in her abuse of him had warped and scrambled his perception of himself. Tragically, all the young women he met who became his victims were his surrogate mother; they had to pay the price for what had been taken from him, what he believed he should have been as a man and was not. His unconscious experienced utter humiliation at the warped *jouissance* he derived from contriving at Rose's unbounded sex while he hid in a cupboard with a camera, observing other men shagging the living daylights out of his wife was the spark for his bloodlust.

The question then arises as to why Rose survived? Why should she have had any elevated position that saved and protected her? On the one hand it is easy to say that they were two peas in a pod, that her own warped and dysfunctional upbringing presented a kind of knowing, a therapeutic understanding, an intuitive fellow feeling, a kindred spirit, which would have been precious. More precisely, Fred in his obsession with sex, would have habitually indulged in a continual stream of self-indulgent talk with her. They would certainly have discussed, at length, each other's genitalia, just as the evidence of Caroline Owens revealed them discussing her vagina or Fred requiring Rose to keep a notebook of the size of the penises of her punters, as well as taking photographs of both vaginas and penises. At some early stage in their relationship, Fred would have asked Rose her opinion about the size of his penis. And she would have replied by assuring him that his penis was bigger than her dad's. For Fred, the usurping of the father in this primitive game of bragging rights gave him a sense of security and attachment to Rose that was unobtainable anywhere else. But Fred would not have just let the subject go. He would obsess and revisit this prospect and needed to know for sure. The only way was to encourage Rose to invite Bill Letts into her bed, even after she had started living with Fred, even after Rose had given birth to Fred's children. And so, Rose continued to regularly have sexual intercourse with her father.

Fred's experience of nurturing in his formative years through childhood within the family of the farm labourer and his wife would be the phase in which formed what Lacan described as the 'Symbolic' domain of subject relationships; whether within the immediate family or the wider local community. And notwithstanding intergenerational dysfunction and aberrant sexual tendencies in the West household, the rural traditions remained a strong influence, and the family accepted without question their lowly place established within the order of landowner and workers, Church and State, of time observed deference to the law and authority.

Country people knew their place; they worked hard tending the land and animals; their lives remained consciously close to the changing seasons and the customs and festivals that came and went in time-honoured observances of the established order. This was Lacan's big 'Other', the overarching moral authority, the outward standard of conduct which intuitively subjects were expected to observe. These standards conflicted with the amorality of desire, that primitive urge emanating from the so-called 'Real', the terrifying void in Fred's unconscious. This departure from the objective moral standard was also endemic within the West house. It is true that some of Fred's siblings were blindly innocent bystanders, but the reality was a disparity between the dictates of the socially enveloping traditional mores and the private sexual urges. This had several devastating impacts on Fred. He developed an intuitive public deference and obsequiousness, presenting as a disempowered castrated vassal, yet inwardly sexually charged as pubescent testosterone surged through his body. This enabled him to develop a chameleon-like capacity for deception. On the one hand, this duplicity acted initially to severely repress his desires. This resulted in fantasies about girls that soon became more and more elaborate. With the encouragement of his father displaying overt sexual dominance in harassing young woman, as well as schooling Fred in the wonders of bestiality with sheep, not to mention his mother's corrupt designs on her firstborn son, the fantasies became progressively perverted and came with a template, a passport to act them out. Perversion manifested itself in psychopathy.

For such a creature to thrive would necessitate an open, liberal permissive society, that was nevertheless male-dominated and institutionally saw the objectification of women as benign and complimentary. It required a society where young people felt empowered to branch out on their own, be independent, move freely and emulate some bohemian dream of communes, hitchhiking, experimentation, Dionysian intoxication. In England, the 1960s and 1970s offered a libertine revolution of the young. There would be casualties, but none more tragic or undeserving of their fates than the victims of Fred and Rose West.

VII.

In the years I acted for Rose, I was drawn back to reviewing the combined evidence of their offending. While the only conclusion can be that they were both integrally complicit, I do believe that Fred and Rose were very different people, who operated at different levels, fulfilled different functions in their repertoire and fundamentally there was a divergence of sexual interest between the two of them that Fred was aware of but not Rose.

For Fred, his own participation in the act of sexual intercourse was a brief and unspectacular event. His desire was to be the voyeuristic puppet master as others interloped as agents to the mechanics of sexual acts that Fred could watch and film or have Rose report to him later. It is doubtful that Rose got any additional sexual satisfaction from knowing that Fred was in the cupboard watching and recording. They were *tête-à-tête* with sadomasochism. There is no doubt they both had a great capacity for cruelty with Fred being cold, calculating and totally lacking in empathy, while Rose was animalistic; like showing a red rag to a bull, she would reach a critical point beyond which there would be an emotional eruption, the violence of which is difficult to imagine. In such a state, Rose became a killer. The eruption would then subside, and she would return to normal as though nothing had ever happened.

Fred was capable of extreme anger, but he was a coward and a bully. He did not fight with men.

As his brother Doug told Marian Partington in 1996: "Fred would never defend himself in fights. We always had to bail him out." He would retreat into his amiable, feeble, feckless, garrulous persona until, that is, he had a naïve young woman in his snare; only then did he become a monster.

Most alarming is the realisation that Fred's depravity went way beyond even the voyeurism, the bondage and the sadomasochism. They were still only the antipasto for what Fred was really driven to. While Rose imagined that Fred, reluctantly, as the man in the house, took upon himself the unpleasant necessity of having to dispose of the bodies after the victims had been used until their tragic lives expired; the truth was that this, for Fred, was the main course, the essential *raison d'être* for him. Do not think that by this I am attempting to salvage for Rose some semblance of innocence. The high point of Fred's repertoire, his full unbounded consummation of his dark fantasies, his contented absorption for hours on end during the night was the dismembering of the bodies, severing body parts and all this preceded by a cold, erotic moment of necrophilia.

It was in these solitary episodes that Fred was fully formed as the monster he was. This was the ultimate fulfilment of his fantasy, the *pièce de résistance*, the blossoming black flower from hell. There was a warm contentment that he derived from this; the sense of pride and skill at slowly and methodically disarticulating limbs, decapitating the head, making incisions to inspect the innards, savouring the strong body odours, cutting of fingers and toes, juggling them like charms before putting them in a bag, savouring the sense of excitement, feeling the need to have a piss, but too excited, too enthralled, too busy to stop, so he allows his warm urine to soak his pants.

This was his affirmation of power, his capturing the lifeforce, like stealing a valuable jewel, remembering the thrill of catching a rabbit, wriggling and fighting, then conquered, still and silent. The salivating grin of a man transfixed in the enjoyment of his labour.

This was Fred West, embraced and driven by the undead disembodied organ, the lamella that left him at birth, lurking in the abyss when his mocking mother forced his pubescent face into her dirty, sweaty, menstruating cunt. And then he felt and smelt that sticky, slippery, slimy surface clinging to his mouth and cheek and forehead: *l'homlette, das ding, objet petit a, oo la la, Urrrr...* manifest unconscious desire, the conflicted libidinous blueprint perched in his conscious self; thereafter to direct his darkest, disinhibited fantasies. And this was his recurring revenge. Ad infinitum. Don't forget to snip those fingers, get his willy back from Mummy's hole, what's it, thingamejig, she took it from him, you know, when she made him become her phallus. "They all say it, they all say they just want sex and then like, what's it, they become all lovey-dovey and I lose it like and tell them to fuck off and then strangle them." Busy, busy. The grubby night rat wrestles with its quarry as it plumbs new depths of obscenity. It insists, it will not be stopped, it is the immutable libido, das ding, objet petit a, origin of desire from some terrible unknowable abyss deep in the unconscious, a place we can never know. One sick mother fucker.

Fred constantly created opportunities to mine his warped world. It encompassed the practical guile and exploitative skills of a psychopath to manipulate circumstances and then the available resources to populate the event and orchestrate the repertoire and then after, the cunning to conceal from view and steal away, yet visible in plain sight. First and foremost, he needed a willing accomplice, which he found in Rose.

VIII.

So how did Rose West's psychosexual development become so aberrant and come to dovetail so perfectly with the distorted excesses of Fred's fantasies? Is it possible for two people to independently conjure the same horrendously warped sexual dreams?

Rose was the fifth child and third daughter of Bill and Daisy Letts, a timid child who was slow to develop emotionally. She was born in Northam in Devon on November 29th 1953. Bill Letts had been in the Royal Navy as a radio operator. He had trained as an electrician and was called up to the Navy in 1942 only weeks after marrying. He remained in the Navy for seven years and was deployed as a steward after the war ended. There is evidence that Bill Letts had been diagnosed as a paranoid schizophrenic. It is not clear when this medical assessment was made, but he would not have been accepted into the forces if there had been a diagnosis before he joined. Almost certainly the diagnosis was made in the Navy.

His despotic fury and neurotic control over his placid wife badly affected her nerves and resulted in a transference of his neurosis and soon after marriage, Daisy slumped into chronic depression and anxiety. Bill would, from a distance, dictate to Daisy the rules of the house, covering cleaning and cooking duties and discipline, obsessive curtailment of contact between his children and their peers in the neighbourhood. In the few short months before he went off to war and during periods of leave, Daisy had learnt about the vicious beatings Bill would dish out to impose his will. He frequently knocked his demure, pretty little wife about like a punchbag. She was eventually referred to a psychiatrist, who recommended electroconvulsive therapy, a treatment Bill Letts supported; Daisy was subject to this over many months, including the period of time she was pregnant with Rose.

Lacan, in his reinterpretation of Freudian psychoanalysis, posits three realms of the human psyche. He called them the 'Real', the 'Imaginary' and the 'Symbolic'. They are purely conceptual, linguistic devices rather than some tangible model of the mind. They overlap and interlink with each other. Lacan called the main point of linkage the Borromean knot. Lacan asserted that when this knot was weakened in some way, the results were devasting in terms of serious psychological malfunctioning, whether neurosis, psychosis or otherwise.

In applying the ideas in this psychoanalytic theory to Rose West, it is instructive firstly to look at the 'Imaginary' realm, which is closely associated with the mirror stage in an infant's development. It is the realm of the senses. Even before a baby has an idea of itself as an individual subject, the senses detect visually parts of its body, it can feel its hands and sides and it is acutely aware of its mother, the first signifier of connectedness to another person. Actually, when a child is born, it has no sense of itself independent of its mother. The child looking into its mother's eyes has, in its mother's eyes, a proto-concept of itself, which is then affirmed by the baby's recognition of itself in a mirror.

The mirror self-recognition by the baby is key in the formation of identity and subject, yet the child also realises that the reflection is something else, the child has a dual sense of both subject and object. Lacan describes a Hegelian dialectic in this process with a schismatic synthesis, resulting in the formation of ego and narcissism. Ego here means the conscious way someone projects themselves rather than the 'I' or full subject, warts and all.

Whatever developmental psychology you choose to read, all will concur in the massive significance of the mother in the early development of her infant. They will also concur in the premise that the first tender months of a child's life are pivotal to its future psychological development. Diagnosing and addressing attachment disorders in children finding their way into the care system creates a major caseload for psychologists and social workers.

While epidemiology may inform us that there is no evidence that ECT applied to a mother adversely affects the child in utero, the impact of a mentally ill, anxiety-ridden, postnatally-depressed mother on her new-born baby is entirely another issue and can be irreparably damaging.

Daisy's mental illness will have severely disrupted this pivotal point in Rose West's early psychological development. Instead of the comfort and a loving reflection that Rose should have reaped from her mother's eyes, she would instead have confronted a blank despair, a hollow lostness, an empty, hopeless disinterest. Her mother was a ghostly shell, gripped by the neurotic prescription her schizophrenic husband demanded over the years, first in threatening missives forwarded from thousands of miles away and then, upon his return, enforced by beatings and terror. He required his servile, browbeaten wife to do his bidding like an automaton.

It is a documented general clinical observation that desire is the desire of the 'Other'. An infant's first desire is what the mother desires. In Daisy's case, this was to slavishly accord with her neurotic, bullying husband. Then, when Daisy would not be present at the side of Rose's cot, as the infant realised herself as a subject separate from her mother, Rose would long to see Daisy and wonder what it was that was more important in Daisy's life. She would conclude that it must be something special to replace her mother's interest. In many infants, the mother might be temporarily absent to be with her loving husband, but it could be to shower love on other siblings, or play the piano, or reading or meeting friends. These other activities are seen by the infant as conceptually phallic; they are the substitute phallus. This idea of recognising the symbolic phallus elsewhere is described as castration, a process that is necessary for the subject to properly enter the 'Symbolic' matrix of the social world, to accept the laws and conventions by the omnipresent mediation of the 'Other', to function as a social being. The substitute phallus in Rose's case was some dour mechanical vacant compulsion to restrict, isolate and discipline her children in order to comply with Bill Letts's desire to enforce his neurotic regime. The substituted phallus is here distorted, a sense not so much of pleasure but relief at avoiding grief through acquiescence in the brutal regime of the father.

ECT was a popular psychiatric therapy in the 1950s and 1960s and it was a therapy regularly used in the Royal Navy, where sailors displayed symptoms of mental instability. Bill Letts's medical records from his Navy days have not been accessed, but his diagnosis of being schizophrenic is documented. It is likely he too received ECT prior to his eventual discharge.

In his formative years, Bill Letts was a weakling, who was mollycoddled by his mother, who would also collect him from school rather than let him walk home on his own and as a result he found himself ridiculed and bullied by his peers at school. He was slight and effeminate in appearance. As a teenager, he had been spurned by girls and when he eventually met Daisy, he initially coveted her as a trophy wife, but his neurosis resulted in him beating and controlling her rather than showing love and affection.

There is no suggestion that his being recruited as a radio operator toughened him up. Something sent him over the top while he was in the Navy. On the one hand, the strict rank hierarchy in the forces would have made junior recruits the bottom of the barrel and susceptible to all manner of banter and bull, including being ordered to clean the deck with toothbrushes. At sea, homosexual relationships developed, and weak neurotic junior ratings would be susceptible to what in the 1940s would have been illicit overtures by other sailors. It is possible that a young, naïve, sheltered Bill Letts was the subject of bullying and sexual abuse while serving in the Navy. He dealt with his subjugation by transference to his own family back in Devon, where he asserted himself as the abusive absolute power. Statements by Rose West and her siblings confirm that among Bill Letts's extensive compendium of abuse was a direction to clean the carpets with a toothbrush. He insisted on the house being constantly sparkling and shipshape even though there were eventually seven children living there.

Bill Letts returned to Devon in 1949. Finding work was difficult and had been the reason that he had not been in any hurry to leave the guaranteed pay structure and navy rations which evidently were preferential to civvy street. The demobbed finished article was a selfish and unpleasant man, yet even when unemployed he would present to the neighbours as a dapper, sociable individual.

If the Borromean knot had been loosened in the formation of Rose's formative 'Imaginary' realm, her developmental trajectory was yet to become even more skewed.

The 'Symbolic' realm is a social world, the world of communication, the world of interaction of the subject with everyone and everything recognisable through the chain of signifiers and signification that provide the complex matrix of reality. This matrix is configured by language, words as signifiers but also gestures, people, any phenomena may act to signify meaning to the world in which the subject is immersed. It is strange to muse that the 'Symbolic' realm of the subject is formed before the child is born in the sense that, for example, the expectations, education, role, etiquette and life trajectory will in many ways already be formed for a prince or a pauper. Likewise, it can be redemptive to accept that the 'Symbolic' realm of a subject continues after their death in the memories and artefacts held by loved ones of a life lived, of the achievements and little kindnesses.

It is always curious when a person's Facebook page remains open and active after they have passed away. It is as though some part of the person continues, as an avatar in cyberspace, within the 'Symbolic' realm.

The people nearest to a child are often the first important signifiers in the construction of this matrix that is their world. The violent despot Bill Letts was a major influence. Rose witnessed his arbitrary irrational beatings of Daisy and the other children, yet by pleasing her daddy in whatever way was required, Rose stayed safe. From very early on Bill Letts was grooming Rose, and from those tender years she would progressively be sexually abused, probably without any sense of how distorted her worldview was becoming. The fundamental interdiction against incest was breached at a very early stage of Rose's development. Whatever Rose was doing in the bed she shared with her younger brothers Graham and Gordon she had been taught by Bill Letts and routinely engaged in a full repertoire of oral sex, mutual masturbation and full sexual intercourse. Rose's 'Symbolic' order was thereby corrupted, the Borromean knot was decidedly loose and the theoretical topography of her psyche would screech serious psychological malfunction with severe neurosis, psychosis or sexual perversion anticipated as a result. Yet, even though Rose was called 'Dozy Rosie' and was timid, immature and withdrawn, she nevertheless progressed in the mainstream and did not overtly display any mental illness.

Psychoanalysis posits the primitive fundamental drives in the dark inaccessible place which Lacan called the 'Real'. It is that part of reality that the signifier misses; it is something beyond communicable meaning, something that is left out when the subject is formed in the 'Symbolic' order. It is something residual, that is present but left out of the being. It is a terrifying, inaccessible, unknowable realm, which nevertheless inevitably creates symptoms that can become signifiers in the unconscious. The drives are the erotic, self-preservation and the death drive. There are, in addition, three partial drives: the oral drive, which relates to the breasts; the anal drive, which relates to faeces and the phallic drive, which relates to genitalia. Lacan asserted that the unconscious had a language of signification and that part of the unconscious so accessible by linguistics was in the realm of the 'Symbolic'.

In Rose's case, it is likely that the drive bleeding from deep within the dark recesses of her psyche was that of self-preservation rather than an overt erotic drive. Sex was just the currency she was able to trade to stay safe under the power of her father. Clinicians observe, in any event, that aggression is more usually associated with the self-preservation drive.

Rose did not mature normally. She was a sexually abused little girl, who for a long time remained babyish; she played with dolls when other children had grown out of playing with dolls. Even as a woman, she dressed as a child with knee-length socks and flowery frocks. With the early onset of puberty, she had a growth spurt and became physically larger than the other boys and girls in her class. Soon she adopted the gratuitous violence of her father to seek revenge on the kids that had hitherto bullied her and were bullying her younger brothers. When Fred bought her some sexy lingerie in the early years of their relationship, she sat on her bed at the Letts's home in Tobyfield Road, Bishops Cleeve, cut the fabric into pieces and carried on wearing her schoolgirl underpants.

Rose West, at one and the same time, was both pliable and compliant, but also potentially an extremely violent and dangerous individual. Rose's brain worked in a very different way to Fred's. It is doubtful that she was driven and preoccupied with perverted sexual fantasies. She was an ever-ready nymphomaniac who, from an early age, was programmed to respond to other people's sexual desires. On this level, she would submit herself willingly to whatever anybody wanted to do, no holds barred. This sexual submissiveness meant that with a partner like Fred she was also an agent for the infliction of sadistic sex on other young women.

While Rose West was the agent who used dildos both on herself and on other women, as was graphically testified to by Kathryn Halliday, the spectacle was inextricably for Fred's satisfaction. It is also true that Rose, whose nature had from an early age been sculpted by abuse, submitted to whatever sexual depravity a man wanted to indulge in. Yet in such circumstances, inside her being, she was like a pressure cooker or a spring coil being steadily wound up more and more. The emotional account was balanced when Rose would explode with a level of rage and anger that is hard to imagine. These episodes would often be when she was pregnant, had been looking after her children all day and then was forced to spend the night with one of the big black gentlemen that Fred had arranged for her to sleep with. The payment, if there ever was payment, was incidental to Fred's voyeuristic satisfaction. He would drive round and collect her in the morning. She would be required to give Fred a blow-by-blow account of what she did and what she had done to her. She was on strict instructions to hand over her semen-stained knickers to Fred as she got into the car. Her sexuality remains complex.

In her paper *Perverse Mothers or Mad Wives: A Lacanian Commentary on Nahaleh Moshtagh's The Silent Accomplice: The Mother's Passive Perversion,* Alireza Taheri offers insight into how there is an innate psychosexual conflict in women.

The paper starts by noting the taboo of asserting that the maternal instinct is fundamentally inscribed in nature. It is then asserted that anthropologically it is a more recent phenomenon and apparently not hardwired at the level of biology. To place the matter within Lacanian topology, the use of the 'nature' is replaced with the idea originating in discourse and language. By the same token, Lacan replaces the term 'instinct' with the word 'drive'.

Perversion attributable to the mother and child relationship is based on the idea that in the baby, the mother retains a substitute phallus and in so doing wards off the process of castration and the sense of 'lack' thereby arising. A mother with child is in denial of the lack. She has a sense of fulfilment; a feeling of wholeness. Lacan thereby viewed maternity as intrinsically perverse, but this generalised perversion does not imply that all mothers are perverts. It does, however, imply that a mother who derives too much satisfaction from her maternal role may inhibit the child's psychological development.

In referencing clinical cases, there is a discussion of the role of a mother in the sexual abuse of a child of the family by her husband. In Lacanian terms, it is necessary to establish the type of enjoyment (*'jouissance'*) that the mother derived from the disavowal of her husband's actions.

Within a marriage, a mother may be conflicted by the divergent roles of mother and wife. These are two radically different positions for her, representing respectively the polarity of the masculine and feminine sexual positions. For Freud and Lacan, the mother with her baby as her substitute phallus is a man, but simultaneously, as the wife of a man she is feminine. According to Lacan, the *jouissance* of the feminine is much more powerful than the phallic *jouissance* of masculinity. It is the *jouissance* beyond the phallus.

Lacan used as an illustration the story of Jason and Medea. They were a happily married couple with three children when Jason left the family home to go off with another woman. Medea felt a huge rage which resulted in her murdering the three children. He concludes that behind every mother there is a Medea. The phallic *jouissance* is sacrificed for the greater feminine *jouissance* of being a woman.

It is illuminating that in a letter Rose wrote to her daughter Mae from prison in 2006 in which she was intimating there was no point in future contact, she said: "I was never a MOTHER to you and there is no point in trying to be now."

If Rose is correct in this assessment of herself, then she was indeed always acting with the added force of feminine *jouissance*. Yet, the young Rose West harboured a girlish dream of meeting a man, falling in love and having babies to look after, like her dollies and all the while her sexual leaning was towards women. 'Fellas' she could take or leave. She performed with men for Fred's benefit. Her early promiscuity was because sex was what she knew from an early age and as a pretty, fecund teenager her sexuality earned her approbation with young men. It was and had always been her currency. It appealed to her ego if men liked her and men liked her if they could fuck her. She had come under Fred's influence earlier than either of them were later prepared to admit and Fred was actively encouraging her to go out and have sex with every man she met that wanted it. It is very likely that it was Fred West who encouraged her at the age of fifteen to have a gang bang with highway workers when their van was parked at Jim Tyler's roadside mobile canteen at Seven Springs. Desire is the desire of the 'Other'.

Rose always denied to me that she was a prostitute in the real sense of the word, that is, that she sold sex as a commercial transaction of which the sole *raison d'être* was payment. In fact, she went so far as to emphasise that she went with other men because first and foremost it turned Fred on. Fred would require her to report back to him with a blow-by-blow account of the choice of orifices employed, the size of erections, the number of ejaculations, the positions. He could never ask too many questions. He would pester her for more information just as he would continually pester her to go with some man or other that he had arranged for her to spend the night with. She said that she had a house to run and children to look after and it is entirely believable when she says she often did not want to go out and spend a night 'with some bloody fella'. But Fred was insistent, perpetually, in an obsessive way as a result of which Rose said she would always eventually give in and comply. She said, "If I didn't, he would make my life a misery." By this I took it to mean that he would beat her up. Fred West could not have been scared of Rose West to have so effectively exerted such pressure on her.

The relationship dynamic between Fred and Rose emphasises that he was controlling in setting the narratives as initiated in his warped fantasies. They can be posited alternatively within what Hegel called 'cunning of reason', where the subject is active through the 'Other' and Lacan's idea of 'interpassitivity', where the subject is passive through the 'Other'.

When Fred was active through the 'Other', he would voyeuristically hide in a cupboard with a peephole and a video camera and enjoy the encounter through the agency of one of his West Indian friends, who Fred had arranged to call round to visit Rose and have sex with her. In so doing, Fred also fetishized his wife as a sex object.

When Fred was passive through the 'Other', he sent Rose out for the evening so that he could get on with concreting the basement or helping his neighbour repair a roof. He remained active on other pursuits and was not there in real time as Rose spent the night having sex with a man as arranged by Fred. Again Rose was objectified as a sex doll for the enjoyment of the other man. Fred would nevertheless, the following morning hear all the twists and turns, nooks and crannies, in a blow-by-blow account of the action, as well as receiving Rose's semen-stained knickers.

This communication between subjects operates at the level of consciousness, as Lacan would say in the realm of the 'Symbolic order'. The 'Symbolic order' is mediated by and through a subjective permeable medium called the 'big Other'. This is the voice subscribed to by all the subjects. It might be their God, or a political ideology; it will be a higher regulatory voice, a social morality that exerts compliance with certain norms, whereby in civil society people are nice to each other, they help their neighbours, they might profess belief in God, they might or might not go to church, they demonstrate a strong work ethic. And above all, whatever else might be regarded as subjectively acceptable or unacceptable, the greatest prohibition of the 'big Other' is not to commit incest.

This compliance is expected. Outwardly, if you present to your neighbours as observing these norms, then you are accepted and content within the overarching domain of the 'big Other', even if what you really feel, what you fantasise about, what your sexual urges and preferences are, represent a stark divergence from what 'one' ought to be.

Freud viewed this divergence, which necessitated suppression of feelings, as the basis of neurosis, psychosis or perversion. In his work *Civilization and Its Discontents*, while centred in the old-fashioned values of early twentieth-century Vienna, the calculus of malady consequent upon the gulf between high-brow expected social norms and the wilder varied sexual desires of the citizens was explored. Freud did anticipate a time of liberalisation, as occurred in the swinging sixties, and thereby expected it to be a means of resolution. He could not have anticipated that it would provide the ideal playground for a monster like Fred West.

The 'big Other's' repugnance to incest emanates in the unconscious; it is instinctive, a priori knowledge, a resonating boundary legislated in the dark terrible unknowable domain of the 'Real'.

Freud, in his work *Three Essays on the Theory of Sexuality*, makes the following statements in the section entitled *The Transformation of Puberty*:

"…The closer one becomes to the deeper disturbances of psychosexual development, the more unmistakably the importance of incestuous object-choice emerges."

He further states:

> "…Respect for this barrier (against incest) is essentially a cultural demand made by society…"

In a footnote, Freud clarifies:

> "The barrier against incest is probably among the historical acquisitions of mankind, and, like other moral taboos, has no doubt already become established in many persons by organic inheritance."

Lacan agreed with this assessment but analysed it in terms of it being a linguistic construction. It is cultural regulation through signification in the 'Symbolic order' that declares the interdiction against incest.

Some might argue that the social origin of the taboo against incest so stated is at variance with the notion of its connection to the unconscious, to some primordial instinct curtailing the conscious mind from rendering such fantasies as palatable. In Lacanian terms, a social origin would imply a prohibition emerging from language signification between subjects, something attributable to the Symbolic order. This is consistent with the approach of structural anthropologist Claude Lévi-Strauss. In his work *The Elementary Structures of Kinship*, he stated that it was not biology but rather symbolic structures of kinship, language and the exchange of goods that were the key to understanding social life, stating that kinship systems kept nature at a distance and represent a cultural phenomenon based on the interdiction against incest.

If this interdiction was emergent from the unconscious it might properly be grouped with ideas such as the fight or flight instinct of the reptilian brain, or the hand-closing reflex of a new-born infant, echoing the instinct for primates not to fall out of trees. Darwinian evolution demonstrates how concentration of bad genes through inbreeding results in a failure of the species.

Much research has been done in this area and the Lacanian approach is difficult to resist. If families were separated at birth and the siblings parted from each other and they are then randomly, coincidentally and unknowingly later introduced to each other there is often a sexual attraction. A sexual relationship then may occur in blissful ignorance of the taboo, which clearly cannot operate in such circumstances. It is only the social construction that invents it.

Lacan considers how observance of the unwritten rules ordained by the 'big Other' provide opportunities for exploitation by sociopaths, for example, the exploitation of the notion of love in a relationship.

During discussions with Rose about this aspect of her life, I mentioned to her the content of some of commercial pornographic VHS videos that had been retrieved from 25 Cromwell Street during the 1992 child abuse inquiry and had survived to be available as disclosure in the 1994 murder inquiry. In one of these movies, a young, nicely dressed housewife meets a friend, who is also neatly turned out. They have gone to a restaurant for a meal. They are both happy and sociable and as they chat away the waiter arrives at the table to take their orders. They order pizza and drinks, but on completing the meal they both realise they have no money on them to pay for the meal. Following a brief discussion of their plight, the matter is soon resolved by the pair offering sex to the waiter and promptly proceeds to fellatio and sexual intercourse. At the end everyone is happy and smiling and they drive off in their vehicle, waving goodbye to the waiter.

They then realise that there is something wrong with the car and they pull into a garage to get it sorted out. A greasy mechanic in oil-stained overalls then gets to work with his spanner and solves the problem and puts the bonnet down. But low and behold, the friends do not have the money to pay the bill and offer their bodies for sexual gratification in settlement of the bill. They are then thoroughly shagged across the bonnet of the car.

I asked Rose what she thought of the movie. It was one of those times where her response was thoroughly relaxed and off guard. She smiled and warmed to me and said, "Yeah, those are my favourites as well."

I asked her whether she regarded what the women in the film did as prostitution? She thought it was not prostitution as such. I asked if that was the way she viewed what she did with various men. Her response was, "Well, yeah, that's the way it was. Sort of playing, really, but Fred was insistent."

This I felt was an admission from Rose, at least in part, that the sexual repertoire had an element of simulacra, that the performance was at least inspired by pornography films. How far it is possible to extrapolate from this that the sadomasochism was also inspired and copied from such films? It is my view that Fred had acted out such warped desires at an early stage where it is doubtful that he would have had access to movies and as he was illiterate, he would not have read, for example, the works of the Marquis de Sade.

I had a discussion with a man in Gloucester who had made a statement to the police at the time of the enquiry. His information was not used by them at the trial. He confirmed that Rose did advertise her services and he regularly visited her for sex during the late 1970s and early 1980s. She called herself Mandy. He said he could not relate the Rose he knew to the horrors with which she was later convicted. In a matter of fact way, he stated that she was excellent value for money. At ten pounds a time she was the cheapest whore in Gloucester and always gave value for money, never hurried and would do whatever a man asked, no holds barred. It is evidenced in one of the pornographic home movies surreptitiously made by Fred of Rose in action with a client. No doubt Rose knew the camera was rolling, which interferes with the spontaneity of what is recorded. She is shown to take the lead while sitting on a man lying on his back. She takes hold of his erect penis and with great dexterity twists it around her hand as though she is winding up the propeller of model aircraft and so facilitates the tool's insertion into her anal passage. All in glorious technicolour. The response from the punter: "Cor… fffucking hell."

The video then continues with Rose and the man bonking, interspersed with a topical conversation about the state of the drains in Cromwell Street. Who said romance was dead?

What this now elderly gentleman did not know was that, more often than not, Fred would be hiding in the wardrobe with a peephole and a video recorder. He would also have a microphone relaying the soundtrack of sexual intercourse to the downstairs room.

When Fred was in prison for seven months shortly after they moved to 25 Midland Road, Rose wrote and visited him frequently. Apart from the value the dates have in determining when Charmaine may have been killed, they are revealing on a psychoanalytic level, if Freudian ideas are to be applied.

Extracts of the letters are as follows:

May 22nd 1971

To My Dearest Lover,

I am sorry I upset you in my previous letters I didn't mean it (NO joking). I know you love me darling. It just seems queer that anyone should think so much of me. I LOVE you. Love I don't mind what you make me, because

I know it will turn out beautiful. Darling, I would like to get a horse for our caravan & put it in a showcase. We've got a lot of things to do darling in the next couple of years. And we'll do it just loving each other. Well Love, see you on the 31st. Better not write too much in case I go putting my big foot in it. (Ha Ha!) Sending all my love & heart.

Your worshipping wife,

Rose

There are two aspects to this letter. Firstly, Rose's desire for a horse to go with the caravan that Fred had made her out of match-sticks while in prison. The horse is seen by Freud and Jung as representing powerful, instinctive urges of a sexual and perhaps aggressive nature. In Greek mythology, the horse stands for intense desires and instincts.

More telling of something more sinister lurking within the gushing lovey-dovey tenor of the text is Rose's strong, overstated, obsequious protestation of devotion and obedience combined with a statement of how worthless she feels and how she is up for absolutely whatever he wants. Rose already knows what Fred wants: total sexual promiscuity, threesomes, bondage and sadomasochism at whatever cost. Rose is saying that she has done something, she is expressing some kind of deficit, some concealed truth that means that she owes Fred big time. And she already knows the price. There is also the self-awareness of not saying too much and in so expressing this sentiment she uses the imagery of her 'big foot (Ha! Ha!)'.

It is possible that by this point in time Rose had already beaten the living daylights out of Charmaine. There is a statement made by Stephen West many years later where he says that he witnessed his mother, Rose, beating Heather violently, and when she had Heather on the floor, she brutally kept kicking her in the head until there was no life left in her.

Yet Rose was carrying on with life. She got up in the morning with Anne Marie doing household chores, she got ready to visit Fred, she wrote him a letter, she ate and drank, she looked after Heather, she was prostituting herself to one or two men in the neighbourhood. She was not destroyed. She was not withdrawn and unable to confront Fred. This is how Rose always was, from the beginning to the end, as all the babies came along.

It is necessary to decide whether Rose really did not know anything ever or whether she knew everything from the earliest days? The evidence is firmly against her.

This letter had been preceded by a letter dated May 4th 1971, in which she says:

> …Blinking base people gets on my nerves. Darling, about Char, I think she likes being handled rough. But darling why do I have to be the one to do it. I would keep her for her own sake if wasn't for the rest of the children. You can see Char coming out in Anna now and I hate it.
>
> Love, I don't think God wanted me to go to that dance, Because I didn't go after all. Darling, I think from now on I'm going to let God guide me…

Words and phrases like 'hate' and 'gets on my nerves' have to be viewed with particular severity and potency when uttered by Rose West. After all, she was a woman of relatively few words and if she said something, she meant business. She was not communicating what most people would understand as frustration that might prompt them to react in a less than reasonable manner. With Rose West, we are talking about a level of intense, searing violence that, once erupted, was uncontrollable, total and devastating. Once the pressure cooker blew, that was game over for any hapless young woman upon whom she was unleashing her fury.

It may be argued that Rose could not have killed Charmaine as early as May because it is documented that she took the children to visit Fred at Leyhill as late as June 15th. All the prison records indicate is that Rose visited with two children. There was an assumption that she always visited with Charmaine and Anne Marie, and that someone was looking after Heather. It is more probable that the two elder girls did initially visit with Rose and that, at least from May onwards, it was actually little Heather who visited with Anne Marie and Rose, and Charmaine was absent.

From the statements of Anne Marie West, Caroline Raine and Miss A we know how events would have unfolded.

In a book of awe-inspiring generosity, hope and reconciliation, Marian Partington, the older sister of one of the victims, Lucy Partington, posed the question 'who had bound, beaten and abused Fred and Rose?'

Fred did not use mirrors. Fred did not have tattoos other than the one Rena had inked Fred's upper arm while he slept with the word name RENA in bold letters. Rose did not have tattoos either.

Some modern thinkers have looked at historical events through social structures rather than the drama of individual lives, but the West case must rest on the grossly aberrant trajectories of Fred and Rose West. Ingrained intergenerational abuse might mitigate but does not begin to exonerate. There is a view which I hold in my mind to help me rationalise the saga of misery and horror that had to be unpicked by the authorities through due process of law.

I view Fred and Rose West as rogue children, who never matured into adulthood. They attained the years that admitted them to the club of grown-ups, entitled them to marry, get a mortgage, drive a car, vote, watch x certificate movies; they achieved the physical development in Fred's case to shave, do hard manual work, produce sperm, in Rose's case to get pregnant, run a household and bring the children up, to have sex and be bestowed by society with discretion and choices reserved for mature people.

Yet they were both such damaged people and carried so much crippling psychological luggage with them from their respective childhoods that they were not beings who could properly take their place as mature individuals in civil society; instead they stayed as children and grew grotesque emotional horns and fangs. They each became monstrous travesties of Peter Pan. Psychologists recognise the symptoms of emotional paralysis, where some traumatic childhood event brings a drawbridge down and emotionally suspends the person at a point in time from which they never properly move on, except exceptionally through effective professional psychological intervention and counselling that, of course, Fred and Rose never had. Yet they were sufficiently able to present to the outside world that they were fully functioning adult participants in the performative enactment of the nuclear family, the bedrock of stable society, the essential cement to build sound foundations for healthy living, comfortable echoing moderators of the 'big Other'.

The frightening side to this immaturity is that children can be cruel. Such behaviour unchecked, untamed and unbounded can twist and turn in any direction to any depth. This is even more so when you have two rogue aberrant subjects, who in their puerility and immature moral vacuity, giggling and posturing, egged each other on and were led nonchalantly by each other, influenced by fantasy or weird pictures of bondage and sadomasochism in glossy pornographic magazines.

I recall reluctantly asking my wife to view with me some of the pornographic material recovered from 25 Cromwell Street. The video in question was of Rose performing 'water sports' and peeing all over a towel. At the time we had several young children, so it was a time when potty training was all too familiar. My wife's immediate response was that Rose seemed like a baby sitting on the floor doing a wee wee. There was for a brief moment a strange juxtaposition of innocent infantile ineptitude and gross adult licentious depravity.

There was always the sense that Rose in the late 1960s and through the terror years of the 1970s, was on the one hand still a child playing at mummies and daddies, except with real babies, and all the while flipping into the *folie à deux* interludes of the utmost sadistic depravity, wherein many beautiful young lives were extinguished. The truth is, Fred was still a little boy who, when he wasn't skinning rabbits in the field the way his dad had shown him, liked to break his little sister's dolls into pieces. In their own sadistic way, both Fred and Rose were still playing with dolls.

Fred and Rose created a family as a front to indulge in abuse and depravity. Heather had a sense of this, and yet Anne Marie, although habitually sexually abused by Fred, did not. The adaptability of children enables then to normalise extreme circumstances. I suspect that as a coping mechanism, Anne Marie remained in denial and may even have, at a subconscious level, shut down certain memories to make life tolerable. While she does not have false memories, her genuine residual fondness for Fred is curious. Her intense dislike of Rose is normal and comprehensible.

There are many photographs of the West children as toddlers and pre-teens. They have happy smiley faces. They are not pretending. And the progeny Fred and Rose spawned, despite everything, as adults, are predominantly peaceful and law abiding. They know and give love to their own nearest and dearest. The human sensitivity expressed by Anne Marie in her many statements bear witness to someone who is empathic and in touch with their own feelings. Is such a capacity immanent and not dependent on the example of parents? It would appear so.

Remarkably, from the many hours I spent interviewing Rose and the dozens of letters she wrote to me, as well as the hundred pages of her proof of evidence, even allowing for the predominant smokescreen that she undoubtedly put up and the persistent stark denial of her guilt, it is my honest view that Rose's fantasies were not unlike those of Heather's. They were simple, uncomplicated, and they lacked narcissistic grandeur and ambition. Her dream was to meet a man she could fall in love with who would take care of her, with whom she could make babies with, take care of them and build a home. She said all that stuff often and could wax lyrically about family life because there was a genuine level where she meant it. To dismiss this and opt, without pausing, for a complete demonization of her personality is to misunderstand her.

Rose's problems were twofold. Firstly, she was irreparably damaged from a tender age by attachment disorder and the sexual abuse she received from Bill Letts. As a child, she learnt that being physically close to her daddy and pleasing him meant that she was favoured, and he would not unleash on her the extreme violence that she regularly witnessed being doled out on her siblings. She was, after all, Dozy Rosie, the one selected by her father for special treatment. At first, she did not even appreciate that she was being submitted to sexual abuse. In this respect, she is not unlike Anne Marie, who was told by her father that the abuse she was being subjected to was normal (but very different to Heather and Charmaine, who got what was going on, found it repugnant and resisted). The trade-off enabled survival; for the price of her self-worth, Rose could buy affection. In terms of cost-benefit analysis, prostitution was a positive career move. And when she met Fred, it pleased him for her to fuck everyone she met.

Secondly, Rose had an anger management problem. When she went to Bishop's Cleeve Comprehensive, she struggled. She was slow, meek and mild; she didn't make many friends; and was withdrawn. In the playground, she was bullied. And then she found herself as one of the girls in her year to reach puberty first. Her periods started; she went through a growth spurt; her breasts became large; her body became firm, strong and fecund. Like any teenager, this was a very hormonal time and when she was menstruating, her moods could be variable. So when the usual suspects in her class tried it on one day, she turned round and gave the erstwhile bullies one hell of a hiding. From then on, girls knew not to mess with Rose in the playground. Rose was also very protective of her two younger brothers, whom she was sharing a bed with and regularly having sex with. If the diminutive Graham or Gordon were ever pushed around at school, Rose would intervene to beat up the boys who were taking advantage.

Rose had the role model of her father who, when he lost his temper, often for no apparent reason, would erupt with uncontrollable violence and seething fury. There is no doubt that Rose had a similar trait.

LOVE AND HATE:

I.

Fred found it easy to talk of love, or more particularly 'making love'. When he was finally arrested and interviewed for serial murder, bizarrely, his 145 interviews were liberally laced with talk of making love. This invariably included a scenario where a young woman was 'coming on all lovey-dovey and saying that she loved him and wanted his baby and then he would lose it and kill her'.

What on earth was this stock narrative all about?

Love and murder obviously went together very easily for Fred West, as did his stark distinction about him making love to the girl, as opposed to the girl declaring that she loved him and wanted more than just sex, which would create an impossible conflict with Rose, his true love, and this thereby sealed the girl's death warrant. This, of course, was Fred's wholly fictitious narrative, given as some kind of justification for killing. Let there be no mistake that what Fred and Rose West did to their victims was an entirely unilateral, unnegotiated, objectifying, dehumanising, abominable orgy of mindless lust. And irrespective of their own history of abuse, they chose to do what they did.

According to Lacan, 'love is giving what we do not have to give'. If that is so, then Fred was very much at home in trading false promises and deception. But Lacan's cryptic statement deserves some more consideration.

He means a love that is really about receiving, satisfying a desire and not giving at all. This can be distinguished from the kind of love of saints and martyrs described by St Thomas Aquinas; the selfless love which is about unconditional giving and not expecting or requiring anything in return. It is a love offered equally to your enemies as much as those who are close to you.

The problems start when you try to associate love and sex. Apparently they are not the great bedfellows we imagine them to be. The idea of love as giving something we do not have, alarmingly, in psychoanalytic terms, is associated with a generalised use of the word 'perversion', where more precisely it means the symptom arising from the suppression of a drive. In this context, love is identified as a culturally fabricated artifice to give a civilised, morally heightened value to the erotic mechanical urge for sexual relationships. In fact, historically, anthropologists will point out that from the mists of time, love and sexual relations have rarely had anything to do with each other. The idea of this romantic courtly love was the more recent creation of Renaissance poets and scribes and is as much a fiction as the chivalrous integrity of knights of old and the Arthurian legends.

Thereby, courtly love is performative with all the ingredients of false gestures in which giving is really about satisfying lust. Likewise, historically the connection between marriage and love has always been tenuous, where even today in many cultures, marriages are arranged. Lacan does not disavow this negative view.

In ancient matriarchal societies, where property was held communally, women would have sexual relations and sire children by as many men as they chose; there was no need for attachment to one man, there was no nuclear family. Significantly in such cultures, women were in no way materially or economically dependent on men. There are then cultures such as the Eskimos, who regard it as polite to let a guest sleep with their wife for the night. In patriarchal societies where property is owned by men and they are the breadwinners, women are dependent on men and it matters that the children born from her are his.

The irony is that the West household was a confusion of a free-living matriarch giving birth to other men's babies, who happened to be dependent on a male breadwinner to bring home the corn and provide shelter for the brood. And it was a household where the supposed matriarch enacted out such a role at the behest and direction of the man. Rose insisted to me dozens of times that she did what she did with other men because Fred wanted her to and if she did not, he would keep on and on and even beat her into submission. So the matriarch was not really the matriarch?

It is true that Rose was herself forceful and evidently took the lead in cruelly disciplining the children. She also received payment from men for sexual services. However, it is known that the West Indian men she slept with did not pay her, although they would bring gifts. And the other punters were only ever charged about ten pounds a time. I have this on good authority from discussion with one of her former clients. It is unlikely that such sums would have been more than pin money for a large family. It has to be concluded that the construct was to satisfy some strange desire in Fred to share his wife in order for him to get voyeuristic sexual gratification.

While every marriage is different, the institution ought reasonably be expected to embrace the idea of at least aspiring to a lifelong commitment, where people invest all that they are in each other, their futures, their wealth, their efforts and energy, and yes, an unavoidable emotional attachment that makes the union intimate, personal, captivating, exclusive, something jealously protected by both parties, a matter of reciprocal pride between a couple. All these things are sustainable through love. Yet these intuitive expectations were clearly distorted or absent in the case of Fred and Rose West. Can a man really have strong intimate feelings for his wife and yet demand the sexual commodification of her body for any man who wanted her?

It is a line of thought that revolves back to the interminable question: what is love?

Can we at least start by saying that Fred and Rose's gushing protestations to each were not really love, that it was a false love or a conditional love?

Slavoj Žižek, in his book *How to Read Lacan*, when discussing empty gestures and performatives, says as follows:

"...Recall the everyday situation in which my (sexual) partner says: 'Please, I really love you. If we get together here, I will be totally dedicated to you! But beware! If

221

you reject me, I may lose control and make your life a misery!' The catch here is of course, that I am not simply confronted with a clear choice... somebody who is ready to damage me if I say no to him cannot really love me and be devoted to my happiness, as he claims. So the real choice that I face belies its terms: hatred, or at least a cold manipulative indifference towards me."

And so this 'conditional love' is not really love at all, even if the partner imposing the condition deludes himself that it is. Fred's love for Rose was conditional in this way. Rose accepted unconditionally this conditional love. She would do whatever he wanted to guarantee her long-term relationship with him. Fred had dark, warped libidinous fantasies. Rose was willing to participate in all the depraved and lurid permutations of the sexual deviancy conjured or made manifest in Fred's consciousness. Rose discussed with me on numerous occasions how, even if she was tired after looking after her babies, Fred would insist that she went to some overnight venue for sex. She said at times that she would protest and say no and yet he would persist and persist, even threaten her with violence until she capitulated. And from very early on in their relationship, Rose was in way too deep to back out.

Rose was not so gushing in her protestations of love, although in her early letters to Fred she put in writing in an express and assertive way her declaration of love for Fred, as indeed he reciprocated for her. Fred also often used the word 'love' both in his written statements including letters between himself and Rose while he was in custody at Leyhill in 1971. Rose reciprocated with protestations of love to Fred in her letters to him at that time, but beyond that, the word 'love' did not routinely issue from her lexicon and was rarely vocalised by her. His final missives shortly before his suicide were in a similar mould. Lacan intimated that the written protestation of love had a greater authenticity than the verbal declaration, which often feels glib and convenient.

II.

The Cambridge Dictionary defines the word 'hate' as an 'extremely strong dislike'. It is 'the opposite of love'. Neither of these statements really seem to meet expectations.

To explore the word 'hate' in relation to Fred and Rose West is to anticipate something much more virulent, wild and untamed. It is difficult to imagine a mindset of someone gratuitously torturing, abusing, murdering and then dismembering the bodies of innocent young women being categorised as an extremely strong dislike.

And to simply describe 'hate' as opposite to love creates two further problems. Although not very Lacanian, for those predisposed to romantic or religious metaphysics, it is to diminish the idea of love as a transcendental phenomena, a cosmic force capable of elevating humanity to aspire to some Platonic notion of perfection. Alternatively, if you subscribe to the Lacanian view of love as a myth, then you would need to subscribe to 'hate' similarly as a myth.

Lacanian psychoanalysis posits love and hate as closer than we might feel comfortable with. They both emanate in the 'Imaginary' realm of the human psyche as sensory phenomenon. Love also necessarily overlaps with the 'Symbolic', with the matrix of socialisation, through signification and language. Hate on the other hand, which Lacan describes as an extension of love, is not embraced by the 'Symbolic' register, but rather is exposed to the 'Real', to the dark, terrifying unknowable part of that is not reducible to communicable meaning in the development of human psyche.

Much of the academic study on the psychology of hate is concerned with dysfunctional political positions that lead to conflict, terrorism, war and eventually genocide. The author Lobsang Rapgay PhD, a former Buddhist monk and an assistant professor and researcher at UCLA, says as follows:

"The problem is, we know very little about the nature and workings of hate and what we as a people can do about it. While anger can be resolved and fades with time, hate at its extreme is an enduring, inflexible state, an all-consuming set of raw emotions. If hate is left unchecked, it intensifies from intolerance to a wish to annihilate the other. Hate strips us of our humanity. Hate eliminates the ability to show empathic concern for the injustice done to others. Hate numbs the guilt and shame that we should feel for our prejudiced behaviour. Most importantly, it eliminates our ability to understand why we feel this hatred and how to eliminate it by addressing the real issues that gave rise to it. It strikes at the core of our humanity."

He further states:

"The underlying insidious presence of contempt and disgust – a deep dislike for the other who is considered unworthy of respect or attention – appears to play a major role in intensifying fear and anger into a vicious, annihilating feeling of hate. Disgust of another instinctively makes us recoil and distance us from them (Taylor, K., 2007). Contempt is a disdain associated with the other being less worthy and inferior and, therefore, not entitled to certain rights and opportunities that are reserved exclusively for the 'ins' (Sternberg, R. J., 2017). Extreme hate, unfortunately is deep-seated and cannot be easily overcome."

These quotations taken together provide an insight that leads back into the issues of early attachment and sexual abuse of both Fred and Rose. Those deeply negative feelings were the mirror and manifestation of what had been signified to them about themselves. It is possibly easier to make this diametrical construct in the case of Rose. I suspect that Fred's psychopathy is from some darker, primal place; his recurring desire to indulge himself in a complex barbaric fetish in the dismemberment of the dead bodies of the young women he had killed suggests something beyond hate. He was devoid of empathy. He may not have felt anything about anybody, so he was incapable of hate. A man with no emotional spectrum, while he may experience extreme anger, simply does not have the feelings to engender hate.

With Rose, hate is more tangible, the word is more intelligible and possesses more meaning. This is not to say she did not have an antisocial behaviour disorder and was a deeply conflicted woman.

Morality and the Problem of Evil:

I.

Philosophical and psychoanalytic discourse on morality can appear outlandish, far removed from a conventional wisdom in the evolving zeitgeist of contemporary society. Some may view the ideas as inverting civilised notions of decency, even at risk of lending a weird validation to the horrific self-indulgence of the Wests.

The fundamental prescription for human relations is that of the Golden Rule: "In everything, then, do to others, as you would have them do unto you. For this is the essence of the Law and the prophets." (Matthew 7:12.) This basic tenet underlies all the great religions of the world and is implicit in the Rule of Law, of even-handedness, the equality of all persons under the law, the safeguard of democracy and individual liberty in a modern secular nation-state. Kant's Categorical Imperative elaborates the notion, in that it states you should only do something if you would want that action to be a universal moral law. It also states that you act morally because it is moral to do so, not due to any other secondary motivation. For Immanuel Kant, the point of morality is to make a world where everyone can be moral together (a kingdom of ends); if you are killing people, you obviously are not working to that goal. Strictly, Kant's morality is not just about treating other people as you would expect other people to treat you, it is something rational and universal. It is a priori to what others do.

To assert knowledge to be a priori is to indicate a transcendence, to have one foot in the realm of metaphysics, to require a faith akin to religion. This inevitably conflicts with philosophical notions that demand empirical proof and logical rational argument. For psychoanalysts, dreams are not messages from God but rather signification from the unconscious. The aim is to understand the symptom and not pass moral judgement.

Friedrich Nietzsche, an arch-critic of Kant, argued that morality does not, as philosophers since Plato have claimed, originate in a knowledge of universal principles. He viewed morality as purely historical, a compendium of values derived from all the accidents and incidents of human activity and interaction and therefore not a revelation of timeless truths.

In *Beyond Good and Evil* and *On the Genealogy of Morals*, Nietzsche essentially rationalised morality as originating in power struggles among people and therefore not legitimate and even harmful.

In a letter to Oskar Pfister, Sigmund Freud wrote as follows:

"...I am dissatisfied with one point: your contradicting my sexual theory and my ethics. I grant you the latter; ethics is far from my interest and you are a pastor. I don't cudgel my brains much about good and evil, but I have not found much 'good' in the average human being. Most of them are, in my experience, riff-raff, whether they proclaim this or that ethical doctrine or none at all..."

Ethical constructs were incorporated into Lacan's work, *Seminar VII: The Ethics of Psychoanalysis*. They were also controversially dealt with in a paper he wrote in 1962 entitled *Kant with Sade*. Here Lacan brought together the highly respected philosopher of moral duty, who led a quiet life of utmost rectitude with the dissolute and debauched Marquis de Sade, whose written works were regarded, even in the 1960s, as obscene, degrading, offensive and not at all suitable for publication. What was there to compare? On the one hand, intellectual moral reason and on the other, a vivid and corrupting abundance of every sexual perversion imaginable.

Lacan saw the necessity to locate his method of analysis of patients' experiences, as identified through a process of signification, within an ethical context because he was aware that all human experience has a moral meaning. This is based on the notion of the undeniable will of the person. As philosophers from Aristotle to Kant have pointed out, there is always a will. In all individuals at the level of personal experience there is an exercise of will. Both Fred and Rose West exercised will in their actions, although arguably Rose's will was subservient to that of Fred's, whose will designed the actions carried out.

Lacan asserts that in asking 'what is your will?', the answer is 'to act in the name of the Good', which is what Aristotle and Kant would assert. However, Freud discovered a new dimension in psychoanalysis to the notion of 'Good'. At the level of the individual, what is good is not a universal good which is true for everyone but rather a good that is true for only one person. Lacan calls this a kind of good 'desire'. But there is also something else, which is neither good nor bad, called 'enjoyment' or satisfaction. Lacan called this *jouissance*. It is something each individual has to deal with.

Lacan then recalls the Kantian duty not to give up on your desire (to do good); except for Lacan, in the realm of the unconscious the maxim not to give up on your desire is individualised (to do what is good for you). There is inevitably, however, a divergence between desire and *jouissance*, which creates an ever-present tension in everyday personal life. They can become powerful, tormenting opposites. Desire and satisfaction must be submitted to will: to will what you desire or not will what you desire and deny yourself satisfaction. And the instability of the divergence means that what might give satisfaction today is superseded by a will to some more extreme satisfaction as a right, ad infinitum, so plummeting the individual to the depths of some greater 'Evil'.

At this point, Lacan brings Sade into proximate discussion with Kant. The only book of Sade's that Lacan referenced in his essay was *Philosophy in the Boudoir*. The boudoir is the room between the salon and the bedroom; it is a space conceived by Sade. In the instinctual crudity of the West household, it may approximately equate to the room, with the drinks bar, the jar of burnt semen-stained knickers, where Fred might retreat for a relaxing sniff while he watched on the VHS viewer something from his collection of hard pornographic films, or listen on the intercom to Rose having sex in the top floor bedroom. In the room were also triple-x top-shelf magazines and storage cupboards of sweaty bondage suits, whips and dildos. This is not to assert that Fred West was in any way into philosophical discourse.

In Sade, the will to satisfaction becomes a duty and a right; sexual satisfaction cannot be repressed or prohibited. In the text, the schoolmaster, Dolmancé, ably assisted by the school mistress, Madame de Saint-Ange, teaches the fifteen-year-old school girl, Eugénie, everything there is to know about sexual enjoyment. The exultation is that anything goes in pursuit of satisfaction, whether sex is with a man, woman or child and whether it be with mother, father, brother or sister. If Eugenie wants to kill her mother, then it is all right to do so and her teachers will join in to help her. Before they murder her, they decide they want to subject the mother to all kinds of 'satisfactions'. Dolmancé, who is the most perverted, says that killing is too final and that if the mother was still alive then the suffering would be more enjoyable, so he devises a plan to take the mother to be with a man suffering from smallpox, so that her death will be drawn out over many months of immense suffering. At the end they say, "Now, let's go and have dinner."

This juxtaposition of Kant and Sade constructs a parallel between the Kantian imperative to act in accordance with a universally accepted moral way, to do 'Good', with Sade's fictitious duty of satisfaction, to do 'Evil'. Lacan refers to Sade's maxim, "I have the right to enjoyment over your body, anyone says I can." This emphasises that, just as Lacan says desire is desire of the 'Other', so this is corrupted in Sade's fiction of the right of satisfaction, as the satisfaction of the 'Other' ('anyone says I can').

Referencing *the Philosophy of the Boudoir* in Kant avec Sade has a frightening resonance with Fred and Rose West, but it is certainly not the case that Lacanian ethics incorporate the idea of a duty or right to satisfaction.

The Cambridge Dictionary defines 'evil' as 'morally bad, cruel, very unpleasant'. A narrow meaning of evil is concerned only with the very worst and most morally reprehensible forms of action. There are evil-sceptics who argue that the concept of evil should be abandoned because it lacks explanatory power and therefore is a useless concept. The concept of evil would be explanatorily useful, if it were able to explain why agents of morality, i.e. human beings, are capable of conceiving and performing certain terrible acts. In opposition to this, there is a school of moral revivalists who maintain that the concept of evil is essential to any moral discourse.

The sceptics resist this by contending, as we have seen, that useful discourse becomes sullied by religious and supernatural notions of evil, that metaphysics impedes sound rational and empirical enquiry. Apart from not offering insight beyond demons and flights of fantasy, the concept of evil is actually dangerous in that it can be falsely applied to facts, events and situations in a subjective way so as to absolve some people and condemn others. This might be the situation with war through the ages where the victors write the history. At a political level, grotesque inversions of what is good and what is evil do occur, such as the justification of carpet bombing an innocent population, the stoning to death of adulterous women, throwing homosexuals off of rooftops or the internment and genocide of ethnic minorities, wherever the authority of the state validates for its citizens a distorted prescription of what is an appropriate moral order.

At the level of the individual, to the extent that 'what is good is what satisfies my desires', the Marquis de Sade was setting out a similar prescription, but by no stretch of the imagination should there be any risk of misinterpreting the dreadful and inevitably destructive harm of such a distorted view, where the word 'evil' clearly has a place as a useful adjective.

In *Eros and Ethics*, Marc De Kesel considers the thought underlying Jacques Lacan's cryptic reasoning regarding ethics and morality. Lacan arrives at a perplexing conclusion: that which, over the ages, has been supposed to be 'the supreme good' is in fact nothing but 'radical evil'; therefore, the ultimate goal of human desire is not happiness and self-realisation but destruction and death. And yet, Lacan hastens to add, the morality based on this conclusion is far from being melancholic or tragic but results in an encouraging ethics that, for the first time in history, gives full moral weight to the erotic.

While this may assist in the identification and treatment of symptoms on the psychiatrist couch, there is no way that psychoanalysis, whether Freudian or Lacanian, would implicitly wish to give succour to the destructive immorality and depravity of a Sade or the Wests or any other predisposed psychopath. On the contrary, it might be hoped that in ensuring that psychoanalysis does not become a hostage to a world view of normative values, by remaining rigorous, scientific and non-judgmental, it may, in addressing such extreme perversions, facilitate the avoidance of such catastrophes.

II.

The human condition guarantees an insidious weave that works within the solemnity of religious and state institutions even as they espouse high moral rectitude, which in reality is impossible to fulfil, destined to be defeated by the flawed aberrant straying of mere mortals. When Fred West was growing up in Much Marcle, he identified himself as lurking in the shadows of an immutable moral order where titled men in fine clothes inhabited important positions in the community, men beyond reproach. He was conditioned to be obsequious. In his mock deference to the time-honoured traditions of church and state, to the superiority of the country gentry, to the lord of the manor, he was acutely aware of his own station in life, as a lowly child of a farm labourer. The West family would, at least outwardly, conform, attain a sense of belonging and acceptance in unquestioning attendance at church for traditional festivities, occasions hardwired into the collective rustic psyche, as inevitable as time and nature, of the seasons, essential rituals like asking God for a good harvest.

Remember how the public recognition of these essential moral bastions contrasted with the base instincts and aberrant lust secreted in the restless monotony of the close-knit hovel in which Fred was nurtured. This was the irreconcilable divergence within the 'Symbolic' order that was presented to the young Fred West. It was a divergence that arguably honed his instinctual facility for cunning, duplicity and deception.

It would be so much easier to rest the case there with clear lines, the path of righteousness, following the guidance of religious elders of the church, against the lostness of succumbing to wayward and aberrant lustful thoughts. Yet, I am bound to recall the view from my office window at 4 Pitt Street and to the saga that unfolded in tandem with the initial months of the West case.

There had been a change of bishop in 1992 when the much-loved bishop John Yates retired and he and his wife vacated the residence. The new bishop was a Benedictine monk, who had taken a vow of celibacy. His name was Peter Ball. Apparently, he had a brother who was also a monk and a bishop; both had gone to Cambridge and received Blues for table tennis. I regularly saw him coming and going, wearing his brown monk's habit and sandals with a cord around his middle. He was a small, wiry bespectacled, bald and wizen man. He would usually acknowledge me with a catty grin, displaying spiky teeth interspersed with gaps. He had a car that he would sometimes use to drive himself, but more often there was a young man, probably late teens or early twenties, smartly turned out usually in a suit or blazer, who appeared to be his constant helper, chauffer, aide-de-camp, acolyte in Holy Orders, general dogsbody.

I never regarded the comings and goings as particularly strange, but within a few months of Bishop Ball being installed, rumours had started flying around the sedate, conservative, cathedral environs. It was, however, with surprise if not amazement, when Vernon Daykin, on seeing the Bishop arriving at his front door with his young aide-de-camp, turned to me and said, "He's an odd one, keep away from him, there is something going on there."

The next I heard about the matter was when I was in my local pub, the England's Glory, when a local solicitor came in for a drink. He was at that time the Diocesan Registrar. He told me that he had been called down to the police station because the Bishop had been taken into custody after being arrested on suspicion of sexual assault on a number of young men, including the young man who we regularly saw coming and going from his residence. While the solicitor did not go into detail, he said it was strong stuff.

It transpired that the Bishop regularly, no doubt to the strains of Gregorian Chants and for the greater glory of God, made young Christian men get their kit off and lie prostrate on the floor while he cleansed them spiritually by whipping their firm, fleshy young buttocks. Hallelujah, praise ye yah, must be better than ping pong.

Of course the Bishop had vehemently denied any such suggestion, but the police had told him that if he admitted it, he would exceptionally be given a police caution and the matter would not end up in the newspapers. Bluntly, the Diocesan

Registrar had told the old monk that if he did not make an admission and accept the caution, he was looking at five years in prison. The Bishop was shipped out and replaced very soon thereafter.

It is a story ripe for philosophical deconstruction and worthy of Lacanian analysis. The idea of a comparison between a bishop and Fred and Rose West ought to echo the same outrageous grab as Kant and Sade, yet in the hands of Bishop Ball the Kantian mantra to do good was tainted by a secondary self-serving motive in furtherance of Lacan's individualised 'Good' for the purpose of the cleric's personal *jouissance*.

Fred and Rose never expressed a view to me on such a local *cause célèbre*, which in itself is informative. Fred had frequently distracted his police handlers over the years by pointing out who was dealing drugs locally; he was clearly not averse to pointing the finger at other transgressors. By the same token, he was keen to boast openly about indulging in any kind of sex, especially if it was sadomasochistic and involved bondage. I suspect he may have had some admiration for the old bishop.

Morality constantly morphs and is mediated, not by God, but by ever-shifting values from one epoch to the next. And it is not that far into the dim and distant past that men were executed at Gloucester prison for stealing a sheep or pinching grain to feed their families and a young woman was hanged for allegedly killing her new-born infant. In the sacred grounds of Gloucester Cathedral, there is a memorial to Bishop John Hooper, whose protestant sympathies saw him burnt at the stake in 1555. A witness account recalls as follows:

> "The fire went out three times as the reeds and wood were damp... but when he was black in the mouth and his tongue swollen that he could not speak, yet his lips went until they were shrunk to the gums, and he

234

knocked his breast with his hands until one of his arms fell off, and then knocked still with the other, what time the fat, water and blood, dropped at his finger ends, until by the renewing of the fire his strength was gone and his hand did cleave fast in knocking on the iron upon his breast. So, immediately bowing forwards, he yielded up his spirit."

And Edward II, who is buried in Gloucester Cathedral, was ceremoniously dispatched from this world at Berkeley Castle a few centuries earlier in 1327, allegedly by having a red-hot poker shoved up his rear passage. This particular wholly unroyal treatment was reserved for traitors and homosexuals. A king would normally in such unfortunate circumstances expect to be accorded the dignity of beheading.

All this was in the name of religion, all accepted as just and expedient in the preservation of the moral order in the prevailing notion of civilisation at those moments of human history. Beyond this could there ever be a personal satisfaction detectable, a psychosexual motive by any person wielding power on behalf of church and state? Well, where, as Louis XIV stated, "L'état, c'est moi," the satisfaction of the state becomes a very personal matter. It was, after all, common for kings to decide the manner of an execution, whether a condemned person would be hung, drawn and quartered or merely beheaded. In extreme cases, crucifixion was a possibility. These barbaric practises continue in many parts of the world.

Psychoanalysis has little time for religion. Put bluntly, it posits religion, along with other cultural and intellectual pursuits, whether in art or science, as an elevated and ornate substitute for the sex drive. Man is driven by the pursuit of happiness, of optimising pleasure and minimising displeasure, the so-called 'pleasure principle'.

In *Civilization and Its Discontents*, Freud identifies on the one hand, humankind's innate aggression, which he asserts serves the ego through self-preservation. Ultimately, he ascribes to this a so-called 'death drive', while on the other hand, he ascribes the sexual drive to the preservation of the species. In nature, man's unbridled libido reigns free, until, that is, he is inevitably overwhelmed by other forces, whether they be stronger competing humans, other creatures or the diverse forces of nature. In this perfect savagery, a man has a right to do whatever he likes, yet his reality soon persuades him to cede some or all of his freedom to a social order wherein his choice of partners and opportunities for sexual intercourse are curtailed as his compliance with the laws of the community is a prerequisite for protection by the group from dangerous forces of nature for which there is good reason to fear.

This is the rationale Thomas Hobbes gives for the social contract in *Leviathan*, ceding some freedom for the protection of a ruler, later revisited in Jean-Jacques Rousseau's *The Social Contract*, where the necessary check on individual freedom was supposedly to be enforced by the collective in the name of all individuals. In Fred West's underprivileged and uneducated world as he grew up, his unwitting sense would have been of an order of Hobbesian proscription, rather than a modern liberal permissiveness that might have been dreamt of as the desired outcome of Rousseau's democratic vision. Whatever it was, the decade of the sixties presented Fred West with a landscape awash with naïve waifs and strays rejoicing in the freedom of the age and trusting in the effectiveness of the state to protect from harm.

Interestingly, Freud asserted that the first curtailment of the unbridled libido was civilisation's interdiction against incest.

So should we blame modern civilisation for serial killers?

The unmitigated death drive has been around a long time. Wholesale rape and murder would have been commonplace in a world of savage freedom, although Rousseau and others would argue that savages were not innately badly predisposed to their neighbours unless, that is, they had competing objects of satisfaction. There is also the curious concept extrapolated from the idea that in nature there is non-ownership of property by applying this to the physical integrity of the individual human body, whereby no one, in proprietary terms, is perceived as owning their own walking, living flesh and bone, which remain at one with nature. This seems perfectly reasonable in the acceptance of the pecking order of the carnivorous food chain. And, weird as it may sound, philosophers argue that prior to Descartes, the modern concept of individuality in a human being was nebulous at best. Foucault reminds us to be wary in evaluating earlier epochs by our own local nuanced standards. Nevertheless, human instincts for self-preservation and highly charged libidinous intent militate strongly against innate primitive philosophical notion of not really owning one's own body.

As the charming historical anecdotes above attest, the rulers of civilisations, ostensibly out of higher duty on behalf of and for the purpose of maintaining order in the state, assumed the role of mass killer and still do. And so the mantle of serial killer appears to have devolved from the savage, through despotic rulers of the civilised world to the new breed of autonomous, dangerous, psychopathic products of modern democratic states, the carriers of a diseased human psyche, warped and shaped by curtailment and suppression of libido, whose actions are thereby the symptoms of any manner of neurosis, psychosis and perversion.

Within a few weeks of Bishop Ball's departure, Rose West was my client. With hindsight and without making any judgment on the propriety of either decision, I compare the preferential way the Bishop was dealt with, with the way some of Fred West's workmates were dealt with after they agreed to assist the Crown by making witness statements, even though in so doing meant confessing to indecently assaulting some of the Wests' children at Fred's invitation. The bargain was that they would thereby receive cautions rather than be prosecuted for the sexual assault of children.

These were workmates from the Wagon Works, who would call round at 25 Cromwell Street for breakfast before giving Fred a lift to the factory on the Bristol Road. The children at this time had beds in a space adjoining the kitchen extension. It was, in the view of the police, a necessary bargain to gather evidence and in the general surreal scheme of the West case, a few indecent assaults seemed pretty tame anyway. The Bishop's bargain saved his own skin and the reputation of the Church of England.

8.

FRED: THE NOOSE

I.

From a conversation I had with the West's third daughter, Mae, in 1994, she explained that her dad had told her that he would be OK with custody because he had done time in the late 1960s/early 1970s and that what mattered was to prepare a comfort pack to have with him. Mae understood this to mean tobacco, rollies and some money so that he would not need to wait for relatives to send a postal order before he could buy anything. Fred's previous prison experience had been as a younger man serving a sentence of a few months at Leyhill, which was a category D open prison, where the regime, by comparison to that imposed on a category A high security prisoner is very different. So his expectations so based were really over-optimistic.

It is true that while he was interviewed by Gloucestershire police over the Cromwell Street murders, his detention was within the custody suite of Gloucester Police Station at Bearlands, Longsmith Street. He stayed there for six weeks with his own cell, regular visits, any materials he wanted, frequent fag breaks, meals and washing facilities as required. Fred was safe and well looked after. There were no jeering inmates in adjoining cells baying for his blood. Given the extreme circumstances, he was as content as might reasonably be expected. The custody officers applied the duty of care owed to detainees with utmost diligence.

It was most unusual, probably unique, for any detainee to remain at a police station for such a period of time. Police Station detention is governed by the Police and Criminal Evidence Act 1994 of the codes of practice made pursuant thereto. Suspects normally cannot be detained for more than twenty-four hours without being released with or without bail. Exceptionally, in more serious cases, investigating officers can apply to the magistrates' court for extensions to enable further expeditious enquiries and interviews. They have to make a strong case to justify such extensions. That had been the situation on a spring evening in 1994, when I addressed the Gloucester Magistrates' Court to oppose the application after Rose had answered her bail and the police applied for further time to interview her.

Fred West had actually been charged with three murders, but there was still much for the police to put to him and it was a lot more straightforward to have him retained in police custody, even though HMP Gloucester was only a stone's throw away on the other side of the tall prison wall at Bearlands. The problem of moving prisoners is not at all straightforward and on every occasion, the essential protocols and procedures have to be followed relating to clearing cells, checking property, body searches, completing paperwork and deploying detachment officers, including a driver, even to move a prisoner less than one hundred yards. Then the whole process occurs in reverse after each interview for the prisoner to be processed back into the prison system. And the problems would not end there, as every time a prisoner is checked out of a prison, his cell is cleared and becomes available for a new prisoner coming in. This might have meant that after every police interview, Fred would have been delivered to another prison, possibly hundreds of miles away. Expedience in his case clearly required that the sensible option was for his to remain in the Gloucester Police Station custody suite.

But once he had been charged with all twelve murders, he was moved to HMP Winson Green, Birmingham and this traumatic watershed was made more disruptive by the sacking of his original solicitor, Howard Ogden, who had allowed himself to be tempted into a tell-all book deal promising grossly inflated sums of money, even while he purported to continue to act for Fred. The new defence firm, Bobbetts McCann, were hard-nosed, no-nonsense professionals from Bristol, who, while not a very large firm, nevertheless operated on a different scale to the legal aid sole practitioner they had replaced.

Efficiency broadly requires deployment of staff to specific tasks. It is not reasonable to be at a police station all night and then the following morning having to deal with a client's trial or a bail application or cover a court duty list. Besides, managed allocation of delegated tasks enables specialisation, which should translate into optimal efficiency and better outcomes for clients. That is the theory anyway.

For this reason, after months of dealing with a close coterie, comprising of Howard Ogden and his wayward ex-client sidekick, Scott Canavan, whom I later had to injunct via the Attorney General to prevent publication of his handwritten notes, which he had negotiated the sale of for a fee of £100,000. In the meantime, Janet Leach, the accidental

241

appropriate adult, remained a constant feature in the Fred West entourage. Fred was now represented by criminal lawyer Tony Miles, who delegated parts of the job to other members of his firm. Representatives who attended the prison to obtain proofs would not be the same faces that would then be seen at court appearances. Fred would have felt a further of loss of control; his sense of being able to manipulate those representing him would undoubtedly have diminished. He had already lost control of Rose's case as I, much to his chagrin, was independently representing her.

It was also deeply disruptive for him, as the scenario Fred had chosen to present over hundreds of hours of interviews was significantly upended. Initially, he had chosen to exonerate Rose and purported to accept all the blame himself; although even then he still sought to mitigate his culpability with explanations of accidents and mishaps during consensual sexual antics resulting in dire unintended consequences.

At an early stage in the investigation, I believe Fred and Rose had embarked on a strategy of damage limitation. They had both realised that the game was up regarding Heather and disclosure by Fred to that murder would, they optimistically believed, curtail further police investigation. And even then, Fred still endeavoured to extricate himself by trying to exert pressure on his son Stephen to accept culpability for his sister's death. As the strategy unravelled and counts on the indictment loaded against Fred, his already flaky sense of reality started to disintegrate.

If anything tangible could be drawn from Fred's digressive waffle about dastardly deeds, it was that Fred was a creature of habit, whose modus operandi made him such a horrendously persistent serial killer. There was no scope for flexible departure from the mechanical routine, no digression from the articulated fantasy. While Fred West's warped mind was possessed of the most florid and sadistic sexual deviancy, his imagination was ultimately curtailed by his limited intellect so that the scenarios were necessarily repetitive, involving ideas and paraphernalia derived from pornographic movies and magazines. That the plasticity of his mind was restricted in this way may, in terms of his efficiency as a serial killer, have at the same time been both a strength and a weakness. Put simply, Fred could not cope with the volte-face, even where his case was now complete denial, blaming Rose for everything. His was in a cut-throat defence against his wife and it seriously unnerved him.

Now in his solitary place, he was resolved to do as suited him. Yet through all this dislocating mental turmoil it cannot be discounted that in the lostness of those early New Year's hours, Fred West was enacting something he had often in sombre moments rehearsed in his mind.

The evidence for this contention is surprisingly transparent and verifiable. Mae often commented on how over the years Fred had an inexplicable preoccupation with the news. He would arrive home from work in his dirty, scruffy overalls and his intuition, even in preference to watching pornography or sitting and listening over the intercom to Rose writhing and groaning in amplified, stereophonic, orgasmic ecstasy in the upstairs boudoir, was to switch the news on. Mae, as a young child and then as a teenager, would sit there with her siblings as he would flick through the channels catching national and regional new bulletins.

This was all the weirder because Fred had absolutely no interest in politics or current affairs. His sole interest outside of work was warped sexual fantasy. Yet he watched and listened attentively as though he was anticipating some earth-shattering statement that must somehow have involved him personally.

Was part of the thrill an investment in eventual notoriety? Would a depraved narcissistic psychopath so calculate this as the pension for his evil career as a serial killer?

He must have experienced an unnerving anxiety many years earlier with the high-profile police enquiries relating firstly to Mary Bastholm and then later to Lucy Partington. One wonders what mix of emotions flowed through him as he listened to updates on the news? Would he have had an adrenaline rush? Was he fearful of detection? Did it excite him or make him angry? What sort of discussions would he have entered into with Rose about the large-scale police operation?

These are questions that Rose is still capable of answering.

Whatever it is, it can be confidently stated that the prospect of either discovery or getting away with it absorbed and preoccupied him.

Fred in a bizarre way publicly signposted his outrageous proclivities on many occasions, recalled in numerous statements, where he would spurt out the most disgusting and outrageous propositions to workmates or neighbours, only for them to be dismissed by normal people as the pathetic, dirty-minded ramblings of an ineffectual, anonymous little man whose limitations meant that he missed the social cues of more or less polite society by uttering fantastical deviant garbage.

II.

It is the early hours of New Year's Day, 1995. Fred West sits alone on the bed in his cell at HMP Winson Green. He has been on remand for nine months awaiting trial for the murder of twelve young women and girls. His wife, Rose, is also on remand awaiting trial for the murder of nine young women. She is held at HMP Pucklechurch.

Fred listens to the prison officers' footsteps as they occasionally pass and peer through the small peephole in the solid metal door, but he knows from the months he has been on remand there are always a few rowdy disruptive inmates that preoccupy them. He also knows that the staffing levels have reduced even while he has been there; initially there was an officer parked outside his cell, but that soon stopped. And Dr MacMaster has now reported that he is not a suicide risk. He asked for his light to be subdued so that he could sleep and that was not an issue.

Besides, it is Christmas-time and there is only a caretaker shift manning the wing at night. He will not be disturbed by the prison officers now until the morning. Fred is furtive and busy in his solitary space: a place he has been so many times before in the dead of night, a nocturnal creature hidden from view, cutting and scrubbing, collecting and trimming, bloody and sweating, digging and scratching, sifting the soil burying the spoil, hard at work, active and assiduous in the production of destruction. The languid weeks of depressive stupor have been lifted. The world is still dark and the clouds heavy, but resolve brings hope. There is relief in oblivion.

The silence of the night has only occasionally been broken by the banging of a door or a solitary distant shout of a frustrated inmate. And the new year has arrived. The shards of light flicker into the morbid cell, footsteps on the landing, doors clanging, prisoners attending their ablutions, noisy whistles and a skeleton crew of prison officers to maintain order. Fred keeps his head down. Fred briefly ventures out to collect his grub. He keeps his head down and snarls as the occasional inmate mate jeers and heckles him. He creates an aura of unapproachability, smelling of body odour, tobacco and fart, but underneath his grimy skin the dishevelled little man is lost, empty and frightened. Back in his cell he perfunctorily consumes his plate of food. One eye peers through the miserable peephole in his cell door, blinks and moves on. Fred has no wish to engage with others.

He feels a strange kind of mild elation, a curious uplifted spirit. In the dead of night, his depression had hit the depths of paralysing despair and in that hopelessness, the mind spirals with morbid thoughts, making focus and action impossible. It is well recognised that it is only as someone stirs from the grim nadir that there occurs the motivation to do the final act, to implement the act of self-murder.

He thumbs in a thoughtful way over the coarse texture of his woven blanket, testing his stitching, pulling at the cord, gripping the plait, checking the strength. He loops the hairy DIY rope and makes a neat knot which enables the chord to move through freely. He plays with the sliding noose, pulling it and then loosening it. He spits on the fibres, then wets them further from a cup of water nearby. This would make the noose tighter, more ungiving. He recalls the knots he had been taught as a young man for a time working on river boats on the Severn. His mind flashes with the recurrent use he made of knots and bindings he used on his trussed-up victims in the cellar at Cromwell Street. In his mind the bindings were closely associated with the pleasure he derived from his depraved activities. Even now, something fetishized and erotic stirs in him as he strokes the stitched cord of sheet and blanket. He is proud of his workmanship; he pleasures in the feel of the binding. Slowly, he places the noose around his neck, still gently feeling the coarse hairs of the strands, licking the rope, placing his nose next to it, smelling it as though it conjured some remote and distant memory.

He moves the laundry bags into a heap by his window. He climbs on top of them. He loops the cord through the bars on the slits of a grill high on the wall. He closes his eyes and pushes the bags away. The cord grips his neck, but the knot did not impact with sufficient force to break his neck outright. Instead he hangs there, choking, gurgling, gasping, struggling to find some non-existent foothold or hand grip on the wall to hold onto, but to no avail. He continues to wriggle and croak. His face is bloated and red, his eyes bloodshot, the cord squeezing tightly and unremittingly into his grisly neck. After about five minutes, his legs stop moving, his arms drop and he hangs there limply. Fred West is dead.

The inquest heard that Fred had collected his New Year's Day meal of pork chops and eggs at some time after 11:30am and gone back to his cell by about 12pm. The indication is that he ate this meal, as no food was reported as being present in the cell. A prison officer cursorily checked on him through the peephole in the cell door sometime after noon. When the next routine check was carried out at 1pm, the peephole was blocked because Fred's body was hanging limply across it on the inside. When the prison wardens got to him, he was still warm and they tried to revive him, but the prison doctor declared him dead at about 1:15pm. The window of opportunity to have carried out the suicide suggests that he probably hanged himself at about 12:45pm.

The news travelled incredibly quickly. I recall Alan Smith of the Press Association telephoning me before 1:30pm to ask me if I had heard anything. I stated that I had not, to which he intimidated that there was an unconfirmed report that Fred had done himself in. The story was still vague and he was looking for details. Alan Smith was a highly professional journalist, who always needed full verification of any story he was going to syndicate. His reputation depended on it. How he had that information, possibly even before the police and certainly before the rest of the media cohort, I do not know.

III.

On January 9th 1995, *The Independent* reported as follows:

> "The Bishop of Hereford, the Rt Rev John Oliver, said yesterday that he could see no reason why Frederick West should not be buried in his village church.
>
> "The parish council of Much Marcle in Hereford and Worcester voted to ask the parochial church council to refuse permission for West's burial at St Bartholomew's if it is requested. Councillors fear his headstone may be desecrated and many villagers are upset by the idea of West resting in the same churchyard as their relatives.
>
> "But Dr Oliver, who may have to rule on the issue, told Radio 4's Sunday programme: 'I think there is a difference between someone who is convicted and someone who isn't. They are two different cases. But I think in either case there would be no reason why a person should not be buried in a churchyard. Nobody is outside God's mercy or the possibility of God's forgiveness.'"

As it turned out, the good people of Much Marcle had their wishes met and on March 29th 1995 at Cranley Crematorium in Coventry, Fred West's body was cremated. As the coffin rolled into the oven, a scuffle broke out between a couple of newspaper journalists. Stephen and Mae West were present, and Anne Marie arrived a little later. Several months later as the trial at Winchester Crown Court moved towards a conclusion, Stephen and Mae, early on the Saturday morning of November 4th 1995, scattered Fred West's ashes on the graves of his parents, Walter and Daisy West, in Much Marcle cemetery.

9.

ROSE: THE GILDED CAGE

At the time of her conviction, while it is true that the sentencing judge, Mr Justice Mantell, stated that if he had his way she should never be released, he uttered those words in the knowledge that at that time, determination of sentencing was a matter for the judiciary and could always be subject to appeal and parole. There was a guiding principle that in all cases, as there must be some element of rehabilitation, it should be recognised that people can change and if true remorse and contrition is demonstrated, then it should be possible for them to be reintroduced into society. That absolute principle changed in 2003 when the question of whole life tariffs was considered in Parliament and the conventional wisdom dictated that individual cases where the extent, severity and depravity was of such magnitude, then it had to be assessed whether the perpetrator could ever have any prospect of release. In the case of Rose West, the Home Secretary of the time, Mr Jack Straw, determined that her crimes were so appalling that she would never be released from prison.

Decisions as to whole life terms in a limited but growing number of cases remain a political call decided by the Home Secretary of the day.

In my view Rose does not have a predisposition to suicidal thoughts. If she did then there would have been many opportunities over the past twenty-five years to realise any such morbid design.

I regard as an aberration the overdose she took in August 1992 after her children were taken into care and she was rushed to hospital to have her stomach pumped. It may, of course, have been prompted by her sense of impending doom that it was only a matter of time before her and Fred's horrific secrets would be revealed. This had, nevertheless, been a serious attempt at suicide.

That Rose has chosen to live incarcerated, serving her sentence, knowing in her mind the things she has done, pilloried in the press, reminded of the abomination and suffering she was jointly responsible for, one wonders what her mindset really is?

As far as is known there has never been a recurrent serious attempt by her to end her life.

HMP Durham has a strange configuration. It is constructed of a dark grey, granite-like rock. It is mainly a male prison, but within the perimeter walls across a square, there is a secure, secluded building, a compound within the larger compound, isolated from the rest of the establishment and within its walls is the female wing, 'F' Wing, or, as affectionately known by the Geordie prison officers, 'She Wing'.

It is true that Rose wasted no time in finding friendship with a number of women who were serving prison terms at the same time. These tended to be older women usually convicted of murder and on long sentences.

The friendships were genuinely supportive and often sexual. They could also be unstable and end in resentment. Rose's first paramour was the Moors murderer, Myra Hindley, who happened to be on the hospital wing at HMP Durham at the same time in 1995 and early 1996. Hindley was there because she had 'fallen over' in the exercise yard of 'F' Wing. It was prison policy that a new inmate who was a lifer would first be assessed on the prison wing. This assessment entailed psychiatric and psychological examination, as well as a physical check-up. Rose remained on the hospital wing for about a fortnight. Myra Hindley had already been in hospital for a couple of weeks.

Rose explained to me that Myra's bones had become brittle and that because of the diagnosis of osteoporosis, the slightest impact could result in a fracture. Hindley had said that the condition was aggravated by reason that for years she was served leftover wartime rations of powdered egg and milk with the prison food. It sounded plausible at the time.

Visiting at the time, I recall that Rose was quite taken with Hindley, impressed by her knowledge and ability. Rose said that Hindley had studied various Open University courses. Her comments were slightly cryptic and cautious, which was a tendency with Rose that I had noted on many occasions. It had made getting express instructions on particular issues sometimes difficult.

She said, "Yeah, Myra, she's all right, we get on, I want to see how it goes."

This was a reference to a flowering, albeit short-lived, lesbian relationship.

After Rose was moved off the hospital wing, Hindley remained in there for a week or so longer before going back to her cell on 'F' wing. At the time, the prison regime on the female wing had a policy of open association. This meant that during the day, the cell doors remained open and the prisoners could come and go within the confines of the wing. In addition to various allocated tasks such as cleaning or in the kitchen, there were also classes available, either education or more practical pastimes. Rose is very good with sewing and she joined a sewing group.

All the inmates were there because they were serving long sentences or on remand for very serious matters. As Rose said, "There ain't no kids kicking off on the wing."

So for the most part, the women on the wing just wanted to get along, serve their sentences and have a quiet life. Human nature being what it is, particularly when you have people locked up serving lengthy sentences, there would inevitably be occasional arguments and petty rivalries. I never saw any evidence that this got out of hand and certainly never erupted into a riot. If it had done, then the privilege of free association would soon have been withdrawn.

When I visited a few months later, Rose's opinion of Hindley had changed dramatically.

She was saying, "You have to watch Hindley, mind. She is very manipulative. You don't realise it, but she gets you doing stuff for her. Oh, she's clever, all right. She's flippin' dangerous, that one. She ain't going to take me for a cunt again."

And so heralded the end of the romance. I did wonder whether Hindley had had earlier dalliances that had not gone well and accounted for her 'falling over' in the exercise yard, which by all accounts happened with some frequency?

Hindley's plausibility and persuasiveness had, at an early stage in the investigation, been flagged up to me when I received a telephone call at my office in Pitt Street in May 1994 from a charming old man by the name of Lord Longford. We chatted for a while and he stressed to me how he firmly believed that 'Myra' had served her time, whatever her culpability, that she was a reformed character. He then explained that with Rose

West, we needed to be on the same side and work together. I remember thinking that the conversation, though entirely sincere, was misplaced as Rose had not at that stage been convicted of anything and strenuously denied the allegations against her.

I politely stated that it might be something we could, if need be, discuss at a later time. We never did. The dear old 7th Earl of Longford, 1st Baron of Pakenham, decent human being, champion of penal reform, innately altruistic and devout, passed away in 2001.

Sue May was a kind and dignified lady from Manchester, who was serving a life term for the murder of her aunt, whom she had been looking after. The aunt had been beaten to death. The place had been ransacked and the evidence pointed to a break-in that had gone wrong. May explained to me how she had discovered the aged aunt and then found herself being arrested and charged despite being of good character and protesting her innocence. May was convicted and served twelve years. She told me she was innocent; I believed her and still do. At the time her solicitors were working on her appeal. She died of cancer about six years ago. The prosecution had failed to disclose exculpatory material to the defence. Sue was a beacon on 'F' Wing, a source of strength, compassion and support to the other inmates whether on remand or serving life sentences, as most were. And she was caring and supportive of Rose.

Sue's close friend was Linda Calvey, the 'Black Widow', so called because it was said that all her lovers either ended up dead or in prison. She was serving life for murdering her then-lover Ronnie Cook. She had paid a hitman to kill him, but when he chickened out at the last minute, she picked up the gun and shot him herself. OK, she was getting through them. Previously she had served a long stretch for armed robbery. You could say she was a down-to-earth, no-nonsense cockney from the East End of London. When Ronnie Kray died, she arranged a big bouquet of flowers to be sent to the family. She was part of that close, East End, old-time community. If you were in, you were in, otherwise best keep well away.

Rose had told Sue and Linda that I had an interest in art and so on one visit I was touched when they presented me with a book on painting techniques with a message on the inside cover signed by the pair of them.

Then there was a tough Maori woman who, to help make ends meet, flew into London to accept work as a paid assassin, which involved bumping off a couple of men, including shooting one while he was lying on a trolley bed in the hallway of a hospital. Apparently, contract killers are sometimes brought in from outside cities to work in areas where they are unknown to the police and criminals. Two men hired the Maori hitwoman for £7,000 to murder a London roofing contractor with whom they had a business feud. Te Rangimaria Ngarimu, twenty-seven, was jailed for life in December 1994 for shooting her victim four times in the head and body.

Then there was the petite bespectacled daughter of a mafia boss, Marisa Merico, who looked so meek and mild, like she would not say boo to a goose. She faced extradition to Italy from Lancashire. A one-time mafia 'princess' who lived an anonymous suburban life in Lancashire faced extradition to Italy to finish a jail term for money laundering. She was the daughter of a Blackpool chambermaid and one of Milan's leading gangsters; she fled to Poulton-le-Fylde after her father and husband were arrested in 1992. She had been arrested by British police in 1995 for smuggling £1.9 million of mafia money across Europe in a baby's cot. She spent three years in Durham prison before being extradited to Italy, where she served fifteen months of a six-year sentence before being released on a legal technicality. Italian state prosecutors wanted her to serve the remainder of her sentence and lodged an application demanding her extradition. Her case was heard at Durham Crown Court while Rose West was awaiting trial.

Durham Prison is attached to the back of the Crown Court. When the young lady went on trial, the security around the court was immense. She was regarded as a Category A prisoner and therefore an escape risk. The authorities believed that associates would try and spring her. Police armed with automatic guns vigilantly guarded the outside main entrance to the court house. A helicopter circled overhead. It livened up my routine visit to see Rose.

The Home Office Prison Service seems like a law unto itself. Prison regimes change quite frequently. This may be because of the philosophy of a new prison governor or more likely because of central government funding. Whatever it was, after a couple of years, Rose wrote to me saying that all was not well. Classes had been curtailed. There were fewer prison officers on the wing and the ones that were there were far less friendly and accommodating. Rose had also had the distress of several impromptu cell searches. She found these particularly upsetting as it meant removing all possessions, clothes, bedding, toiletries, photographs and then watching as a detachment of prison officers turned the cell upside down and even sent in sniffer dogs. When there was no perceived reason for doing this, it became an oppressive and unnecessary step which Rose felt was gratuitous punishment just for being there. This was a destabilising time for her. She had resolved to hunker down and get on with serving the rest of her life sentence. She had no expectation of parole.

The cell searches were either triggered by a malicious rumour of some sort or otherwise had been incorporated into the regime by the then prison governor.

For a while, things got better and Rose was able to get on with her sewing, but this respite was short-lived because overall conditions deteriorated. A prison review had deemed it appropriate to house long-term prisoners and short-term prisoners together on 'F' wing. Rose was soon writing to me with worries about the number of unprovoked incidents which she was having to endure.

She said, "The thing that really pisses me off is that it is me who then has to clear out my cell and start again."

Disruptive incidents escalated. One young offender tried to set Rose's cell alight; she had to constantly watch over her shoulder and be careful that her food was not tampered with.

During the period from 1994 to 2004, I received many letters from Rose in prison. I often wondered about Rose's handwriting. I make no claim to be a handwriting expert, but recall a case where I retained an expert, known as a graphologist, to give evidence in a matter some years before the West case. In this case, my client, a respectable middle-aged lady and the wife of an army officer, was accused, by way of the most depraved correspondence, of harassing another woman. The content went into great detail, using the most profane old English to describe the kind of lesbian sex my client desired to engage in with the victim. It was one thing for the expert to identify characteristic similarities in samples of handwriting exhibited in court, but the learned judge became amused and incredulous when the expert then started to present to the court a character profile based on the handwriting. This was viewed as a pseudoscience, the validity of which was questioned and the jury were cautioned against accepting too literal an interpretation of what the expert presented.

With that caveat I would ask the reader whether he or she would reasonably be able to discriminate between the fluent script of a literate older person and that of a child who has recently learned to write or, for that matter, of an illiterate older person who has never mastered basic grammar, syntax and spelling? And by the same token, would you be able to detect the handwriting of a naïve young girl in her early teens, whose writing is rounded, large, upright and clear with all the 'i's dotted and the 't's crossed with good spacing and adherence to rules of grammar and spelling expressing herself in simple, uncomplicated statements?

This last option is the description I would give to Rose West's handwriting. It has always been the same in the hundreds of pages of letters and statements prepared in manuscript by her that I have read. To me it is as though the person writing the letters is frozen in a state of juvenilia, a point in her life where there was pride and progress in her literacy and simple written style. And likewise, the content. Even when asked to address the most extreme allegations of brutality and sexual deviancy, what Rose wrote, if not a denial, would be some girlish explanation that seemed to glance across the grave adult content that needed to be addressed. There is an irreconcilable chasm between the grim luggage Rose undoubtedly carries in her mind and the preponderance of innocent girlie sentiments expressed in her juvenile scrolls. These are the jottings of a young woman who was still playing with dolls and preferring to wear baggy childish knickers and bobby socks when her 'teenie bopper' classmates were wondering about buying lipstick, wearing stockings and miniskirts, and finding out who was Top of the Pops. Yet Rose, the bullied, emotionally vulnerable, babyish girl, who was early to puberty among her peer group and in weird contrast to her arrested emotional development had for years been engaged in sexual activity with her father.

In our DNA, there are remnants of the earliest life forms on Earth. As it is, we share over ninety per cent of our genetic make-up with other primates. To take another analogy, consider a geologist extracting a column of soil and rock for sampling. His findings provide a picture of our history, of when the climate was arid and the land parched and sandy, when there was water and a plentiful diversity of pollen, when there was some massive disruption in nature, perhaps a super volcano erupting or a giant asteroid hitting the planet. We are constituted by what we came from.

As Freud states in *Civilization and Its Discontents*, "In the realm of the mind... what is primitive is so commonly preserved alongside the transformed version which has arisen from it," and, "...it is rather the rule than the exception for the past to be preserved in mental life." This might appropriately be termed as a palimpsest of the psyche. Psychoanalysis starts with the symptoms, the aberrant manifestations and then traces back through the deviant trajectory.

In categorising the letters I received from her, I would divide them into two. The first sort related to how she was coping with the vagaries of prison life, perhaps the opportunity for sewing classes had been curtailed, perhaps she had been taken off of kitchen duty, perhaps she felt victimised by too many unnecessary and disruptive prison searches. Often she would complain of physical altercations with some of the young short-term inmates who would deliberately try and pick a fight to enhance their kudos within the prison. Normally, she would be asking me to intervene, make a complaint to the prison governor and request that I visit her. I hasten to add that Rose contacted me because she wanted a legal resolution according to the prison rules as she realised the alternative would have resulted in severe sanctions. Rose did not fear any of the threats from younger inmates. On the contrary, she told me in no uncertain terms that if they got to her she would fight and give them 'a good fuckin seeing to'. It was evident to me that when it came to it, Rose was tough, uncompromising, capable of looking out for herself physically and would be the last to back down. This significantly contrasts with Fred, who was a meek, cowardly little man who was scared stiff of getting into a scrap with another man.

It is a long train journey to Durham and the attendance and time costs had to be justified to the Legal Aid Commission, which they usually were. At that time, the minutiae of prison law, where there was some legitimate point of dispute, were usually funded without endless form filling and explanation. In any event, for much of that time I was collating information for an application to the Criminal Cases Review Commission, where occasional attendance on the client would always be properly considered.

The second type of letter I would receive from her would be to inform me of some long-distance romance with a pen pal. There were many such instances and the ones she told me about were always with men. In addition, when I would visit, she would explain that she had received a steady stream of letters from writers, film producers and journalists wanting to visit her to assist in their research towards a new book or film. Invariably she would dismiss these missives without second thought and without needing to ask my opinion. However, on affairs of the heart she would usually write to tell me of her most recent paramour by proxy.

Among the curious mix of suitors, I recall an early overture by a convicted sex offender who, shortly after she commenced her whole life sentence, became her pen pal and clearly pressed the right buttons before offering his hand in marriage. As I recall, the budding romance was soon nipped in the bud, not least because Rose discovered that true facts about her long-distance lover were not quite as he represented in his correspondence. I guess, in any event, Home Office clearance for visits would have been problematical what with his curfew and tag and the like.

And then some years later there was the infatuated rock star. Rose, I think for a moment, was smitten. Her notoriety and inaccessibility had landed the replacement bass player from the 1970's glam rock band Slade. I suspect Noddy Holder might have had a word to two to say to the musician along the lines of *My Oh My*, *Lock Up Your Daughters*, *Gudbuy t' Jane*, *Mama Weer All Crazy Now*, *Cum on Feel the Noize*, not to mention *Merry Xmas Everybody*.

The bass player backed out when he realised somehow his private life was damaging the band and in any event Rose announced that 'she wanted to give that young man his life back'.

I could never understand the motley crew of chancers that beat a path to Rose's mailbox. I am aware of the many women who are similarly drawn into relationships with lifers or prisoners on death row in America. There is maybe a dark, seductive allure and exclusivity in progressing such a relationship? They are invariably doomed. They are, by their nature, impossible.

Within the literature, both Freud and Lacan deal with this curious dance by Eros, the suggestion being that people embarking on such romances are displaying a kind of neurosis because deep down they know that the person who is the object of their sexual love (imagined or otherwise) is unobtainable. As civilisation places curbs on the liberty and free-flowing instincts of human beings as a price of social organisation and protection, this invariably inhibits sexual expression and this inhibition can be identified as the source variously of neurosis, perversion or psychosis. This does not mean these symptoms have to be so extreme as to disable. The energy of the libido is invested in other pursuits, in work and improvement, in satisfactions derived from religion, science or art. Even the ritual of courtly love serves as a socially constructed barrier to the essential satisfaction of the sexual desire. In the case of suitors of the hopelessly incarcerated, such barriers to the fulfilment of the pseudosexual adventure seem to be implicit, perversely built into the nascent fanciful origin of the idea.

I was aware of Rose's preference for women. Her lesbian tendencies were well-documented throughout the case. There is a strange parallel between the way she was ultra-critical of her daughter Heather for supposedly being lesbian, and yet she freely, and with Fred's blessing, regularly indulged in lesbian relationships. And here in prison, Rose was and is known to have a succession of women lovers, yet, apart from Myra Hindley, she never mentioned any of these to me in her correspondence? If there were pen pal lesbian romances, she chose not to disclose those to me. Inside the prison walls, the lesbian sex was happening, intense and committed while it lasted. These dalliances would only be made known through information in the press derived from other inmates or comments by off-duty prison officers. Yet she felt the need to tell me about the offers of marriage from men she had never met and who would never have any chance of getting through the twelve locked prison doors by which they could gain access to the supposed object of their desire?

Was this a game she was playing? Was there some narcissistic trait at play? Did the situation flatter her ego? In her mind did it offer her some kind of control? Perhaps it was all of these, but it would still be necessary to question whether her quandary as to what to do was sincere or simply another deception to obfuscate the truth?

I also have to consider whether she had formed any attachment to me. Was any part of this charade to test my feelings about her? Rose was certainly well-disposed towards me, possibly her demeanour softened when I was about. I have no delusion that she ever wished to bear her soul to me; her guard remained firmly fixed. I always made a point, as I would with any client in prison, of avoiding tactile contact with Rose. I was always friendly and professional. On greeting her, I would shake her hand. Her hands were the hands of a working woman, not delicate, but quite large, reasonably firm and rarely clammy. These were the hands of someone who was used to hard graft, whether it be sewing and needlework, cooking, sharpening the kitchen knives or working as a cleaner on the Brunswick campus of the Gloucester College of Arts and Technology, which was her part-time occupation when she was first arrested in the summer of 1992. They were also the hands of a torturer and murderer.

When we met she would smile, was usually calm and polite. She appreciated me taking to the trouble to visit. Most requests for visits by others, she either ignored or turned down, or in some cases, these were refused by the governor.

I do not believe she ever made any overt advance towards me. There was one occasion when I visited and I recall, for some reason, that there was no space available in the visiting room. Legal visits necessitated the confidentiality of a separate consultation room rather than mingling in the visiting hall. As it was, the women on 'F' Wing had entirely separate visiting arrangements from the men who occupied the main part of Durham prison and the designated accommodation was restricted within a confined area. As a result, a prison officer directed me to the chapel as this would afford a place where matters could be discussed in confidence away from other prisoners. The corridor that led to the chapel was on the wing and so there was no requirement for a prison officer escort. As we walked towards the chapel door Rose announced she needed to use the toilet and suddenly disappeared into a side-door, which I realised she did not close before proceeding to relieve herself. In an unwitting momentary glance, I caught sight of Rose with her pants down sitting on the toilet and smiling back at me with her eyes beaming through the large lenses of her black-rimmed glasses. I quickly moved away and concentrated my attention in some other direction until she reappeared, and

I was able to discuss the business for which I had visited. While fleetingly embarrassing, I do not believe that this was an old-fashioned 'come on'. There was no grit in the eye and besides I cannot imagine a less seductive manoeuvre.

I ceased acting for Rose in 2004. Since then, she has moved from HMP Durham to Long Newton, which is also in County Durham. I am aware that she has pictures of cats on her cell wall and that for some time she was allowed a budgerigar in a little cage in her room. I think of the budgie as safe and as secure in its incarceration as indeed Rose was. The chirpy little bird represented Rose's own strange contentment confined within her own gilded cage. I say gilded because she was fully aware of the unrelenting scrutiny and physical risk she would be at if she was ever permitted to venture onto the 'outside'. Now, after twenty-five years in custody, the outside must seem like a very alien space. Inevitably she has become institutionalised. I know Rose accepted prison as the location of her being, as her domain and her domicile. In her mind she made a reasoned, realistic and sensible choice. The all-female environment also suited Rose's lesbian preferences, as her various relationships verify. She can sew and knit, prepare meals, adorn her cell, watch television, make her cell space pretty much as she wants it. She said that she wanted to make a life for herself behind bars, that she had no wish to confront the media mayhem that would follow her around and visit her children if she was released.

Where would she live? What peace would she get? What hell would it create for both her and her family?

These were the questions Rose posed in her letters to me, when she decided that it did not matter what conclusion the Criminal Cases Review Commission arrived at. She actually told me in 2002, after I had prepared a detailed application, that she did not wish to have her case reviewed because she felt that she could make a life for herself on the inside, and anyway, she would never get any peace on the outside and neither would her children. She adapted well to life in prison.

When you consider what Rose's last memory of freedom was like, her choice makes more sense.

She had had her children taken away from her, the dreadful happenings at Cromwell Street had been revealed to the world, intimate details of her sordid private life and her cruel abuse of her children were headlines, she had to keep moving from one safe house to another, and she had good reason to fear a lynch mob. 25 Cromwell Street, the place she called home, was demolished. And for many in her family (although not all), life on the outside had been a veritable disaster, a chaotic, dysfunctional spiral of misery.

I do not know what strange machinations of the mind enable Rose to neatly pack away the horrific knowledge of her years with Fred West. It is something she seems to be able to do. They are memories she locks away as thoroughly as the twelve electronic gates behind which she now dwells.

While she can exercise some control over those memories, she could never contain the constant threat of vengeance by ill-disciplined vigilantes, who would see it as their right to seek her out and physically tear her apart if she was able to venture out onto the street. She well knows that freedom is a relative thing and in prison she has the protection of the regime and a duty of care must be accorded to her.

10.

EPILOGUE

Over the last twenty-five years I have done my best to forget about the West case and move on with my life and career. I had a family to support and the clients of my law practice to look after. I have other interests in art and science. I was a member of the Law Society's Art Group and a founding member of the Gloucester Stuckists. I studied for degrees in science and engineering with the Open University and attended Birmingham Institute of Art and Design to complete a master's degree in Fine Art. This desire to move on I believe was echoed in the overall collective psyche of the Gloucester community where there was a palpable wish to try and draw a line under the horrific revelations of 1994/95.

It was a spontaneous and arbitrary moment when I decided one morning as I woke up after the Christmas festivities of 2018 to write a book about the West case. It is true that Howard Sounes had contacted me in November about an interview for a television programme he was working on. That required me revisiting the events from years earlier, but I have over the years given dozens of interviews to television reporters, journalists and writers, and never once felt the need to pen my views on the client and the case. And yet when I sat down and started writing, I could not stop.

I found that there was much to say: my personal take, a perspective that had not already been covered, so many ideas and questions that I felt had not been answered. There was a cascade of free-flowing thought, things that had not really gone away, things that remained unresolved. It made me realise, as a lawyer, something that must similarly apply to people in many occupations. While we can galvanise ourselves and move on to the next case or incident, with a new set of disturbing facts and remain professional and stony-faced, resolute, mature and of firmness of mind, yet we are really not dealing with a lot of personal inner turmoil?

And once a book started to take shape and the many ideas and pieces of information coalesced, I realised there was a need for further self-reflection on the impact of the case, not just on myself and my family, but in a wider context, in particular the victims and their families. This presented a responsibility to reflect on the way I had written the book and how I might address the sensibilities of anyone affected by the case who might read it.

In order to be open to new and imaginative ideas, which may not be pleasant or palatable, but should nevertheless not be excluded for that reason, it is necessary to avoid being hidebound by conventional moral judgments on what is tasteful or right. This is just as true for art as it is for philosophy or psychoanalysis.

The case generated many hundreds of witness statements, the majority of which did not form part of the evidence at Winchester Crown Court. Most people I come across in Gloucester either have some personal anecdotal soundbite or knew someone who had at some time a connection, however tenuous, with some aspect of the case: a family member, a victim, a location. This prompted me to recall my own teenage years out and about in the pubs in Gloucester and Cheltenham. Could, I wondered, unbeknownst to me, on some random occasion, ever have seen Fred and Rose West? My mind wanders back, and I recall a spring evening in 1973. I am with my brothers and some friends. We are having a drink in the packed courtyard of the New Inn on Northgate Street, Gloucester. In the background a jukebox is playing *Albatross*. Across the chattering noisy vista, amidst the strangely democratic mix of hippy types in Afghan coats and their wafting scent of petunia oil and marijuana, intermingled with well-scrubbed 'smoothies', could my eyes have fleetingly glanced the apparition of a strange young woman loitering in her ultra-short, floral mini skirt and knee-length schoolgirl socks, bizarrely exhibitionist, psychosexually toxic, behind large, dark-rimmed glasses, her gaze deranged and unfocussed, her olive pallor blurred by a strange aura of distorted pride, emanating from her flickering, icy hot, intimidating demeanour? She stands still and haughty, posing as some kind of trophy, amidst a group of beer-swilling men on a weekend night out in their loons or bell-bottoms, gaudy shirts, flared jackets and platform shoes.

Could I, on a routine Saturday afternoon sojourn into Cheltenham to do some shopping and meet some friends, have walked past an old green Austin Van awkwardly parked on the promenade with a dishevelled little gnome offering an unofficial taxi service to any innocent young woman?

There is a kind of guilt trip in this 'what if' narrative. How might there have been more vigilance?

Could things have been different? And if I feel like that, then there must be hundreds of people, including many police officers, social workers, teachers, friends and family who must feel so with greater intensity.

Yet I do not regret representing Rose West. She had as much right to proper legal representation as any other citizen. She was already my client and I had a good working relationship with her. I did my professional duty in adhering to just and fair principles that everyone is entitled to a fair trial based on the law and facts of the case. I have often been asked in relation to criminal practice generally, how is it tenable to continue to act for someone if you know they are guilty?

Well the first thing to stress, is that the question one really needs to ask is, "…if you know someone as guilty 'as charged'?"

In the West case the evidence was compelling that she was involved in serious sexual abuse, that she was married to a self-confessed serial killer, that she shared in his sado-masochistic perversion, that she had on occasions a foul temper. Should all that smoke automatically condemn her?

If I thought writing a book may be cathartic, as it progressed it did not feel that way. Revisiting the facts of the investigation magnified feelings of sorrow and horror at the dreadful fate that befell so many young women, who should have been enjoying the happy times on the cusp of their lives. The burden of the loss, the unknowing and the imaginings of close family and friends of the victims about the plight of their loved ones must be unbearable. With or without a religious faith, it can only be hoped that time affords some healing and that all those affected can in some way move on with their lives.

It is humbling to read Marian Partington's long, painful and seemingly impossible journey towards healing and forgiveness. At one point, she reaches out to the tormentors and killers of her dear sister in the following empathic paragraph:

"Everything that the Wests did to you, Lucy, tells me something about what was done to them in their childhood. The Wests abducted you, either by force or deception. (Who abducted their childhood?) The Wests stole you from us. (Who stole them, or didn't miss them when they had gone?) They gagged you. (Who wouldn't let them speak? Who didn't listen to them? How early were they silenced? When was their truth negated? When did they become invalid?) They strung you up and raped you. Were you conscious or unconscious from now on? (Who immobilised them and played with them as sexual objects?) Did they kill you directly or did you die alone? (Who killed them and their sense of sacred self?) They dismembered and decapitated you. (Who fragmented them and demolished them?) They disarticulated your joints. (Why were they emotionally inarticulate?)"

There also must be deep sense of collective sorrow that there are likely to be other victims that we simply do not know about. Young women whose existence was snuffed out without a trace, never to be seen again and no one asking where they had gone. It is true that there is a national database of missing persons, but a large number of the cases which go back over many years have never been solved and may never be.

I recall the volte-face when, at the conclusion of Rose West's trial in Winchester, Superintendent Bennett announced that he believed there were many more victims and that the search for more remains would continue. This statement would not have been made without the approval of the Chief Constable. The prospect would also have required a necessary input of central funding. Within days, there was then a precisely worded announcement that the police investigation was at an end, that it had been brought to a satisfactory conclusion and that on the basis of existing information, the matter was closed.

Gloucester City Council had to decide whether to commemorate the tragic victims of 25 Cromwell Street in some way, but ultimately decided to demolish the property and replace it with a path through from St Michaels Square.

Gordon Burn, in his book *Happy Like Murderers*, describes the dismantling and demolition of 25 Cromwell Street and the encasement of the basement and foundations in concrete almost as though describing a Rachel Whiteread installation, with all the symbolism emphasising the collective need to make inaccessible the dark secrets that imbued the subsoil. I saw this as a signifier of Rose and Fred's perpetuating unconscious, of still necessitating the scrutiny of discourse into the dark psychological foreboding that haunts the place; the untameable, enduring, undead lamella, the disembodied organ that persists beyond death, the severed hand that freely moves in horror movies, the cat's grin in *Alice in Wonderland* that continues after the cat has gone.

There was a flurry of activity in the years following the West case as local authority contractors seemed to be forever digging up the roads in the centre of town from the Cross into Northgate, Southgate, Eastgate and Westgate Streets and replacing the old concrete with stone block paving. They commissioned statues commemorating Gloster Aircraft Corporation and new sculptures such as the Glover's needle in the docks. There is also the elaborate, tall, sculptural steel structure on the Kimbrose Triangle at the bottom of Southgate Street completed in 2010. It commemorates Gloucester's Saint Kyneburgh.

The story goes that in the late seventh century, a Saxon princess by the name of Kyneburgh wanted to give herself to God, but her family had arranged her marriage to a local prince. Kyneburgh ran away to Gloucester. Some say she was actually the sister of a king and became abbess of the city's new abbey of St Peter. Whatever it was, when her family promised her in marriage, she hid herself in Gloucester and found work with a local baker. The wife of the baker became jealous and when the opportunity arose, murdered Kyneburgh and threw her body into a well just outside the city walls. It is said that the plaintiff wails of the saintly lady can still be heard in the cold depths of a dark stormy night.

The modern installation represents both the city wall and the well. When I pass the intricately positioned layers of flattened metal that define the contours of the work, I see them as a representation of human skeletal bones. Perhaps the installation should also signify absence through incorporation of incongruent voids, of layers that should be present but are not. Is the Kyneburgh installation also a way to remember the Cromwell Street victims?

As I revisited the material, I recall seeing a rat scurry along the fence at the bottom of our garden. It had an unnerving resonance. I mention this for a number of reasons. It is true to say that these rodents, though grisly and disgusting, are also clever and, apart from anything else, can hide by secreting themselves in tiny irregular spaces often within arm's reach of humans. They do this by a capacity to dislocate their backbones, enabling impossible contortion. In considering the West case, I realise that it is perhaps impossible to see human beings as the monsters that a very few really are. In this human connection, the dislocation remains unseen, there is an anamorphosis, where the desire to deceive is met with a need by reasonable people to assume normality and what is presented by the offender is a re-adjustment of a horrible distortion mediated and mirrored so that truth is the resulting casualty. The 'unseenness' of the real image presents an ongoing grave risk of harm. Fred and Rose West were accomplished liars. The full extent of their weave of concealment of evil has even now yet to be properly unpicked and may never be.

There is another resonance (actually with many members of the animal kingdom) in that rats do occasionally kill their offspring, but when they do, they eat them. Research is ongoing in this area. It is uncertain whether the cause is natural or pathological, whether it is infanticide or cannibalism, whether it is stress related or a matter of adapting to scarcity of resources. It can, of course, and often is both. Many zoological articles and papers also rightly remind us of the fact that infanticide is commonplace in humans. And it is necessary to be reminded that human beings are routinely capable of acts of cruelty, aggression and kill each other, sometimes on an industrial scale. How might this be categorised: pathological or a question of resources?

The word 'resource' in zoological terms is about food to sustain the group, to preserve body mass and energy for hunting or foraging to survive. And sick offspring are likely to die naturally and almost certainly will be unable to keep up with the group as they move on. The economy of the natural world and considerations of fundamental survival appear to have little time for helpless passengers. The word 'resource' becomes more nuanced in human beings. While it still fundamentally relates to sustaining the group, the existential sense of sustaining would include the removal of threats, not just from famine, but from others. In particular, the sanction of wider social authorities within which the group exists, that if informed of unacceptable pathological aberrations would curtail those practices by apprehending the offending members of the sub-group or family. What is normal is a relative concept. Acts of killing the young can be regarded as acceptable and necessary in civil society. The broader use of the word 'sustaining' is equally applicable to legal abortion and also may encompass warfare based upon ideological differences or national rivalry or ambition.

Is it out of context to consider the behaviour of the Wests as some intriguing extrapolation from the science of the natural world? Human beings are so much more complex, with behaviours mediated by sentience. Descartes declared to the effect, "I think therefore I am," although Lacan did challenge this and was more likely to say that 'The Other' thinks therefore I am, but then Lacan also said that the book writes the author (perhaps an unhelpful digression at this juncture). Whatever it is, if humanity means anything, there must be an implicit universality of mutual accord and respect even when, as is often the case, those basic standards are not observed. Humans are able to make independent ethical and moral choices, exercise individual responsibly for their actions, irrespective of societal injustices in their nature and nurture. If the courts were to recognise that defendants are merely the inevitable sum total of negative experience or chemical imbalance whether self-induced or not, then eventually culpability for their actions would be extinguished.

As a closing thought, I proffer the honest belief that if Rosemary Letts had not met Fred West she would never have become a murderer, let alone a serial killer, but not so of Fred West; he was already fully formed as a sexually deviant killer. Rose West was the pliable vessel ripe in her already groomed and nascent predisposition to energetically play her part in the gross excesses of Fred's perverted fantasies.

RECOMMENDED PAINTINGS FOR THE READER TO VIEW:

Francis Bacon – *Painting 1946* (1946)

Hieronymus Bosch – *The Garden of Earthly Delights* (1504)

Gustave Courbet – *L'Origine du Monde* (1866)

Salvador Dali – *Dream Caused by the Flight of a Bee Around a Pomegranate a Second Before Awakening* (1944)

Salvador Dali – *The Skull of Nudes* (1951)

Salvador Dali – *The Persistence of Memory* (1931)

Salvador Dali – *The Disintegration of the Persistence of Memory* (1954)

Salvador Dali – *Madonna of Port Lligat* (1949)

Salvador Dali – *Female Nude* (1928)

Salvador Dali – *The Invisible Man* (1929)

Max Ernst – *The Angel of Hearth and Home* (1937)

Max Ernst – *Oedipus Rex* (1922)

Henry Fuseli – *The Nightmare* (1781)
Nicolai Abildgaard – The Nightmare (1800)
Paul Gauguin – *Spirit of the Dead Watching* (1892)
Paul Gauguin – *The Lost Virginity* (1891)
Théodore Géricault – *Anatomical Pieces* (1819
Francisco Goya – *The Disasters of War* (1810–1820)
Frida Kahlo – A Few Small Nips (1935)
Man Ray – *Merry Wives of Windsor* (1948)
Paula Rego – *Snow White and Her Stepmother* (1995)

TEXT REFERENCES AND READING LIST:

Dante Alighieri – *Dante's Inferno* (1320)

Ansell, Pearson & Large – The Nietzsche Reader (2005)

Lionel Bailly – *Lacan* (2009)

John Bennett with Graham Gardner – *The Cromwell Street Murders* (2005)

Professor David Ormerod QC – *Blackstone's Criminal Practice* (2016)

Gordon Burn – *Happy Like Murderers* (1998)

Jane Carter Woodrow – *Rose West* (2011)

Marc De Kesel – Eros and Ethics (2009)

Marquis de Sade – *Philosophy in the Boudoir* (1795)

Diagnostic and Statistical Manual of Mental Disorders, Fifth Edition (2013)

European Journal of Psychoanalysis (2017)

Jill Evans – Hanged at Gloucester (2011)

Sigmund Freud – *Civilization and Its Discontents* (1930)

Sigmund Freud – *The Interpretation of Dreams* (1899)

Jean-Louis Gault – The 'Truth' of Kant's Moral Law: Fantasy and the Limits of Enjoyment (2003)

Thomas Hobbes – Leviathian (1651)

James Joyce – Portrait of the Artist as a Young Man (1916)

Jacques Lacan – Seminars & Ecrits (1953-1981)

Brian Masters – She Must Have Known (1996)

John Milton – Paradise Lost (1667)

James R O'Shea (ed.) (2011) – Kant's Critique of Pure Reason (1781)

Gavin Parkinson – Surrealism, Art and Modern Science (2008)

Marian Partington – If You Sit Very Still (2012)

Lobsang Rapgay – The Psychology of Hate (2018)

Philip Roth – Sabbath's Theatre (1995)

Jean-Jacques Rousseau – The Social Contract (1762)

Howard Sounes – Fred & Rose (1995)

Keir Starmer QC (LAG) – European Human Rights Law (1999)

Alireza Taheri – Perverse Mothers or Mad Wives? A Lacanian Commentary on Nahaleh Moshtagh's 'The Silent Accomplice: The Mother's Passive Perversion' (2016)

Geoffrey Wansell – An Evil Love (1996)

Anne Marie West with Virginia Hill – Out of the Shadows (1995)

William Wordsworth – Tintern Abbey (1798)

Michael Zander QC – The Police and Criminal Evidence Act 1984 (1990)

Slavoj Žižek – How to Read Lacan (2006)